OOTHECA WOLLEYANA:

AN ILLUSTRATED CATALOGUE

OF

THE COLLECTION OF BIRDS' EGGS

FORMED BY THE LATE

JOHN WOLLEY, Jun., M.A., F.Z.S.

EDITED FROM THE ORIGINAL NOTES

BY

ALFRED NEWTON, M.A., F.L.S., ETC.

PART I. ACCIPITRES.

LONDON:

JOHN VAN VOORST, PATERNOSTER ROW.

M.DCCC.LXIV.

[*Price* £1 11s. 6d.]

Wolley

OOTHECA WOLLEYANA:

AN ILLUSTRATED CATALOGUE

OF

THE COLLECTION OF BIRDS' EGGS

FORMED BY THE LATE

JOHN WOLLEY, Jun., M.A., F.Z.S.

EDITED FROM THE ORIGINAL NOTES

BY

ALFRED NEWTON, M.A., F.L.S., ETC.

PART I. ACCIPITRES.

LONDON:

JOHN VAN VOORST, PATERNOSTER ROW.

M.DCCC.LXIV.

PRINTED BY TAYLOR AND FRANCIS,
RED LION COURT, FLEET STREET.

TO

THE REVEREND JOHN WOLLEY, M.A.,

OF BEESTON, NOTTS.,

AS AN ACKNOWLEDGMENT OF

HIS GENEROSITY

IN FULFILLING THE LAST WISHES OF

HIS SON,

THE NATURALIST WHOSE LABOURS

ARE HEREIN RECORDED,

THIS WORK IS INSCRIBED

BY

THE EDITOR.

20TH NOVEMBER, 1863.

PREFACE TO PART I.

Reserving, until the completion of my duties as Editor, a detailed introduction to this work, it is yet necessary for me to prefix to the portion of it which first sees the light a few words in explanation of my motives in publishing it.

The late Mr. John Wolley, after spending nearly all his life in the pursuit of Natural History, died, as is well known to ornithologists, at the early age of thirty-six years. Shortly before his death, he requested that his Oological Collection, the formation of which had latterly been his chief occupation, should be handed over to me; and this wish was fully carried out by his father. As soon as I heard of the desire my deceased friend and fellow-traveller had expressed, I began to consider how I could best make use of the valuable property which was to be entrusted to me; and after consulting on the subject with Mr. P. L. Sclater, the Secretary of the Zoological Society of London, I came to the conclusion that I should be most advantageously serving the interest of Ornithology by publishing from Mr. Wolley's note-books a complete Catalogue of the contents of his Egg-Cabinet. Mr. Wolley's life had been one of so active a nature, and his death was, until a few weeks before it took place, so entirely unexpected, that he had

had but few opportunities of making known to the world the
results of his labours. To prevent these results from being
lost to science was my main object; and it appeared to me
that this would be effectually attained by the compilation of a
Catalogue such as the present, which should embrace as far as
possible all the information he had gathered, whether extracted
from letters addressed to his friends, from fragmentary diaries,
or from detached memorandums, as well as that which was
contained in his 'Egg-book,'—this latter being the principal
record of his experience, and having been, with some few exceptions, most carefully kept for many years.

In preparing this work for the press, the plan I have adopted
has been to bring together systematically all the notes relating
to the same species, and arrange them for the most part in the
order of the time at which they were written. I have not
scrupled to add an account of such specimens as I have lately obtained, and of those which were included in the joint collection
formed by my brother Edward and myself, prior to its incor-
poration with the contents of Mr. WOLLEY's cabinets. In
doing this, I believe I have only acted as my late friend would
have wished; for I am sure that, in leaving his collection to
me, he expected that I should continue to make it as perfect as
I could. These interpolations, however, are in all cases typo-
graphically distinguished from Mr. WOLLEY's text; so that
there is no fear of my words being mistaken for his.

I regret being unable to give even an approximate estimate
of the extent of the 'Ootheca Wolleyana.' I am well aware
that uncertainty on this point will be as unfavourable to myself
as it may be inconvenient to the public. I shall endeavour to

publish the Second Part of the work on the 1st December next, and this I hope may contain the whole of the *Clamatores* and *Oscines* which I shall have occasion to include. Mr. WOL-LEY's collection was confined to European species: it has been my intention to extend its limits to those of the western half of the Palæarctic Region, as being a district more naturally defined.

The subjects from which the plates have been drawn are, in every case, solely illustrative of the collection as it now stands. I must here return my best thanks to all the artists who have assisted me in their production, and especially to Mr. Wolf, whose liberality in placing at my disposal the paintings from which three of the engravings have been taken, and whose kindness in superintending the execution of the rest, are only equalled by the faithful effects of his marvellous pencil.

A. N.

MAGDALENE COLLEGE, CAMBRIDGE,
APRIL 1864.

OOTHECA WOLLEYANA.

NEOPHRON PERCNOPTERUS (Linnæus).

EGYPTIAN VULTURE.

§ 1. *One.*—Tangier, April 1845.   From M. Favier's Collection, 1846.

Hewitson, 'Eggs of British Birds,' pl. i.

ONE day, during my stay at Tangier, September 1845, after an inquiry about some monkeys, I was taken by Hamet, my guardian Moor, to a *patio* (courtyard) round which lived in apparent harmony a Jewish. a Moorish, and a French family.   The latter consisted of a solitary individual, who dealt in monkeys, and who also skinned boars' heads, jackals, ichneumons, and other trophies of the Consul's shooting-parties.   He showed me a quantity of birds' skins, well preserved, and, as far as my knowledge went, correctly named from a copy of Temminck's 'Manuel' that he greatly prized.   Upon my asking for eggs, he produced some; and he assured me that all of them that were named had had the mother killed over them.   Every egg that I knew was correctly named, with the trifling exception of a Goatsucker's, marked *Turdus merula*; and so I was fortunate enough to procure eggs of the Little Bustard, Stilt, Pratincole, and Bee-eater.   The only eggs I felt in doubt about were four, marked *Cathartes percnopterus*.   I fully believed that this bird laid a white egg; and I did not think it could be so small as these.   However, M. Favier (for that was the Frenchman's name) assured me that the old one was killed off one of the nests, was bought by Mr. Sandford, and is now in England.   I was also shown a nestling young one.   The eggs were taken in different years, as the dates 1843 and 1845 on them testified; two single ones; the other two,—each, as he said, "half of a complete nest."   In fine, he "gave for false" all that had ever been written about the egg of this bird, asserted that it was unknown in Paris or in London, and that

B

he intended to publish a book himself.   However, in the then state of my finances, I declined his price, "sept piastres fortes d'Espagne," *i. e.* seven dollars.   I heard well of M. Favier, and that he was patronized by the late much-lamented British Consul, Mr. Edward Drummond-Hay.   On my return to Cambridge I consulted Audubon and other authorities.   I found that the eggs of the Black Vulture of North America (a bird not far different in size from the *percnopterus*) are small, and marked with large irregular dashes of black and dark brown towards the larger end; that they never exceed two; and also that they are more elongated, as well as sharper at the smaller end, than those of the Turkey Buzzard (Ornithological Biography, vol. ii. p. 51, and vol. v. p. 346).   Hence, notwithstanding the authorities quoted by Mr. Yarrell, and the figure originally given by Mr. Hewitson[1], I thought the egg of the *percnopterus* might follow the tendency of other Vultures' eggs—of the Black Vulture according to Audubon, of the Turkey Buzzard according to Wilson, of the Bearded and the Griffon Vultures according to Temminck—and be a coloured one.   This last difficulty removed, I thought there was scarcely room for doubting the authenticity of M. Favier's eggs.   I accordingly wrote for the two most opposite varieties of them, and, by the kindness of several friends, I received them safe.   On opening the box, they looked so like some large Hawks' eggs, that my doubts revived, and were not dispelled until, in consequence of an accidental inquiry put to me by Mr. Wilmot, that gentleman furnished me with an account of what he already knew on the subject; and I was also favoured with a sight of a drawing made by M. Moquin-Tandon from a specimen at Toulouse.   This drawing is evidently taken from an egg similar to mine, and intermediate in size between them; at one end it is somewhat pointed, at the other end blunt.   One of my eggs (that figured by Mr. Hewitson, and the subject of this note) is inclined to be peaked at both ends; the other, taken in April 1843, which I have given to Mr. Wilmot, is considerably less, and almost a perfect oval.   This would come very near Wilson's description of that of *Cathartes aura.*

M. Moquin-Tandon's communication, dated "Jardin des Plantes, Toulouse, Sept. 6, 1843," was as follows:—"L'année dernière, du Crau d'Arles, on découvrit deux nids, contenant chacun deux œufs: deux furent déposés au Musée d'Avignon.   Cette année, sur le Pic de St. Loup, près de Montpellier, on a trouvé un troisième nid de cet oiseau : il ne contenait qu'un œuf."   M. Favier, in a work in his hands

---

[1] [This figure was in plate i. of the 'Eggs of British Birds,' 1st ed., which was subsequently cancelled by the author, to be replaced, as above quoted, by a figure of the subject of the present note.—ED.]

that has not yet seen the day, states that " the *percnopterus* makes its nest at the end of March, in the crevices and in the caves of rocks, usually in inaccessible places in a perpendicular cliff. It lays in the month of April, one or two eggs of a variable form. It hatches at the end of May; and the young (always one or two in number) are not of age to take their flight until July." The " one or two eggs " agrees with the account of M. Moquin-Tandon, and of that given by Bruce (Travels to the Sources of the Nile, App. p. 164); but the time spent in the nest does not come up to the " four months " of Bruce, though, from the small size of the egg, we might expect it to be long. The Condor, the Black Vulture, and probably most Vultures, appear to lay two eggs only; and it is also said of them that they make no nest (Darwin, ' Zoology of the " Beagle " Voyage,' part iii. p. 4; Audubon, ' Ornithological Biography,' vol. ii. p. 54). Does our bird form its own nest? In Barbary, the Egyptian Vulture probably breeds only in the mountains of the interior, as it was not known to Mr. John Drummond-Hay, then Her Britannic Majesty's Consul at Tangier. Mr. Hewitson writes, " I have not the slightest doubt of the authenticity of this egg." From Mr. Wilmot I have heard also of two other eggs of this bird,—one laid in some Zoological Garden, and figured in Lefèvre's ' Atlas des Œufs des Oiseaux d'Europe,' the other brought from Egypt by a Scotch physician. I should add that M. Favier's account of the nidification is partly worded after that of Temminck (Man. d'Orn. i. p. 10)*.

[M. Moquin-Tandon has some very instructive notes on the nidification of this species in the ' Revue et Magasin de Zoologie ' for November 1857, p. 491.]

§ 2. *One.*—Tangier, April 1845. From M. Favier's Collection, 1847.

O. W., tab. 1. fig. 3.

This egg I bought, among some others, of Mr. Williams of Oxford Street. I saw M. Favier's marks on nearly all of them, and I did not doubt they were all from him originally. From the writing upon it, it is evidently one of those I saw at Tangier.

* A curious geological event happened in consequence of M. Favier's oological inclinations. A huge mass of sand-rock was pointed out to me, underneath which were said to lie the remains of four men who had been engaged in robbing a nest for him, when the mass gave way and rolled upon them. It had been undermined for several years by the crumbling away of the clay on which it rested conformably; and as it is the last feather that breaks the camel's back, so the weight of these four men determined the moment of the fall of the huge cliff. All the powers of Tangier could not get them from beneath it.

§ 3. *Two.*—Tangier, 3 May, 1846. From M. Favier's Collection, 1847.

O. W. tab. 1. fig. 5.

Received from M. Favier, 21st February, 1847. There cannot be much doubt now of the authenticity of these eggs. I saw one with M. Lefèvre in Paris in 1846, and another at Geneva in the same year, both similar to these. The latter showed much of the ground-colour, *i.e.* the white shell. The best-marked of the two specimens under consideration is of a similar red, in the spots, to the other eggs. I have had, further, a satisfactory assurance from M. Favier that *Aquila nævia* is not found on the Barbary coast.

§ 4. *One.*—Tangier. From M. Favier's Collection, 1847.

O. W. tab. 1. fig. 1.

I have had much doubt about this egg. Mr. Henry Milner says it is exactly like his Osprey's taken in Scotland; it is also very like Mr. Yarrell's egg of that bird.

[This egg was bought of Mr. Williams with the one before-mentioned (§ 2). Mr. Wolley is certainly right in saying that it resembles an Osprey's: indeed, as far as I know, it might be taken for one; but I can well understand, after having now seen so many, it being that of a *Neophron*; and Ospreys' eggs must be less easy of access in North-West Africa than those of the Egyptian Vulture.]

§ 5. *One.*—" Pyrenees, 1855." From M. Parzudaki's Collection, 1856.

Sent to me with other eggs by M. Parzudaki, 28 March, 1856.

§ 6. *One.*—Valley of the Medjerdah, near Souk Harras, Eastern Atlas, 25 April, 1857. From Mr. O. Salvin's Collection.

O. W. tab. 1. fig. 4.

The Medjerdah is the river that flows out at Utica. This egg, Mr. Salvin states, was taken in the upper part of its valley by a Frenchman named Lafosse, a collector of minerals and such things.

[Mr. Salvin's notes on the nidification of this species are published at length in 'The Ibis,' vol. i. p. 180.]

§ 7. *One.*—Kef Laks, Eastern Atlas, 15 April, 1857. From Mr. O. Salvin's Collection.

The spot just mentioned is a sort of plateau, with rocks falling away all around: the cliff whence this egg was obtained faced the east. It was taken by an Arab near the camp. The nest contained one egg, which was very fresh.

§ 8. *Two.* — "Pyrenees." From M. Parzudaki's Collection, 1858.

About the 25th February, 1858, I selected these two eggs, as extremes in point of size, from a number brought by M. Parzudaki to London,—one being a very large and one a very small one, and yet, he says, undoubtedly of the same species. If I understood him rightly, they are from the Pyrenees, and not Algeria, and from the same tract as the Lämmergeyer's I got at the same time.

§ 9. *One.* — Khifan M'sroutun, Eastern Atlas, 24 April, 1857. "W. H. S." From Mr. W. H. Simpson's Collection.

There were three eggs in this nest. Wherever the initials of my friend Mr. Simpson appear, they imply that the egg was taken by his own hand, or actually as he was looking on and identified the species. Hence this is a very interesting specimen, besides its being rather a variety. One day, while he was away from the tents, all his eggs got wetted; and most of the Vultures' were seriously injured, as they remained unlooked to for several days.

§ 10. *One.*—Gala el Hamara, Eastern Atlas, 25 April, 1857. From Mr. Tristram's Collection.

O. W. tab. 1. fig. 6.

From a nest of two fresh eggs. It formed Lot 11, at Mr. Stevens's rooms, 9th February, 1858.

§ 11. *Two.*—Kef M'slouta, Eastern Atlas, 2 May, 1857. From Mr. Tristram's Collection.

These two specimens were from the same nest; one is small and very curiously coloured.

§ 12. *One.*—Kef Gh'tar, Eastern Atlas, 22 April, 1857. From Mr. Tristram's Collection.

O. W. tab. 1. fig. 2.

Given to me at the same time as the preceding two, in the autumn of 1858, by Mr. Tristram.

[§ 13. *One.*—From Lord Lilford's Collection, 1855.

Bought at Vienna.]

[§ 14. *Two.*—Medjerdah, Eastern Atlas, 6 May, 1857. From Mr. Tristram's Collection.

A complete nest of two eggs, brought by M. Lafosse.]

[§ 15. *One.*—Kef Laks, Eastern Atlas, 17 May, 1857. From Mr. O. Salvin's Collection.

This egg is one that was collected by Arabs for Mr. Simpson, on his return from Aïn Djendeli.]

VULTUR CINEREUS, Gmelin.

CINEREOUS VULTURE.

§ 16. *One.*—" Les basses Alpes, 1856." From M. Parzudaki's Collection, 1858.

M. Parzudaki said this was from *" les basses Alpes."* He did not tell me in whose writing the name on the egg was.

GYPS FULVUS (Gmelin).

GRIFFON VULTURE.

§ 17. *One.*—Knowsley Menagerie, 14 March, 1849.

Hewitson, 'Eggs of British Birds,' Ed. 3. pl. i.

This egg was presented to me on the 15th March, 1849, by Mr. Thompson of Lord Derby's menagerie. It was laid the day before. I saw the Griffon Vultures with another Vulture, or Eagle, in the cage, and I was told the Griffon laid an egg (or two?) last year, and another this year. She was preparing the nest. They were supposed to be barren eggs; but why, I forget—whether both the Griffons were females, or what? I did not inquire whether the egg might not possibly be a hybrid; but no one suggested it was so. It was cracked when I first saw it at the keeper's house. It was quite fresh when I blew it, and the contents had a musky taste. Lady Cust has presented an egg of this bird to the Liverpool Museum, no doubt from the same quarter. A few days before I went to Liverpool I had written to M. Auguste Lefèvre, of Paris, to bespeak four eggs of the Griffon Vulture.

§ 18. *One.*—From M. Lefèvre's Collection, through Mr. H. F. Walter.

§ 19. *Two.*—Pyrenees (?), 1856. From M. Parzudaki's Collection, 1856.

Taken, as it seems, this year. M. Parzudaki told me how that the first season he offered large prices for a few, then there came more, till this year he had a great many.

§ 20. *One.*—Kef Gh'tar, Eastern Atlas, 14 April, 1857. From Mr. O. Salvin's Collection.

From a cliff facing the north at Kef Gh'tar, long. 5° 20′ E. of Paris, lat. 36° 15′ N., near Ras el Alia, marked in the map of the province of Constantine, published by the French Government in 1854. Mr. Salvin shot a bird near this rock, and states that this species hardly ever lays more than one egg, a single exception only occurring to his knowledge. The nests, some six hundred feet above the river, are about the middle of the perpendicular part of the cliff, and built of sticks. The birds sit hard, and soon come back to their nests.

[Mr. Salvin's notes respecting the nesting of this species a republished in 'The Ibis,' vol. i. p. 178.]

[§ 21. *One.*—Balkan Mountains (?). From Lord Lilford's Collection, 1855.]

[§ 22. *One.*—Gala el Hamara, Eastern Atlas, 15 April, 1857. From Mr. W. H. Simpson's Collection.

Brought from Algeria by Mr. Simpson.]

[§ 23. *One.*—Kef M'satka, Eastern Atlas, 8 March, 1859. "P. L. S." From Dr. P. L. Sclater.

One of the few egg-treasures obtained by Mr. Sclater during his short trip to Algeria and Tunis in 1859. It was taken in his presence.]

GYPAETUS BARBATUS (Linnæus).

BEARDED VULTURE.

§ 24. *Two.*—"Pyrenees, 1857." From M. Parzudaki's Collection, 1858.

Without inscription till I wrote on them, from a memorandum of what M. Parzudaki had told me concerning the eggs I received of him. He particularly said these were not from Algeria, but from the Pyrenees.

AQUILA CHRYSAETUS (Linnæus).

GOLDEN EAGLE.

The Mountain Eagle, as in Scotland it is generally called, still breeds in some of the more remote districts of our island, as well as of Ireland. Last year (1852) I knew of five nests that had eggs in them in different parts of Scotland; and undoubtedly there were at least as many more of which I did not hear particulars. In the Orkneys there was for a number of years an eyrie in the interior of one of the islands. In Shetland I have not been able to obtain any proof of the existence of this bird, and it is certainly unknown in the Færo Islands and in Iceland. In Norway it is common, and, with the Sea Eagle, is so numerous at, from a statistical account of the premiums paid each year by the government for the destruction of beasts and birds of prey, as published in the 'Athenæum,' No. 1267 [for Feb. 7, 1852 (p. 179)], it appears that, in the five years ending December 1850, there were paid for altogether no less than 10,715 Eagles! The Sutherlandshire Expedition of Naturalists mention [Edinb. New Phil. Journ. xx. pp. 158, 159] the number of Eagles that had been paid for between March 1831 and March 1834 to have been 171, besides 53 nestlings or eggs! Shortly after that time the Association for the destruction of vermin was dissolved, and the breed was kept down only by the individual exertions of the large sheep-farmers, who generally gave five shillings for each egg or young one, and ten shillings for every old bird; and great satisfaction they had in dashing the former against the ground. Still so many remained, that in one district in the south-west of that county a clever gamekeeper trapped fifteen Eagles in three months of 1847,. and about as many in the winter of 1850-1, almost all of them being Mountain Eagles. In other parts of Scotland more frequented by south-country game-keepers, they have been already almost exterminated, except in those wild tracts preserved as Deer forests, upon several of which the proprietors take real pleasure in seeing them circling overhead, ready to gorge themselves with the " gralloch " as soon as a Stag has been cut up. For, whatever may have been said to the contrary, they are great carrion-eaters, as Scott well knew :—

> " That Highland Eagle e'er should feed
> On thy fleet limbs, my matchless steed."
> [Lady of the Lake, Canto I. Stanza 9.]

But the Trossachs is no feeding-place for the Eagle now, as it still was in Sir Walter's time ! Only a few years ago a friend of mine saw no less than nine of the two kinds collected round a dead horse, within gunshot of the window of his father's house. This habit of theirs gives sad facilities for their destruction. In Wales there were Eagles not long ago : but the only account I know of a nest in England which can with certainty be referred to the Golden Eagle is Willughby's of the one in Derbyshire ['Ornithologia' (1676), p. 19] ; for the nest on the rocks near Plymouth [Mag. Nat. Hist. ser. 2. vol. i. p. 114] is more likely to have been a Sea Eagle's.

I have in different years carefully examined some eight or nine distinct eyries of this bird in Scotland, and seen the old sites of a good many more. It always, in this day at least, takes up its quarters in some mountainous district,—never, as far as I have seen, in sea-cliffs, but for the most part in a warm-looking rock, ˙ ˙˙ clothed with vegetation, and by no means very wild and exposed. Still there are exceptions. I have seen several very high rocks selected ; and in these cases the nest was generally near the top. In one instance I know of a nest halfway up a very bleak mountain ; but then it is in the front part of a little cave, from which the occupants enjoy the most magnificent prospect. Into this nest one walks almost without climbing ; at all events, two dogs followed our party into it. They are often in places remarkably accessible. One nest, in a very low rock, was upon a grassy ledge, into and out of which I vaulted with the greatest ease

from the top of the rock ; and three nests of other years, in different
spots in the same ravine, within a hundred yards or so, were all
accessible without ropes. Another, which was described to me by a
most accurate person, who offered to show it to me, was on the ground,
at the foot of a rock on the rise of a hill ; and near it, also upon the
ground, was an old nest of a former year. This was some hundreds
of miles away from the pair of Golden Eagles in Orkney, which one
year allowed an old woman to walk by chance into their nest and carry
off the eggs in her apron. At another eyrie, into which I had climbed
with some difficulty, I was enabled to find a very easy path out, by
following the ledge where I saw that some sheep had been not long
before. The eyrie from which I took the pair of eggs figured by Mr.
Hewitson [Eggs B. B. ed. 3. pl. iii.] was in a bad part of a great
and perpendicular crag, under a very sharp shelf beyond a ledge,
whence we could use the ropes. Its support was small, and the mass
of the nest was consequently large. A few yards from it, on either
side, were old nests of former years, one of which had been recently
repaired, and was connected with the occupied one by a continuous
platform of sticks. One eyrie is generally in a corner protected from
the wind on one side ; and the rock overhangs more or less, so as to
shelter it, but by no means so as to hide it from a gun above. The
platform of rock is often very broad ; and when it is also flat, there
are not many sticks used. It has for the most part some kind of
vegetation upon it, and generally more or less of the broad-leaved
grass called *Luzula sylvatica*, which, with other plants, often extends
in a green stripe a long way below the nest, owing to the richness of
the soil,—a mark by which an experienced eye can, from a great
distance, detect an old eyrie on a mountain, some years after it has
been disused. There is sometimes a sapling tree at the edge of the
platform in front ; and in the Derbyshire nest [described by Willughby]
it was no doubt the lower part of the bole that helped the rock to
support the fabric. A nest is generally five or six feet in its greatest
width, considerably less at the top : sometimes the mass of materials
would fill a cart, but in other situations there is no great quantity.
The very largest of the sticks used may be an inch in diameter, but
most of them are less. Upon these is laid freshly-gathered heather ;
and in one instance large sprigs of Scotch fir, broken off for the
purpose. The top part is composed of fern, grass, moss, or any other
convenient material, but principally (and, as far as I have seen, invariably) of tufts of *Luzula sylvatica*, which, by the time the eggs are
hatched, are still fresh and green towards the outside of the nest, but
dried up in the centre with the heat of the bird's body, [so as to look]

like little flattened pine-apple tops. Once I saw this in a great measure replaced by tufts of a kind of *Carex* or *Nardus*. The hollow of the nest is never deep; but whilst the eggs are unhatched it is often pretty regular and sharp at the inner edge, and it is not more than a foot from the back wall of rock, close to which the soft materials are generally packed. There is little interlacing of the materials; but the whole structure, whilst it appears loose, is yet so firm that it scarcely springs at all with the weight of a man.

The nest is repaired each year; and I have no doubt, from Willughby's description, that the one found in Derbyshire had been used more than once. But it is usual for the same pair of Eagles to have several favourite sites in different quarters; and they frequently repair them all before making a final choice of the one in which to lay their eggs. What determines them it is difficult to say. One forester thinks it is the way the wind blows when they are ready to lay; another, that the sight of a human being scares them. A third possible and very singular cause has once occurred in my own experience: it is the generation, in the lining of the nest of a preceding year, of myriads of fleas, exactly like those that trouble mankind. I do not know whether a fourth reason for giving up a favourite place may not occasionally be a forcible ejectment by even a less power than man. I have seen in a simple rock an old eyrie, which had been subsequently occupied as a nursery by a Marten; but I think there must have been a previous desertion in such a case. Still a few of the best places are inhabited uninterruptedly. I have seen one which it was said had never been empty for fifteen successive years until four years ago; but it was again used in 1852. Some old shepherds have told me that they and their fathers had seen two eyries relieve each other every two years or thereabouts. The same birds will select very different situations. I am told of a pair that alternate between a crag quite impregnable and a corner into which a child can climb. In these days an altogether new place is rarely thought of. It is quite sufficient to visit the four or five known stations in a district, in one of which the Eagle will be found. Long experience had made many Highlanders believe that the supply of Eagles was inexhaustible; for if one of a pair was killed, the survivor was sure to bring a fresh mate the next year; but most of these persons have by this time found out their mistake.

The eggs are laid very early in the year, often with the country under deep snow. The hen sits very close; and, accordingly, that is the sex which is most frequently murdered at this season; but if anything happens to her, the cock will take her place for a time, but not so as to succeed in rearing the young, for he too is often slain in his turn. The very clean condition in which the eggs are mostly found, even when just hatching, shows that she can scarcely have left the nest since they were laid; and yet it is not till there are young ones that much food is seen lying about. So closely does she sit when "closking," that it is only the sight of a man's eye, or a bit of stick or stone about her ears, that will make her fly off; but when she does so, it is generally in considerable alarm, and perhaps with a low cry, taking care to appear no more till her enemies have retired. I have heard of an old man, and another time of a woman, being attacked by the birds near a nest; and a person told me that once, when quite alone, and in some difficulty on a very ticklish rock, the Eagles tried to knock him off with their wings. Such a thing never occurred to myself; and from conversations with persons who have been at scores of nests in former days, I am disposed to believe it is a rare event. When the eggs are taken, I have never heard of a second laying that year. More than one supposed instance of their being removed to another spot, in the claws of the parents, has come under my notice; but the propensities of Hooded Crows, and other sources of error, make me hesitate to consider these accounts as proved.

There are from one to three eggs in a nest; I do not know of an instance of four; but two is the usual and proper number. Last year I had three eggs, all fertile and nearly ready to hatch, out of one nest; and Mr. Salmon mentions that he knew of three young ones in a nest in Orkney [Mag. Nat. Hist. ser. 1. vol. v. p. 423]. In all other cases where I have heard of three eggs, one was addled; and it was thus in a nest where I found two young ones with a rotten egg. This was white, whilst one at least of its fellows had been highly coloured; but pure-white eggs are not always bad, as I know for certain in two instances. One infatuated Eagle I found sitting on a solitary egg, which, though addled, had some colour on it. The eggs are laid at intervals of a few days, and are hatched in the same order. In two pairs, I know which of the eggs was hatching first. Of the pair figured by Mr. Hewitson [Eggs B. B. ed. 3. pl. iii.], the one represented by the uppermost figure had already been chipped, whilst the other had not nearly arrived at the same condition. In another pair, an egg, crowded with faint freckles, was hatched certainly several days before its companion, a purely white one, would have been. There is often a remarkable difference, and yet a family likeness, in twin eggs. Again, in an undisturbed eyrie, where you find pale eggs one year, you may expect to find them still pale the next. The healthy triplet I have above spoken of were all very pale, and they came out of the nest which had the white and the freckled egg the year before.

The eggs of this Eagle vary exceedingly; those in the plate I have just referred to are the highest-coloured ones I have seen, but are very useful as showing the *beau idéal* at which a considerable number appear to be aiming, and it requires only a very little stretch of the imagination to resolve them into their varieties. The markings, still preserving the intensity of those of the upper figure, are frequently more evenly distributed over the egg, in spots of greater or of less dimensions, sometimes thickly scattered, and sometimes very remote from each other. In some eggs there is a beautiful arrangement of the colouring matter into closely crowded streams or drops, which reminds one of the " golden rain " of a firework,—a variety also to be seen in eggs of the Buzzard and Sparrow Hawk. In others the spots are very minute and of a reddish-purple hue, gradually collecting together, and slightly increasing in size, till they almost coalesce in the centre of the large end. Again, the egg is thickly dusted all over with one colour—a yellowish-brown—in several degrees of intensity, and in this form is very like eggs of the Iceland Falcon. One wholly-coloured egg of Mr. Walter's reminds me of the more even and uniform specimens of the Peregrine Falcon and Merlin. Of eggs with the markings all very faint, and as it were foreshadowings of those on the varieties to which I have alluded, I have seen a good many examples; but it must not be supposed that highly-marked eggs are uncommon. I am convinced, from a considerable and quite unselected number of Golden Eagles' eggs which I have seen, that well-marked specimens are the rule, not the exception. The egg which I should be disposed to choose as most typical is such a one as that figured by Mr. Hewitson [Eggs B. B. ed. 3. pl. iv. fig. 1]. There is a purple or lilac cast about it, and the markings are agreeably shaded and blended together. I have repeatedly seen eggs more or less like it, and it has a character in common with the beautiful example formerly represented by him [Eggs B. B. ed. 1. pl. ii. fig. 1]. The one taken out of the same nest with it has as much colour, but of quite a different kind, being somewhat of the Iceland Falcon type. The tendency of markings to the large instead of to the small end is to be found in the eggs of many kinds of birds; but it is so frequent in Golden Eagles' as hardly to deserve to be called a variety in this respect. A remarkable egg in Mr. Wilmot's cabinet has very fine dots, one or two small blotches, and some long straggling lines of the same colour near the larger end. In short, eggs of the Golden Eagle may be found representing those of all our other birds of prey in succession, even including the Egyptian Vulture.

In shape, the egg of this species varies in different specimens; but the lower figure of the pair represented by Mr. Hewitson [Eggs B. B. ed. 3. pl. iii. fig. 2] is most typical. This same egg is perhaps of about the average size. I have two very large ones, out of one nest; they are of a long-elliptical form; one is 3·26 inches by 2·38 inches, the other is 3·13 inches by 2·38 inches. The latter is of the purest white, the former like a well-coloured Iceland Falcon's.

The eggs are hatched in Scotland about the end of April. In three nests I have found young ones just coming out on the 23rd April, the 27th April, and the 1st or 2nd May. These are provided by nature with a little white "diamond" on the convex part of the beak to enable them to break the shell. They remain chirping inside for some time after they have made a little window to get a taste of fresh air; and in the meantime the long threads with which they are covered begin to dry, and to burst their thin delicate envelopes, that they may be converted into a forest of snow-white down. It is a curious sight to see in the middle of a huge nest these little powder-puffs holding up their tottering heads, overgrown and watery-eyed, to peck feebly at an intruder. Here I will leave them, only whispering of their capital larder, which the Irishman and (in the case of another species[1]) the African have each in their own country learned to share. The Scotchman did so too, till one day, finding a dead "serpent" ready for him, his indignation got the better of his prudence, and he knocked the "uncanny beasties" on the head. I must, however, add that Reynard also will put in his claim; and that he may not have to travel too far for his supper, he will probably make his earth in the immediate neighbourhood.

But still one word more. Is it not worth an effort to save the last remnant of this noble race—the bird which so many of the greatest nations of the earth, both ancient and modern, have taken as their emblem—the very highest type of swiftness, of energy, and of power? How many people of England, France, or Switzerland itself, ever saw an Eagle on the wing? and how many have longed in vain for such an incident even in the heart of the Highlands! Of the Scotch themselves, how many would now know an Eagle's quill from a Turkey's if they saw it in a chieftain's bonnet, and in a land where its feathers were once scarcely less prized than they still are by the Indians of the Fur-Countries?

Fitzjames's cap was trimmed with Heron plumage; and it was the Falcon that watched the chase from her cairn; but what a number of ideas the Eagle supplies in Scott's glorious poem, and in all truly

---

[1] [*Aquila bellicosa*, Daudin. *Le Griffard*, Levaillant, Ois. d'Afr. i. tab. 1. *Aquila armigera*, Rennie, 'Field Naturalist,' vol. i. (1833), p. 44.—ED.]

Highland stories! Is not the value of a few lambs and fawns a cheap price to pay for its preservation? for it is only here and there that an Eagle is not contented with Hares, and sometimes a Grouse or a Ptarmigan: just as with Foxes, it is but a few individuals that bring the bad name on all their race. But if it be too late, as I fear it is, to hope for the Eagle's prolonged existence in Scotland, now that the railways tie London to the Grampians, and the salmon-fisher, the grouse-shooter, and the skin-collector, as well as the sheep-farmer, all give great rewards for its destruction, we may still go to see it in foreign lands, and we must try to console ourselves with the utilitarian reflection that the number of destructive animals in a country is the measure of that country's civilization![1]

§ 25. *Two.*—Sutherlandshire, 24 April, 1848. From Mr. W. Dunbar's Collection.

Of these beautiful and highly-marked eggs, Mr. Dunbar says in his letter dated 21st June, 1848, " The Golden Eagle's eggs are both from the same nest. The eggs were two in number. The nest was placed in a rock about two hundred feet high, in Sutherland. The nest was about eighty feet from the bottom of the rock, and composed of large sticks and stumps of strong heather, with moss. The old bird, a female, was shot; I have her now preserved, and she is a very fine specimen."

The following year I heard that the nest in which these eggs were was easily accessible, on the east side of the mountain.

Further particulars respecting the locality whence these eggs came are given by Mr. Scrope in his ' Art of Deer-stalking,' p. 865.

---

[1] [The foregoing paragraphs were written by Mr. Wolley in the spring of 1853, for the use of Mr. Hewitson, who was then preparing the third edition of his well-known ' Eggs of British Birds.' A slightly modified version of them was accordingly communicated to that gentleman, and he has given copious extracts from it (*op. cit.* pp. 10–13). I have here introduced the notes from the original manuscript now in my possession. Some verbal discrepancies are consequently observable between the two accounts; but these are so unimportant that I do not think it necessary to reprint the passage from Mr. Hewitson's pages, though he has most kindly given me permission to quote in this book all the information furnished to his last edition by Mr. Wolley,—a favour of which I shall not be slow to avail myself in most cases. It must be remembered that these notes contain the general results of their author's experience only up to the time above-mentioned. A more extended knowledge of the habits of the Golden Eagle, especially as regards its nidification in trees, in some points altered Mr. Wolley's opinion; and a case of *four* eggs being found in a nest has been recorded by Capt. Orde (Ibis, 1861, p. 112.—ED.]

§ 26. *Two.*—Sutherlandshire, 27 April, 1849.   " J. W. *ipse.*"

Hewitson, 'Eggs of British Birds,' Ed. 3. pl. iii. figs. 1, 2.

We started from the inn with two men carrying the sixty-fathom ropes which I had had made in the town. We rested at a place where the foreman was anxious to get rid of Eagles, and sent for the shepherd, at whose house we had been the day before, and who was to follow us. We heard many different accounts—how that the foxhunter killed one Eagle a few weeks ago, &c. Some were willing to mislead us, others not so, but all agreed that the nest was inaccessible.

We reached the crag after a walk of some eight or nine miles from the village. It is a very high cliff, overhanging a large loch of the same name. A small birch wood slopes from it to the water. We saw an Eagle fly, and settle again at the top of the cliff. Arrived at the shepherd's house, he agreed to come with us, and his son was to show us the nest; but afterwards the old fellow turned coward and would not come near the edge. Having returned under guidance of the shepherd's son to where we saw the Eagle, I made out the nest with the help of my glass, but I could not point it out exactly to my companion. However, he was to remain below with the boy, to signal to me where it was. Having reached the top in about half an hour, I tied myself to the thick rope, and proceeded, gun in hand, over a ledge to an undercliff of from ten to twenty feet wide, along which I walked some forty or fifty yards. I leaned over the edge, and saw the sticks of the nest some little distance to my right. I got up, shouted and made all the noise I could; but no Eagle came out. I saw one soaring silently at a great height. I had been led to believe that there was only one bird belonging to the nest; so, after all the noise I had made, I took it for granted that this was the one. I shouted for the little rope, and tied a stone and a piece of white paper to it, for my companion to signal when it was opposite the nest. However, I found afterwards that he could not distinguish it. I could only just make him out to be waving his cap, he was so far below. No sooner was the stone over the edge of the rock than out dashed an Eagle close to me, within five yards, and with one low cry of alarm flew away to the right, down the valley. Evidently a Mountain Eagle, as the shepherds had all called it (it looked rather "ring-tailed") : I was not altogether sorry at having laid aside my gun.

All was now finally planned. The men wisely thought it would be better to have the stake driven and everything done upon the ledge. The shepherd, being an old man, did not dare come down. After a //

little difficulty (for there was no depth of soil), we fixed the big stake firmly above a very steep slope, some yards from the edge of the rock; then a stake for the little rope twenty yards to the left of us. Having spliced the rope to the stake upon which I was to sit, and tied myself in, explained all to the men, and agreed upon the signals, I proceeded over the edge, which, to my horror, I found almost as sharp as a knife, being a kind of mica-schist. I now felt how stupid I had been in forgetting to bring the leathern tubes I had had made; for the sharp edge, besides wearing the rope, caused great friction and difficulty in hauling up. No sooner was I over the rock, with the little rope in my right hand, than I saw the nest, with two eggs, beautiful, and very different from each other, about five feet to my left as I faced the rock. I could just reach the ledge with my fingers and unshod toes, and so, having cried "Stop," I hung, with the rope bearing me backwards towards the abyss, in a position both cramping from the muscular exertion required, and highly nervo-excitory from the feeling of danger or insecurity, unfounded though it might have been. On looking at the eggs in the nest I at once saw a hole in one, as if the old bird had dug her claw into it in her hurry; but on further examination I found it had a young one in it just hatching, and giving vent to low cries, which accounted for the high state of "closking" in which I had found the mother. I reached the eggs and put them in the box with tow, which I had lashed under my right arm, and I put some of the lining of the nest in my pocket. It was very large, something like a Rook's highly magnified, and lined with a kind of *Luzula*, much of it quite green, and apparently recently placed around: the middle was dried up*. About six feet to my left, and with the embankment of sticks continued to it, was another platform, with fresh stuff on it—perhaps a nest of last year, or a roosting-place for the other bird. Ten or twelve yards to the right, and not exactly on the same ledge, was another old nest. A few white feathers (Ptarmigans') and white fur (Mountain Hares') were all the remnants of prey that I saw. I was able to communicate with the men by shouting, as I was not more than six feet from the top of the rock, and one of them had descended to the edge. It was fortunate; for had there been wind, as in the morning, I could not have been heard; nor, as it was, could I have been heard further down. The little-rope signals had entirely failed. The eggs

* This *Luzula*, which I believe to be *L. sylvatica*, grows plentifully on the damp mountain-sides and ledges of rocks. The Eagles pluck and use the whole plant, which is something like the top of a pine-apple; and when dry, the leaves remind one of Russian matting; but they are not long as in specimens gathered in woods.

c

having been carefully tied up, I shouted to ascend. The first pull, they told me, was very hard; but I assisted them by climbing myself, and in half a minute I was high and dry, and we shook hands all round: we had finished our " wee drop " of whiskey before. During this time the Eagle did not appear, though it had again come within two or three hundred yards before I went down, but without scream- ing. All agreed that no man had ever been there before. My com- panion and the boy, tired and cold, reached the top of the cliff just in time to congratulate us on our success. In going home I put the eggs alternately in my breeches' pocket to keep them warm, for I was anxious to save the life of the young. In the evening I liberated the hatching one by an oval opening, and the egg is as good as ever. This is the one with the fewest marks upon it: and it must have been laid and sat upon several days before the other; for when I opened that in the same manner, part of the yelk was not yet absorbed. I put the young bird from the first egg before the fire; its down soon dried, and it became like a powder-puff: I kept it as warm as possi- ble, but it died in two days: perhaps I tried to feed it too soon; or it might have been neglected while I was out. The other one I put in spirits. The down on the legs, as far as the division of the toes, proved them to be Golden Eagles. The eyes were not open. The " diamond " on the beak, as in other young birds, used for making the hole in the egg, was very conspicuous.

P.S. 6th April, 1852.—Mr. H. F. W***** has this day, for the second time, made me a *bona fide* offer of twenty pounds for this pair of eggs.

§ 27. *One*, with the half of another.—Sutherlandshire, 4 May, 1849. " J. W. *ipse*."

O. W. tab. iv. fig. 1.

On 1st May, 1849, I looked in vain for an Eagle's nest, though the birds were said to be daily seen about. I caused huge stones to be pitched down every hundred yards or so. In past years a pair had built in at least four different spots about. A man had climbed to three of the places this year and found none in use. He gave one egg to a gentleman, probably the late Mr. Charles St. John, when he called at his house[1]. The rocks are wooded like the range of the High Tor in Derbyshire. Next day, after harrying a White-

---

[1] [The following year Mr. Wolley heard that this nest, for which he had sought so much, had been found, a few days after he left the ground, with a young bird, which the finder killed in the nest, shooting the hen Eagle also!—ED.]

tailed Eagle's nest, we proceeded to visit a noted breeding-place of the Golden Eagle. Here the young ones were destroyed last year by the shepherd's fox-hunting party; but no one had succeeded in climbing into the nest. As we approached, we saw no cock bird to encourage us; but several Eagle's feathers were lying about. I saw a nest which was only twenty or thirty feet from a point easily accessible. Having reached it, I threw stones; but no bird appeared. I climbed up with considerable difficulty into the nest round an angle of the rock, where I could hardly worm my way, and then only by digging my fingers into the matted rhizomes of *Polypodium vulgare*, without which I must have fallen over. In the nest, which appeared to be that of last year, I found a foot of a Red Deer fawn. Resting on my hands and knees, I felt, as I thought, a lot of flies crawling on my hands. On closer inspection I saw they were fleas, and my arms and legs were swarming with them. I beat a retreat; but the point that was before so difficult was far worse in going back. I lay down, my feet first, and got round safe, though the rock pushed me out so much that the weight of a bullet would have overbalanced me. One of my men standing on a ledge below helped me down the last part. Then for the fleas! With the help of flint and steel a fire was made with moss and heather, and I stripped to the skin. Luckily the day was as hot as could be, and it was very pleasant with a plaid coat over my shoulders. I afforded much merriment to my men and to myself, telling them I was in the dress of the Highlanders before the kilt was invented. After an hour or two's hard picking and smoking, the clothes were handed over to me, one by one, as I sat at some distance, and I extracted a few score more, but still put many around me*.

This nest was in a situation similar to the others—a platform in a corner, with rock overhanging; but I was too much frightened at the fleas to make the leisurely examination I had intended. I saw a curious rock-plant, that I did not observe elsewhere, in two places here; it had a large pink flower.

Having cautiously extinguished the fire, we made for the corrie, where the Eagle was said always to build. We presently saw one sailing from round the far corner; but he took to circling, and appeared to be hunting, as he gradually went out of sight. We telescoped the rock

* Lady Franklin afterwards told me of a notorious nest of fleas in a bell-tower, I think, at Constantinople, into which she went in spite of warning. I have heard of a similar swarm having been met with amongst the shavings in a new house at Rome; and an adventure of my own among the loose leaves under the fig-tree at Tangier is a fourth instance.

in vain. The men were sent to the top to pitch stones down; and a fearful sight it was to see the huge masses bounding and whizzing through the air. My dog " Jock " and I then went under the rock to look for traces, and in one place we saw bones and sticks as if from the nest; but on looking up I could not see it, though I thought it must have been there. We saw Deer, one of which stood at not more than fifty yards. I went on as far as a second loch, round the corner from which two Ravens came to meet me. On firing a shot a female Peregrine left her nest, the male having appeared before. We saw more Deer and a Ptarmigan. Then there was a huge fall of rock, and an alarm of a stone overhead. On returning past the corrie we saw an Eagle again, but after one turn along the face of the rocks it sailed away. We left the ropes in the corrie, so as to make a further search the next morning, and got home about ten to an excellent supper and a noble peat-fire at the lodge. The following day the forester went with us to the corrie; I observed that our guide kept us a long way from the rocks, and he suggested that our ropes should be left on the other side of the valley, where we were to pass the next day. With the aid of a glass he pointed out the sites of two old nests. On the morrow (4th May), we started. The heat was tremendous. The men made straight for the ropes, while I kept to the left and more sheltered side of the valley, intending to re-examine the Eagle-rocks in this corrie. I fired a shot, when an Eagle showed high overhead. I called to the men across the valley; and when they, poor fellows, arrived, we went back to the old place where the two nests had been seen. Climbing up to the right of the nest as I faced the rock, I saw that it was new; but to my vexation I heard the same little squeaks from the egg as on a former occasion (§ 26), showing that the young were hatched. I could not see into the nest; and it not appearing easy of access from that quarter, I went to the other side, where, after throwing down two or three loose bits so as to make a footing round a narrow corner, all was plain sailing.

"The nest is five or six feet across by three or four broad from the angle. The cup or hollow of the nest is a foot from the angle. Foundation made of sticks, of which the largest may be one inch in diameter: top made of heather, of which some is green. Lined with *Luzula*, fern, grass, and moss, chiefly the former: rhizome of it is rather like palmetto. The same stuff is growing all over the shelf, which may be, including the slope to the tree (which is five or six feet below the nest), about nine feet square, or, rather, lozenge-shaped. A shelf at the height of ten feet overhangs to the tree by the plumb. In the nest is a white egg, with half the shell of another (which last is highly coloured) round it, and two young birds in the same state mine was when it died (*i.e.* the one mentioned in § 26): the eyes have a dull watery look: one generally with eyes closed. They peck feebly at my fingers. I read the above to G * * *, who is with me in the nest. He assents to it all: 'it could not be correcter.' The platform of the nest itself (*i.e.* of the top part) is about the width of the cup every way, except towards the rock, where it is rather less; about two feet high outside; the lining may be nine inches in perpendicular depth. The nest is, according to various computations, from fourteen to sixteen feet from the slope of the hill below. The old birds never show whilst we are at the nest. I blow the egg in the nest. It is addled; a sort of sour smell; all liquid inside, and no appearance of chick. I pack the broken shell by placing it on the sound one as I found it in the nest. I do not wash, or, at least, rub, the addled egg, which is a little soiled, but with one or two specks of true colour."

This egg is very like one Mr. Hancock has, as he himself remarked. The two young ones, covered with white down, had large livid feet, with soft, oddly-shaped claws; their legs are downy to the very division of the toes, proving them to be Golden Eagles. They cost me a great deal of trouble, even in the middle of the night following, when I got up occasionally to keep up the peat-fire. They ate Golden Plover that night—the first time, probably, they had tasted anything. The next day they were so nearly dead of cold, that I had to make a fire for them on the moors. They throve and grew till an unlucky journey, during which I either overfed them or they were shaken too much: they became ill, and died, after a lingering illness, between the 20th and 30th of May. They were then much grown, but with nothing on but white down. I preserved parts in spirit.

§ 28. *One.*—Argyllshire, 24 April, 1851. "J. W. *ipse.*"

O. W. tab. iv. fig. 2.

On the morning of 24th April, Mr. Edge and I started, having a horse with the ropes round his neck, and a young man to take care of him. We picked up three other men as we went along. This was about seven or eight miles from our inn; and we left the horse and young man. We walked on a mile or two under a hot sun, till we turned into a corrie on the right. Here we saw an Eagle taking a long swooping flight directly down into a hollow out of sight, without moving its wings, which were brought to a point. Presently we crossed over the entrance of this den, and proceeded silently up the other side. When we got a little beyond where the nest was, we looked over, and there lay the hen Eagle on the nest. We watched her for an instant or two as she sat, with the axis of her body parallel with that of the den, her head towards us—that is, towards the closed end of the den. She stretched her neck a little on one side, saw us, and slowly flew off, sailing or flapping smoothly across the hollow, till at some distance she turned a corner, and, though we kept a good look-out, we did not see her again. We were about twenty yards from her when she was on her nest, and I had time to look at her copper-coloured head and neck, her hazel eye and yellow cere, &c., before she moved; and when she was on the wing, I had a good sight of her spread marbled tail. A fine object she was! On looking at the nest we were disappointed to see only a single egg in it, which did not look a very good one. The rope being tied round me, and a trusty man being next the rock, I descended quite easily by three stages or platforms into the nest, which might be twelve yards from the top, or even less. On one of these was an old nest. All the flats were covered with *Luzula*. The nest was made principally of heather; but there were in it some branches of birch, newly gathered from the tree, apparently within a day or two. The lining was almost entirely leaves of *Luzula*. The hollow, which was well formed, might be two spans in width, and was about one span from the rock, which did not overhang much. In front of the nest was a small Rowan-tree, growing at the edge of the platform. Some time later in the day I climbed almost into the nest from my right hand below, and from my left hand I climbed to the platform above the nest, thus ascertaining that in two directions it might be reached without ropes. I went to the place from which the forester who was with me shot an Eagle some time ago, and last year shot another, which I saw stuffed at his house, from the same spot, getting so close to it that he could have touched it with the muzzle of his gun. He then saw the whole of its body except the head, and sent some one round to clap his hands and frighten it off; but it did not go until after several such noises were made, and it fell some way on the other side of the burn. On another occasion, when a bird was shot at and missed from the same spot, it darted confusedly into the depths below. It was in a wonderfully easy place, six feet from the level at the top of the rock—so easy, that there is almost a highway into it from the left above, and from the right a drop of less than a fathom. It was on a ledge, say four or five feet wide, and flat. I went in at the left and came out at the right. There were two birch-trees and a rowan about it—one of the birches in front of the platform. The nest was of the usual construction, principally heather, untouched this year. Another nest, between this and the inhabited one, was very easy to climb into. I went quite into it, and found a couple of young raspberries growing a foot or two high out of the middle of the old heather-stalks; it could not have been used for several years. The rock behind it was overplumb to a considerable height, and the nest was placed in an angle. All the nests were on the side of the den facing the east, which happened to be the steepest.

The one egg was pinkish in colour and slightly soiled. On blowing it the same evening, we found that it was addled, though so little stale that it could not have been laid a very long time. It floated in water with a small part above the surface. In attempting to account for its condition we were much puzzled. It had been seen nearly a week before; and several days before that, it was not laid.

§ 29. *One.*—Scottish Highlands, 1849.   From Mr. L. Dunbar's Collection.

This finely-marked egg was taken by a shepherd, and came into my possession 4th May, 1851, in its present mutilated state.

10th February, 1856.   I have this day finished mending the above-mentioned egg, strengthening it with many strips of strong yet thin paper secured by the best gum-arabic; also with a brace made of a Hooper's-pen quill laid across inside. It had previously been very rudely mended with poor paper laid on apparently with paste, for insects had eaten it.

> [This egg, in its present condition, is a model of Mr. Wolley's care and skill in treating a valuable specimen. About two-thirds of it remain; but as this includes a complete "show surface," it has every appearance of being quite perfect as it lies in the drawer.]

§ 30. *Two.*—Sutherlandshire, 17 April, 1852.

O. W. tab. ii. fig. 3.

These two beautiful eggs reached me in London on the day on which, three years before, I took the exquisite pair [§ 26] since figured by Mr. Hewitson. They were packed with wool and oat-chaff in a small box with lid and bottom too thin; so that one of them got cracked on its journey. The insides were quite moist when I examined them, as though the eggs were just blown. They were very clean both inside and out; and I had particularly desired my correspondent not to wash them outside. The cracked one, in the process of mending, I have been obliged to touch a little with water. I found the colour (which was slightly "smudged") comes off very easily. The other egg

I have very lightly touched in one or two places where it was soiled with handling. The eggs and the wool in which they were packed have the peat-smoke smell of the inside of a Highland cottage, with its happy recollections : through this smell I fancied I could perceive the scent of the Eagle's nest.

The following particulars, many of which are of considerable interest, were received subsequently from my correspondent :—"3 May, 1852. * * I got the eggs the third day before the date of my [former] letter, being April 17th. They were quite fresh. I should think they had only been sat upon three or four days. The nest was on the side facing the water, being, I suppose, the north-north-east, in a rather rugged rock. I could get within three yards of it without a rope, and I think, if I were ever trying it again, I would go without any rope at all. The rock is about fifteen or twenty fathoms in height, and nearly two-thirds of it under the nest [*i. e.* the nest was thirty or forty feet from the top.—J. W.]. There is no overhanging in the rock. The nest was very large, with some sticks as thick as my arm, lined with heather and wool, with no tree in front. The Eagles have been known to build there for a number of years back in the same spot, and harried almost every year. The first day I tried it I did not see the bird on the nest; nor did I know she was there, till she flew over my head, as large as life. On my return the second day, I could not see her head. I shouted, but she would not rise until I threw a stone. I made an attempt to get the eggs; but as there was no one with me, I had not nerve enough to push on. Then on the third day I started with a young friend with gun and ropes. I shot the Eagle, and then got the eggs by his holding the rope. I could not see the bird from the bottom of the rock, and the head only could be seen from the top. I shot her from below; she flew out of the nest rather hurriedly. She only gave one scream when she felt the smart of the shot, flew about a hundred yards, and fell quite dead. I did not see the cock bird the last day. I did not see any Hares near the nest, nor are there any Ptarmigan on the hill. There was a Raven's nest quite close by . the Eagle's. I did not hear of any Fox being on the ground. You regret, I have no doubt, that I shot the Eagle; but there will be a nest there next season. I never knew (nor did I hear) of an Eagle wanting a mate above a month at furthest."

§ 31. *Two.*—Argyllshire, 20 April, 1852.

O. W. tab. F.

These two very fine eggs reached me at Paddington, 11th June, 1852. The spotted one is of extraordinary size. It has perhaps lost some of its colouring-matter on the side on which it is blown, from the wiping which would be necessary during and after that operation. I have not touched it with water since it arrived. In giving my correspondent a drill last year, I had told him to take care not to wash the eggs. The white one appeared not to have been cleansed at all, as there was a good deal of dirt upon it, which I thought it desirable to remove. I did so with pure water and a cambric handkerchief, touching it very lightly. After this washing, it shows, I think, traces of fine spots and lines, especially towards the larger end. It was not at all stained or deeply grained with dirt, all this being superficial. Comparing it with five other white Eagle's eggs now before me, I cannot hesitate to attribute some faint yellow specks to true marking ; and this is rendered more evident by comparing it with its fellow, the very first stage of whose thick sprinkling the white egg may well be taken to represent. The coloured egg, which strongly reminds one of eggs of the Gyrfalcon, is not unlike one in Mr. Henry Walter's cabinet ; it also belongs to the same class of eggs as the one Mr. Falconer has, laid in confinement, and the fragments which I obtained with a white one last year (1851) [§ 32]. My correspondent's letters of 9th and 22nd June contain the following particulars about these eggs :—"I took the Golden Eagle's eggs from a rock on the 20th April." "The bird flew off, the same as the one at the corrie last year did [§ 28], but a little quicker, and afterwards came round once above our heads, and then we lost sight of her. I could have shot her flying off the nest, but this I did not intend to do. I saw her sitting on her nest from the south side of the rock. I sent one of my men down on the rope from above to the nest, which was from twenty to thirty feet from where we hold the rope ; and down from the nest to the bottom of the rock is about a hundred and fifty yards. The nest was made of different kinds of small sticks and that broad grass you have seen [*Luzula sylvatica*]. There was no game in the nest, but there were some pieces of Hares and some feathers scattered about the top of the rock. The birds were formed in the eggs, but the bones were not thicker than pins."

On 10th April, 1851, the site of this nest, among several others, was pointed out to me. It was on a very high rock ; but my informant said that a man could climb from above so near it as to push the young ones out with a long pole, as he himself had seen done. He had also let a man down with a rope. There was a nest there fifteen years in succession, but not for the last two years, though, on looking with his glass, he said there were fresh sticks, as he could see the green branches, altogether a cart-load, and, at the distance we were, the mass through a glass looked very great. It was necessary to go a long way up the valley before we got to a spot sufficiently near to enable us to distinguish it well. There were no eggs in it then, as a forester reported to us after an examination he had been directed to make[1].

§ 32. *One*, with fragments of another.—Argyllshire, 23 April, 1851. "J. W. *ipse.*"

Mr. Edge and I left our quarters with our guide in a light cart, provided with ropes, &c. Opposite a certain corrie we met the forester, who had no good news for us, as the Eagle had deserted her nest [§ 31] in the rock at the end of it. He went on with us some way further, when we sent him forward to fetch the head forester, on whose ground was the other nest we intended to visit. We also sent our cart back with the driver, and walked on with our guide directly towards the point which had been shown to him as the locality for the principal object of our search. After crossing the river with some difficulty, we reached a spot opposite to the nest, and rested there. The place looked like a small pigeon-hole, in the face of the barest and boldest mountain in this part of the country. On the south side of it, at the entrance of the glen, our guide pointed out another spot, apparently inaccessible, which had been shown to him as a locality for the same pair of Eagles. Presently a whistle announced the arrival of the other party, and we observed with our glasses an Eagle fly into the hole, and soon leave it again. This gave rise to much speculation as to whether it was the cock or the hen. We now began to ascend; and after a long climb up the mountain, over very broken ground, we began to get into the region of the nest. We climbed over a very rough rock or mass of rocks beneath the nest, and then came upon a huge crack in the rock, down which we rolled stones, making a great noise. Still ascending, we were perhaps a hundred yards below the nest when the Eagle left it, flapping slowly, the ends of her wings curling up at each stroke, till she was round a corner to the west, and we never saw her again; but before this we had seen the cock bird high overhead. Then we went down a ravine in which there was a great drift of snow, and up the opposite side, where there was some rather ticklish climbing, till we recrossed on very slippery snow, and reached a succession of ledges or a little track on a level with the nest. For

[1] [During the past summer (1862) Mr. Wolf visited this nest, which then contained two young ones; and I am indebted to him for the beautiful plate (tab. F.) representing it, which has been executed from his sketch by Mr. Jury.—ED.]

some time past we had been finding the remains of Grouse and Mountain Hares; and the head forester was afraid there were young. Great consequently was the interest at this point. We hurried round the corner, and my first exclamation was, "Two or three eggs, at all events!" but another glance showed that there was only one white egg, and a young one hatched within a day or two, lying on its back chirping. The dogs (a Colley and a Terrier) had followed us into the nest and required restraining, as we were all of us at the side of the nest. The nest was in a little sort of cave in the face of the rock, which is ten or twelve feet wide, five or six feet high, and eight or ten feet deep, forming an admirable shelter; but there was a good deal of dripping at the back part, which is overgrown with Ferns (*Lastræa dilatata*), *Marchantiæ*, and Golden Saxifrage. The wet, however, does not fall on the inhabited part of the nest. The depression was slight, lined with a very little *Luzula*, but more of *Carex*-tufts, and the lining was altogether of a good depth. The rest of the nest was made principally of heather, about the usual size, few sticks or none. *Luzula sylvatica* was growing in plenty near it, and principally in a long band for a great distance below the nest, which, our guide said, was usual with Eagles' nests, in consequence of the great quantity of animal matter coming from them; and here, at all events, the water which drips from the cavity must assist to wash it down. Our guide pointed out the same thing at the other station on the same mountain. Half a Hare was in the nest when we went into it; and the men said it would be left to rot there. On taking up the egg, I heard the young one cheeping inside it. I carried it home wrapped in tow in a botanical box; and on warming it some hours after, it again began to make a noise. I carefully cut a hole in the egg, and with some difficulty extracted the bird, slightly cracking the shell in doing so. There was a good deal still to go into the navel, which was open as wide as a sixpence. I poulticed it with a piece of the membrane, and wrapped the bird up in a bit of wet calico, put in a cup covered with a saucer. I took it to bed with me; and it was all the following day kept before a good fire, where it still cheeped vigorously. The egg I mended with paste.

Before quitting the nest we all drank to the health of the young Eagle we were to leave in it. Mr. Edge and I enjoyed the prospect, our guide observing what a splendid picture we should make for Landseer! There was a most extensive view over what looked like a great plain eastward. The rocks in the neighbourhood were most grandly broken up, like those at the back of Quenaig; and it is, of all the situations I ever saw, most worthy of an Eagle. Our guide said they were very rarely met so high up a mountain. Above us, at a little distance, was snow and mist, and a heavy shower was falling, with the sun breaking through it here and there, and shining brightly on the other side of the valley. Below us the precipice seemed far greater than it really is, as the hill is very steep. It had probably not been visited for five or six years.

I picked out of the nest the fragments of the shell which had contained the bird we found already hatched, and have since gummed them upon a tame Goose's egg. They thus show the character of marking that the Eagle's egg of which they had formerly formed part had borne.

On 26th April I re-hatched the young Eagle, whose navel had been gradually contracting as the yelk receded, some urate of ammonia being duly discharged through the opening. The down soon expanded by judicious picking and pulling, each piece being enclosed in a pellicle, which required bursting or slipping off. About noon he opened his mouth and showed symptoms of hunger. Having procured two little birds, I minced up some of the breast with the liver and gave it to him, whereupon he not only readily swallowed it, but pecked at my blood-stained finger, his eyes being occasionally open. He was by this time covered most naturally with the purest white down. Soon after, we started for a long journey, and encountered several severe storms of hail and snow; but as I had him in Lord Derby's little basket[1] in a box packed with wool and hemp, along with two pint bottles which I replenished with hot water at every stage, he did not suffer. He was in bed that night, and the following day lay in a hand-basket before the fire on a piece of flannel; for he is apt to swallow bits of cotton or hemp. However he died on the 28th, and I sent him soaked in spirits to Mr. John Hancock. The characters of the tarsi showed him to be the Golden Eagle.

§ 33. *Three.*—Argyllshire, 23 April, 1852.

These eggs, taken from the same nest and on the same day as those last year by myself, were sent to me by my guide on that occasion, who says that they were taken by the forester who then accompanied me. My correspondent did not receive them till some time afterwards, but they were then not blown. There was a bird in each, of good size, and he broke one in taking out its contents. When they arrived, there were sticking to the pieces of this one tufts

---

[1] [This seems to have been the basket in which Mr. Wolley brought away from Knowsley the Griffon Vulture's egg before mentioned (§ 17), and which had also been of service on another occasion.—Ed.]

of the very characteristic down of young Eagles, which I have preserved. It was in a great many pieces; but I determined to try to
put them together, and I succeeded far beyond my expectations. I
commenced operations by taking the skin off the inside of the pieces
as I fitted them together, and then I fixed on them strips of foreign
letter-paper with very strong gum-arabic. When I had, after three
or four days' work, gathered them into as many large groups, I had
great difficulty in joining them together evenly, but at last succeeded
by relaxing one or two of the paper bands and squeezing one of the
pieces in the direction contrary to that in which it had warped, and
then holding them together until the gum on the last slips was
partly dried.

§ 34. *Three.*—Argyllshire, 1853.

These eggs, two of them being unblown, were received for me during
my absence in Lapland by Mr. Edge, who succeeded in satisfactorily
emptying the full ones. They are from the same nest as those I
took 23 April, 1851, as I am assured in a letter from my guide at
that time.

§ 35. *Three.*—Argyllshire, 10 April, 1854.

These eggs were sent, blown, to Mr. Edge, with a letter, dated
"29 April, 1854," containing the following passages:—"You will
receive three eggs of the Golden Eagle, which were taken on the 10th
of this month. I need not say anything about the place where they
were taken, as you and Mr. Wolley were in the nest when you were
here. I am sorry to say there is not, to my knowledge, an Eagle's
nest within the bounds of my forest this year, as I have searched all
the old places where they used to build. As I told you before, in a
few years there will not be such a thing as a Golden Eagle seen in
Scotland."

[§ 36. *Three.*—Argyllshire, 18 April, 1855. " E. N. *ipse.*"

O. W. tab. iii. fig. 2.

These eggs, from the same eyrie as those mentioned in the four preceding
sections, were taken by Mr. Edward Newton, to whom Mr. Wolley had given
the introductions necessary for enjoying the pleasure, now so rarely within
the power of an Englishman, of taking, with his own hands, in this island a
nest of the Golden Eagle. The following is condensed from the account which
Mr. E. Newton gives of his exploit:—

"On the evening of April 17th I arrived at the little inn, and of course my
first inquiries were for my guide. I was told he had been there that afternoon,
and had left word that he had gone to the hill, and would return a little later.

Meantime I strolled out by the side of the loch, and watched with interest
some fine Black Cocks, birds I had never before seen alive, sunning themselves
on the topmost branches of the old dead Scotch-fir trees. On my guide's
making his appearance, he was very frank, and said how glad he was to
welcome me as one of Mr. Wolley's friends. But it was some time before he
came to the subject of my visit, and then it was only approached cautiously.
' Yes, there were Eagles left, certainly, both Golden and White-tailed, but
in nothing like the numbers of old. He indeed had been their principal
destroyer in those parts; but he no longer intended to be so. In fact, he
had received orders to the contrary; for the proprietor liked to see them
flying, when he came with his friends from the south, though he was desired to take care that the farmers should not have good ground to com-
plain of their number.' My guide had once caught ten or a dozen in as
many days, keeping them alive as a show; and since then it was that their
utter destruction had been forbidden. They were mostly young Golden Eagles,
' Ringtails;' but I think he said there were White-tailed ones among them.
He was not certain, but he thought there was a nest he could show me,
though no one had been near the place for fear of making the birds forsake,
which they would do if they happened to see a man off the road and near the
place; that is, of course, when they were building, for when they had begun
to sit they were not so easily disturbed. There was, besides, another nest,
which he thought I could get. It was in an adjoining forest; but it could be
done without much trouble. To this we settled to go the next morning, and
I accordingly joined my guide at an early hour; and after a walk of about ten
miles, we reached the entrance of a glen celebrated in history. On the road
he showed me the mountain to the left, on which he had found Greenshanks'
eggs, a long way from any water, except perhaps a few springs, such as
are to be found almost everywhere in the neighbourhood. On our right front
·was a loch, the breeding-place of a pair of White-tailed Eagles; but the year
before a shepherd had trapped one of them, and it was doubtful whether the
survivor would find a mate and return again. Black-throated Divers also bred
there, and my guide generally got an egg or two when he was not forestalled
by the ' Huddies.' Here, too, I had my first glimpse of really wild Red Deer,
as a herd was feeding on the ridge to our left, and every now and then one
could be seen standing out clear against the sky. To my companion's more
accustomed eye many were also plain, feeding on the hill-side. They must
have been at least three-quarters of a mile from us. On gaining the entrance
of the glen, where a bare and lofty mountain was in full view, my guide
pointed out to me the site of the nest. It looked like a black spot on the face
of what seemed a perpendicular cliff, halfway up the mountain. The snow in
the gorges extended far below, so that we should have to pass over it before
reaching the nest. A short way further we arrived at the forester's lodge, to
find its occupant gone away for the day. However, his son soon came home;
and after a short conversation in Gaelic between him and my guide, the latter
informed me it was all right, and at about half-past twelve we commenced the
ascent. It was a beautiful day, and the mountain was quite clear of mist.
The snow in the gorges made the climbing somewhat more difficult, as the frost
was not out of the ground. We passed first quite under the nest to the westward, and then began to ascend. We kept to the left of a small corrie, stopping
every now and then to rest, and gaze up at the object of our ambition. When

we had arrived nearly at a level with the nest, and about two hundred yards from it, my guide, with his telescope, spied the old bird's head as she was sitting on her eggs; but as she saw us she drew it in, and he had not time to hand me the glass before the forester gave a shout, and out sailed the first wild Golden Eagle I ever saw. She was almost immediately lost to view by flying round to the eastward. We remained quite still, and in about five minutes she appeared again, high over the top of the mountain. My guide at first thought this bird was the male, but afterwards felt certain it was the same as had flown from the nest; and this, both my companions agreed, was the hen. She made one or two circles, much after the manner of a Rough-legged Buzzard, and then, closing her wings, descended to within two hundred feet of the nest, when, catching a glimpse of us, she soared away again to the east-ward. We then proceeded onwards, crossing the gorge or ravine, where we sank almost up to the middle in the snow with which it was filled. Coming out on the other side, our path was only a narrow ledge of perhaps eighteen inches wide along the face of the rock, a steep cliff of a hundred feet or so. The forester was first, I was second, and my guide last. This narrow ledge led quite into the little cave where was situated the nest, which, as we rounded a corner of the rock, opened to view. There were three eggs, one spotted and splashed with light red, and in look much like some eggs of a Spoonbill, another was suffused over the small end with reddish brown, and the third was nearly white. The cave was about five feet high, perhaps the same in depth, and six or eight feet wide. The nest occupied the whole of it, and, being some eighteen inches or two feet thick, obliged us to crawl in. Once in, however, we could all three sit upright, side by side, with our heels hanging over the precipice. The nest appeared to have been of late well repaired with fresh heather-stalks, small Scotch-fir boughs, and thick stems of coarse grass, with pieces of wool, possibly picked up by accident while sticking to the heather. Inside it was lined with grass and a little moss, with a sprig of myrtle and one of juniper. It was very flat, the hollow not more three inches deep, and about a foot in diameter. There were a few of the old bird's feathers lying about, which, together with the lining, I brought away. The three eggs were placed in a peculiar figure; if I remember right, like this ꞉꞉, with their small ends all pointing towards the entrance. On the roof of the cave were a few small ferns. The first thing we did was to drink to Mr. Wolley's safe return from Lapland, and the health of the Eagles, and then to smoke our pipes. When we had been there a quarter of an hour or so, an Eagle, which my guide de-clared was the male, came again in sight, soaring at a great height above us, and was soon lost in the mist, after which we saw no more of either of the birds. The view at first was very fine. We waited about a quarter of an hour longer, when, a mist coming over the top of the mountain, my guide thought it prudent to begin our descent; and before we were halfway down the nest was hidden in the clouds. But as we were coming down he called out, 'Aye, but there's a mon looking down at us!' I glanced upwards, and there was the appearance of an enormous human figure in a Highland bonnet stooping and looking over the precipice. I saw the joke at once, and laughed, whereupon he was pleased to remark, 'Aye, but you're no' to be cheated. Mind, Donald, ye ca' that "Newton's stane."' We reached home about nine o'clock; and I attempted to blow the eggs that night, but found them so hard sat on that I papered them up, and left them till I got to Elveden."]

§ 37. *Three.*—Argyllshire, 16 April, 1856.

[These eggs were received and blown by me for Mr. Wolley in May 1856, the sender being the person to whom the acquisition of the eggs in the last five sections is mainly due; but, though no doubt the produce of the same hen bird as those, they are not from the same nest, but from one in the immediate district—a corrie north of the corrie visited by Mr. Wolley in 1851 (§ 28). They were taken 16th April, 1856. The sender says he is sure they were laid by the same bird as those in the preceding five sections; and I entirely coincide in his opinion, judging only from their number and appearance.]

[§ 38. *Two.*—Argyllshire, 16 April, 1859.

These eggs are from the identical nest visited by Mr. Wolley and my brother, as before mentioned in these pages (§§ 32–36), and were sent me in 1860 by the person who acted as guide to them on those occasions. There were no eggs in this nest in 1856 or 1857, though in the former year it is believed the hen-bird bred in another spot (§ 37); and it was supposed she had since died or been killed. These eggs, being nearly colourless and of a very different shape to those which have formerly come from this eyrie, I had accordingly thought were the produce of another bird; but my own experience the year after (1861) has changed my opinion, as will be seen in the next section. The eggs have probably lost colour by having been left unblown more than a year in a damp outhouse.]

[§ 39. *Two.*—Argyllshire, 22 April, 1861.　"A. N. *ipse.*"

These two eggs were taken by myself on the above-mentioned day, from the nest which has already supplied so many specimens. I started betimes in the morning, with the same trusty companions who had before guided Mr. Wolley and my brother to the spot. Just as we got in sight of the hill it came on to rain pretty heavily, and continued doing so most part of the day. As the clouds were low, the view was quite destroyed, and I was unable to bring away any distinct recollection of the scenery. When we came to the foot of the ascent we stopped some time, hoping the mist would clear. This it only partially did; but the precise situation of the nest was sufficiently well shown to me. After waiting half an hour or so, we began the climb, and I got nearly up to the first bare rocks before I had to stop for my second wind. Then we went on again, finding the snow very soft, and consequently not slippery and dangerous as it was when Mr. Wolley was there, within a day of ten years prior to my visit; but my heart was in my mouth when I saw the forester looking straight down at a human spoor he could not recognize, for he had just been clapping his hands and shouting to put the bird off, without succeeding. I was dreadfully afraid some one had been beforehand with me, but just as we were preparing for the nasty place, he exclaimed "The Eagle!" and there she was, sailing round to the eastward, and soon out of sight. This set at rest my fears of having been forestalled; and now only the original risk of the eggs being already hatched remained. We had made one or two short halts before we came to the ticklish place, where we had to go sideways on a narrow ledge round the rocks. With my companion's assistance I accomplished it very well, and then all the rest was easy. As we wound round the last corner along the ledge on which the nest is built, the leading guide, to my great joy, called out that the two eggs were all right. I followed him, and was the first to handle them. Crouching on the nest, I kept very still, for the height seemed dizzy enough, until I had packed up the eggs, which exhibited the Spoonbill-like character of yore (one of them hardly marked at all), clearly showing that the original hen bird had not, as we had supposed before, met her death a few years ago. I took out the lining of the nest, and then began to look about me. After my brother's account, and Mr. Wolley's accurate description, I almost felt disappointed at the want of novelty. It seemed as if I had been there twenty times before, as indeed in imagination I had. The only material difference I could remark was that the latter had been able to sit upright in the nest, which I did not find possible. This of course was owing to the nest having had so much added to it during the last ten years; and it is said now to project much more than formerly, which I can well believe. Close on my left hand, as I lay, was some hares' flock, the only remains of prey about the place. The lining of the nest—which I have since given to Mr. J. Hancock—was much as that which my brother brought back in 1855. There was one very " pine-apple " looking tuft of *Luzula sylvatica*. The spring at the back of the nest was hardly dripping—not enough to qualify the whisky with, and the forester had to get some water from the nearest snow-drift. A small tuft of a bright-green plant, which I plucked from the rock at the back of the nest, has been identified for me by Mr. A. G. More as *Chrysosplenium oppositifolium*. Mr. Wolley's description had mentioned golden saxifrage as growing near by. We ate our biscuits, and drank one another's healths, my companions not forgetting that of Mr. Edge or of my brother, with whom they had in like manner sat there, nor I omitting the old Eagle's, to whom I was so much indebted. We had an indifferent view over the moors to the eastward; and just opposite, the clouds quite hid the top of the hill; some of them came below us. After enjoying ourselves for as long as we had time, we came out and began to descend. The forester tried to make out on the snow the spoor we had seen in climbing up, but he was unable to do so. It was fresh, or at least within a day or two. It had evidently not been to the nest, though not far off. He was annoyed at not discovering whose it was, and did not like it being supposed, as my guide thought, that it was his son's; was sure his own " laddie" would do no such a thing as run the risk of disturbing the bird which he knew his father wanted to have left alone. He pointed out a nasty place close by, where a year or two before a Deer had fallen, and had to be taken out. It was in a cleft of a rock; and the feat seemed almost impossible. He only succeeded after a long time, and then by cutting it up where it lay. The descent was worse to me than the getting up, but, with two such careful fellows, I knew the risk of harm was small. Still it was comforting to feel a firm clutch every now and then, and always just at the right moment. We reached the bottom without a single slip. Arrived there, we saw the Eagle again soaring over the hill, and again disappearing in the mist to the eastward. We had seen nothing of her while in the nest, though the man who was holding the pony for me below said she once came within a hundred yards of us; if so, it must must have been above our heads. Here bidding the forester good bye, I trotted off to bait the pony, before rejoining my guide on the road to another nest.]

D

§ 40. *Two.*—Argyllshire, 1853.

O. W. tab. G.

These eggs, already blown, were received and taken care of for me
by Mr. Edge in the summer of 1853. It appears that they are from
a nest in a glen visited by me 15th April, 1851, and in which there were
no eggs that year, though a man on that very day had seen a bird
about the rock. The nest was not directly visible from above; nor
indeed from any place could we see entirely into it. I descended by
a rope, and, looking down a few feet above it, was able to see the whole
of it. It was quite fresh, made of large branches of the Scotch Fir,
as green as if growing, with some heather beneath, and lined with
Luzula. It was a large mass of sticks, and projected from the rock
more than any nest I had previously seen,—there being very little
ledge overhanging it, though there was a projecting sloping ledge
partially covering it towards one side [1].

§ 41. *Two.*—Argyllshire, 19 April, 1855.   " E. N."

O. W. tab. iii. fig. 1.

These eggs were taken on the day above mentioned, in the presence of Mr. Edward Newton, whose account of the nest is as
follows :—

"The next morning we were to visit the second nest of which my
guide to the previous one had spoken [§ 36]. Accordingly about ten
o'clock I went up to his house. He proposed showing me a Deer-hunt,
as he wanted to 'blood' some young hounds, and took with him three
couple. On the way nothing particular occurred. We stopped every
now and then to look round the hills for any Deer that might be near
enough or in an advantageous place, but we saw none. Presently
rounding a corner, some six miles from home, we saw an Eagle about a
mile off, flying low over a hill. Just under that hill my companion
told me the nest was, and soon after he pointed out its position to me.
It was on the side of a small steep ravine, perhaps some sixty yards
wide by twenty deep. This ravine we crossed perhaps a quarter of a
mile below the nest. As we did so, the old bird flew out; she went
down the glen past us, and then soared high away to the westward.

[1] [In July 1862, Mr. Wolf visited a Golden Eagle's nest, which was situated
very near the place of that above mentioned, and was probably used by the same
pair of birds. It then contained one young one; and I have again to acknowledge
his kindness in allowing Mr. Jury to copy the drawing which he made of it
(tab. G).—ED.]

She came within sight twice afterwards, though at a great height. I had a good look at her through my guide's glass; she appeared to me to be a larger bird than the one whose nest I had taken the day before [§ 36], and my companion said so also. A few minutes more brought us just above the nest. It was built in the same place as when Mr. Wolley, in 1851, saw it, situated about fifteen or twenty feet from the top, and, on my reaching over, was, with the two eggs, plainly visible. It was now about three o'clock. I did not go down into the nest myself, but was contented with seeing a man do so; for as the eggs were not to be for our own collection, I did not feel very keen about it, though there was no danger, and the man who was lowered was up again in five minutes. He brought back, with the eggs, as much of the lining of the nest as he could cram into the basket. One of the eggs is white, the other—the finest, I think, I have ever seen—blotched and spotted all over with two shades of lilac and reddish brown. Both are larger and rounder than my former captures. At the top, just above the nest, I found one old casting, apparently of hares' fur and bones; and about fifty yards off, some large white splashes on a high block of granite. No feathers either of the bird itself or its quarry. This is the nest that Mr. Wolley had so often wished to be photographed with the bird upon it; and indeed the operation would not be difficult, as the distance across the ravine could not be more than fifty yards or so. It was somewhat like a crack or rent, and had, so to speak, perpendicular sides, though of course in many places small landslips had occurred, which caused ledges. On one of these the nest was. At the bottom were a few trees, Birch and old Scotch Fir. The hill down which the ravine ran was a gentle slope, covered with short white lichens. My guide told me that he once shot an Eagle from this nest; and on another occasion some one else missed one; but who, I do not remember. On our return home, we came in sight of seven or eight Stags, which were feeding near the bridle-path. The dogs were slipped, and we had a very good chase. They singled out one wretched beast, and had the speed of him all the way; however, though they made several attempts to catch hold of him, it was not until he reached a small burn at the bottom of the valley that he turned to bay, and was at once pulled down. A gillie then cut the Stag's throat, and the hounds got well blooded. The head was afterwards cut off, but was not worth having, the horns being only a foot long. That evening I blew the eggs, which seemed to have been sat on about half their time."

§ 42. *Two.*—Kuusi-niemi, East Bothnia, 23 and 24 April, 1855[1].

These were brought to Ludwig 26th May, 1855. The finder called them Eagle Owl's, but they appear to be Golden Eagle's. He said he took them near Kuusi-niemi—"Six Points," which is between Parkajoki and Kihlangi, below Muonioniska. He further said that the bird was very wild, and that he could not see it. Eagle Owls were in the habit of hooting about the rock where he took the eggs.

§ 43. *One.*—Ketto-mella, Enontekis Lappmark, N. lat. 68° 20'. 30 April, 1855.

Piety climbed up to this well-known nest himself on the day mentioned. It was not a very large tree; but a very big nest halfway up it. A tree with a nest had been cut down there four or five years before. He saw the two birds; they were "Black Eagles." He thinks they have some little white on the tail, but they were certainly not Sea-Eagles. They were shy. There was a young one with eyes formed in the single egg.

§ 44. *One.*—Aberdeenshire, 28 March, 1855 (?). From Mr. J. Gardner's Collection.

O. W. tab. ii. fig. 2.

I first saw this egg in Mr. Gardner's shop-window, January 22nd, 1856. For its history I was referred to Mr. J. D. Salmon; and on going to him, as I at once did, he told me that he got the egg in the spring of 1855, soon after it was received by Mr. Gardner, who subsequently took it back from him (Mr. Salmon). Mr. Salmon was informed that it had come to Mr. Gardner from a gamekeeper in Yorkshire; and the following particulars, among others more precise, were given in writing respecting it. "The egg of the Golden Eagle was taken March 28th. There were two eggs in the nest, on which the old bird had sat about a week. It was built in a Scotch Fir-tree, and was composed of

---

[1] [With respect to the nidification of Eagles in Lapland, Mr. Wolley has remarked (Cat. Eggs, 1855-56, p. 7), "A pair of Golden Eagles is generally to be found at the foot of the several groups of mountains in the interior, building upon some great tree—less frequently on a rock,—the reverse of what we see in Scotland. The Sea-Eagle, on the other hand, is mostly near the coast, or on large lakes, as with us."—ED.]

dry sticks of the same tree, with dry heather, and lined with coarse grass. The nest was at the foot of a mountain in Aberdeenshire. It has been occupied for many years." Having read this, I recollected having heard of a nest in a tree from several people, and, amongst the rest, that Mr. Newcome had himself seen it and the birds, which, he was told, and believed, were Golden Eagles. Accordingly I went again to Mr. Gardner's; and Mr. Salmon was so good as to accompany me. After some conversation of a satisfactory kind, the egg was brought out of the window, and I bought it, having previously observed the cracks near the smaller end. It was said to have been under a glass, and untouched, ever since Mr. Salmon returned it; and that gentleman at once said it was the same egg.

[I have been obliged here to condense very much the account of this specimen, which occupies several pages in Mr. Wolley's note-book, and I am unable, without mentioning other names, to show how great the probability is that it came from the nest seen many years ago by Mr. Newcome. To my mind the evidence is sufficiently conclusive; and I may add that since the egg came into my possession, I have obtained additional particulars highly corroborating the opinion Mr. Wolley had formed. The result is, that it is a very valuable specimen, whether considered on account of its beauty or on account of the situation of the nest in which it was laid,—a situation which appears to be certainly uncommon for British Golden Eagles.]

§ 45. *One.*—Akes-lombola, East Bothnia, 1856.

Brought 6th August, 1856, from the place named above. It was much decomposed inside, and the young had bones[1].

§ 46. *Two.*—Sammal-vara, Kemi Lappmark, 1857.

A. *One.*—11 April, 1857. "J. W. *ipse.*"

O. W. tab. iii. fig. 4.

This beautiful egg, something like those of mine figured by Mr. Hewitson [§ 26], I took from the nest found by Heiki. On 4th April the Wassara lads had told me, at Rauhula, that they had seen an Eagle on Keimio-tunturi as they were shooting wild Reindeer the day before. I called at Keimio-niemi, and left word that Fetto should tell Heiki to look for it. In two days Piety brought word that Heiki had found the nest. He had marked the tree, but not looked into it. On 11th April, the morning after Good Friday, I started with Heiki

[1] [In 1855, Mr. Wolley obtained one egg from this nest, which is now in Mr. W. H. Simpson's collection.—ED.]

and Ludwig for the place. We reached Keimio-niemi about 11 a.m.,
left our deer there, and took to *skidor*[1]. After crossing the arm of
the lake to the east of the promontory, we began to ascend the hill,
Heiki showing us the tall trees near the top where the nest was. It
was a long and difficult climb—in many places an affair of hands and
knees, as the *suakät*[1] would not hold. At last Heiki pointed out the
tree, about twenty paces off; and the bird, with a spring, tumbled out
of the nest over the valley. The cock showed himself on the wing
directly afterwards. The white in the middle of the wing above, and
on the proximal half of the tail, was very conspicuous in both birds.

Once the cock flew near the nest, and disappeared. The tree was a
Scotch Fir (one of the thickest), about two feet in diameter, or nearly
so; thick branches at convenient distances for climbing; perhaps
thirty-four feet high; the nest twenty feet from the ground, touching
the bole, but supported by branches. The situation noble. The nest
just so as to be on a level with the top of the hill, or a little above it
when the snow melts. A grand view over Jeris-järwi, and so on to
Ollos-tunturi and Muoniovara westerly. I climbed up and called out
the good news to those below, "There is one egg." It lay on the off
side of the nest, near the edge of the large well-marked hollow. I
carefully packed it up in the tin, and put in its place an egg of *Anser
minutus* I had prepared, written upon, filled with tallow, and the end
stopped with sealing-wax. The nest was of great vertical thickness,
perhaps seven feet, mended from year to year; the sticks of small
size; the platform by no means wide, lined with living sprigs of Scotch
Fir and a little *lupu* ("tree-hair")—nothing else. A small quantity
of old snow was still clinging to the twigs on the side next the slope of
the hill. The foundation of the nest I guessed to be about four years
old; perhaps it was more. I transferred the egg to another box in
Toras-sieppi, whilst I took Heiki to look if there was anything in the
Jua-rowa nest; but it had not been disturbed since we were there on
the 6th*. Opening the box on the following morning, I found the

---

[1] [Snow-skates.—Ed.]

* 6 April, 1857, I went with a man to the Golden Eagle's nest in Jua-rowa by
Särki-järwi, whence he obtained an egg in April 1856, subsequently sold at Mr.
Stevens's (Lot 8, 23 February, 1858) to Mr. Braikenridge. A bird was killed from
this nest in 1854, whose head and sternum Mr. A. Newton took with him to
England [Osteoth. Newt. *MS. Cat.* No. 256, b.], and whose tail is amongst my
skins [Woll. Don. No. 99]. This *rowa* is visible from my windows at Muoniovara, over the south-west shoulder of Ollos-tunturi. The snow, about two feet
deep, was so softened in the middle of the day as to make the climbing of the
steep hill comparatively easy. It is covered with Scotch Fir-trees to the top, where,
however, they are dwarf; but the nest was in a good-sized one, and so far below
the crest of the hill that I could easily see into it. The tree scarcely differs from

egg cracked—when and how I could not exactly make out. I blew
and mended it. Looking at it afterwards, I found that where the
colour was thick it had a tendency to chip off. The contents were
perfectly fresh, and had the usual flavour of Eagle's eggs.

B. *One.*—22 April, 1857. " J. W."

O. W. tab. iii. fig. 3.

Brought to Muoniovara by Heiki's wife, 25th April, with the egg of
Anser minutus, which, as above stated, I had left in the nest, and
blown at once by me. It seemed to have been two or three days at
least sat on. " J. W." as I saw the bird at the nest, not "*ipse*" as
on the other egg. 15th May, Apo brought word from Heiki, who was
ill, that the egg was taken 22nd April; he also said that the Goose's
egg was cracked in the nest.

§ 47. *Two.*—Argyllshire, 10 April, 1857.

O. W. tab. ii. fig. 4.

Received for Mr. Wolley by Mr. Edward Newton in the summer
of 1857, with a short statement of when and where they were taken.
There were only these two eggs in the nest, which was in a rock, and
does not seem to have belonged to any of the birds mentioned before
in these pages.

[§ 48. *Two.*—Sutherlandshire. 22 April, 1859.

Sent to me by a correspondent, who states that they were from the same
nest. The hen bird was well known to have bred for the preceding ten or
twelve years in one of two places alternately. In 1856 her mate was killed
and the eggs taken, but by whom he was not able to learn. He also adds,

---

its neighbours, and is only some ten paces from the tree that formerly had the nest,
felled in 1854. That tree was said to be more difficult to climb than this, which
is indeed very easy. The nest may be five fathoms from the ground, and a fathom
and a half from the top of the tree, which last is bushy, and almost like a "wind
nest." The nest was on the south-east side of the tree, and had snow over it, on
the top of which were a good many newly-broken sprigs of Scotch Fir, showing
that the birds were repairing it. It seemed to be a considerable mass in depth,
but not in breadth, made chiefly of small sticks. The trees about it grew pretty
close, and it was not visible from the valley. To it may probably belong the
Eagles that frequent Ollos-tunturi, though it is some distance off. The *rowa* has
two heads; the nest was on that nearest Särki-lombola. We saw nothing of the
birds. [The term *rowa*, as used about Muonioniska, signifies, I believe, a rounded
hill, more or less wooded, and of moderate height.—ED.]

while that bird lived, one of the eggs was always plain and the other spotted,
but that ever since they had been both marked alike. Mr. Wolley was pay-
ing me a visit when these eggs arrived; and one of them being somewhat
injured in the journey, he with great patience repaired it so skilfully that it
is now but little the worse.

In 1849 Mr. Wolley visited this locality: he says, "Being without
a guide, I could not find a nest; but there was a cliff, on the summit
of which an Eagle was in the habit of feeding."]

[§ 49. *Two.*—Sutherlandshire, 3 April, 1861.

O. W. tab. iv. fig. 4.

These beautiful eggs were sent to me by the correspondent mentioned in
the last section, and, as he informs me, from the same nest as those he obtained
for me in 1859. "If bred by the same birds," he adds, "is more than I can
ascertain;" but the similarity of markings observable in all four would tend
to the belief that they were the produce of one bird. The specimen figured
was placed in the hands of the draughtsman but a very few days after I received
it, and he has been very successful in depicting its glowing and delicate tints.
Its fellow is more highly coloured still, so as somewhat to resemble one of the
magnificent pair of eggs of Mr. Wolley's own taking, of which Mr. Hewitson
has given an illustration. For this reason only I have abstained from having
it figured here, though well aware that a representation of it would have
greatly enriched the present work. My correspondent wrote that he went
himself and saw the bird, which he could have shot, and that the eggs were
taken out of the nest in his presence.]

[§ 50. *One.*—Sutherlandshire, 11 April, 1862.

I received this egg from the same correspondent as those in the last two
sections; and having regard to its appearance and the district whence it
comes, as well as the information given me, I cannot doubt it to be the produce of the same hen bird as those, though it was not laid in the same nest.
Early in the season my correspondent ascertained that a pair of Eagles had
prepared three nests within the distance of a mile from one another. Two of
them were in the same crag, from the summit of which is visible the rock
whence the eggs he sent me in 1859 and 1861 were taken. It seems that,
on the 10th of April, a shepherd discovered an Eagle sitting on one of these
two nests, and, expecting that she had "dropped her eggs," next day he
procured the assistance of another man, and by means of ropes got into the
nest, which he found to contain this only one. In consequence of being thus
disturbed, the bird does not appear to have laid a second, though my correspondent, in full confidence that she would do so, examined all the sites he
knew of within a circle of forty miles; but the only satisfaction he had was
once seeing both birds on the wing. He adds that the nest from which this
egg came had been deserted for many years past: he himself visited it the day
after it had been plundered, and is certain that its tenants were the same

birds he had robbed before. The egg is a very fine specimen, almost exactly like the highest-coloured of the two in the last section; and is further useful as showing probably that it was the nature of this Eagle to lay her best egg first; for I cannot doubt it would have been followed in a day or two by another, had not the bird been molested.]

[§ 51. *Two.*—Ross-shire, 10 April, 1860.   From Mr. Tristram's Collection.

O. W. tab. ii. fig. 1.

Received by me from Mr. Tristram in the spring of 1860, with particulars of the time and place of their capture.]

[§ 52. *One.*—County Mayo, April 1860.

This egg was given to me 24th September, 1860, by Mr. T. M. Birch, who told me that it was brought to him, unblown, with two others, taken from the same nest, towards the end of the preceding April. The hen bird was also killed from the nest, the position of which was subsequently pointed out to me; and I afterwards had some conversation with the lad who shot her. Mr. Birch sent her to be stuffed by Mr. Glennon, at whose shop in Dublin I saw her, and from whom I obtained her breast-bone (Osteoth. Newt. *MS. Cat.* No. 256, e.). A remarkably fine bird, both from the coppery (not to say golden) neck and marbled tail. An Eagle believed to be her mate was seen and shot at (I am glad to say, ineffectually) by two gentlemen, who told me of the circumstance, a few days before this egg was given to me. Mr. Birch assured me that the other two eggs were as nearly as possible like this one— at any rate not more coloured, except with dirt. He had given them to Mr. Partridge and Mr. Richard Longfield.

The district whence this egg came is described by Mr. Maxwell in his ' Wild Sports of the West.']

[§ 53. *Two.*—Argyllshire, 22 April, 1861.   " A. N. *ipse.*"

O. W. tab. iv. fig. 4.

These two eggs were taken by myself a few hours after, and on the same day as, those mentioned in a preceding section (§ 39). After baiting the pony, I continued along the road until I fell in with my guide, who had taken a short cut over the moor. When we came nearly opposite the hill which contained the nest, we struck across the moor. After fording the river, we began to ascend the eminence, which was indeed but a slight one compared with the lofty height to which we had but just before climbed. In the morning we had seen more than a score of Deer on the very ground we were passing over; but they had all moved away by the time we returned. The hill has two knolls or summits, on the most eastern of which, and facing the north, the nest was situated. There was only a very little snow on the top. Some years ago, an accomplished author and sportsman had tried to shoot the

bird from this nest; but though he succeeded in getting immediately below
and within a few yards of it, he missed her clean with both barrels! After
that, it was for a long time untenanted, and Mr. Wolley never visited it. Last
year a pair of Eagles took possession of it, and hatched off their two young
ones, which my guide, when he went to ascertain if there was not a rotten egg
left, saw flying from one rock to another, the parents "waiting on." We
went first to the western knoll, from which, in former times, the hen could be
seen as she sat on the nest. Here we lay down on the ground and got out
our glasses, but we could not discover her. My guide began to have mis-
givings lest he had been deceived, though a fortnight or so before he had seen
an Eagle sitting about on the rocks close by. We could, however, make out
the nest. The hill seemed to slope up within a very little (about fifteen feet, as
I afterwards found) of the low cliff, on the top of which grew some small birch-
trees. The nest was on a ledge with overhanging slabs, almost like the recess
in which the one I had just come from was situated, but it was more exposed.
We then went on, and, a few steps further, off went the bird, which continued
long in sight, flying slowly away over the lochs to the northward, till we lost
her behind some rising ground. We took the pony to the foot of the low cliff,
which looked very easy until we came to try it. My guide took off his shoes,
and, getting on to a ledge, I, with his assistance from above, and, from below,
that of a lad who had joined us, followed. He then crawled along (for we
could not stand upright) some three or four yards, and peeped into the nest;
but he was not able to see its contents until, with one of my walking-sticks,
he had pulled away some of its outworks. He then, to my delight, announced
that the eggs were unhatched. I had some difficulty in passing him on the
narrow ledge, for I wanted to take the eggs out myself, and I hardly know
how we managed it; but, the lad holding him up from below, he slipped back,
and I raked the eggs out, one at a time, with the handle of my stick, and gave
them to him, he handing them in his turn to the lad, who placed them in a
safe nook below. The ledge suddenly terminated, so that no one could get
into the nest. I then retreated cautiously, for the rocks were very wet and
slippery, besides being overgrown with Polypody and Bilberry, which was not
firm enough to hold on by. My guide then went before and beyond me, so
that I dropped down nearly on the place whence I had climbed up; but
just as I got down I had an awful fright, seeing him fly through the air
past me, and go down the slope at a fearful rate. Fortunately he was brought
up by a big stone before he got very far, and greatly relieved me by bursting
into a laugh. The tuft of plants on which he had been relying had given way
without warning. I had not time to think of the eggs. He must have passed
right over, though a long way above them. He first struck the ground where
my coat and his shoes were laid, and sent them all spinning a long way down
the hill. Fortunately no harm came to him, or to anything. The moral of
this long story is, that a low nest may be far worse than a high one. I confess
I should not have liked it at all, had it been higher up.

The eggs have a rather unusual appearance. The one figured here has a Buz-
zard-like character, with a few rather large markings of deep red, some of them
running into lines, the others roundish; the spots at the larger end on a white
ground, discoloured however by dirt or damp. This specimen I am glad to
have, as there was nothing at all like it before in the series. It was so much
soiled that I ventured to wash it, though of course very carefully. The other

is of a creamy brown all over; but whether from dirt or true colour I do not know.]

[§ 54. *One.*—Särki-järwi, East Bothnia, 15 April, 1861.

Brought to Muoniovara by Heiki's boy Carl, 2nd May, having been taken as above stated. The finder had gone six Swedish miles to look for this nest, and received a suitable recompense accordingly.

Whether this nest belonged to the same birds, or their successors, as those seen by Mr. Wolley (§ 46, *note*), I do not know; but the two localities are very near each other.]

[§ 55. *Two.*—Sutherlandshire, 15 April, 1862.

These two fine eggs were sent to me by a correspondent, who states that it is more than probable that one or both parents were the progeny of the pair of Eagles whose nest Mr. Wolley took in 1849 (§ 26). The nest was in the same range of rocks, and about three-quarters of a mile distant from that one. It had been forsaken for sixteen years previously; but the Eagles had since repeatedly bred in another one, about twelve yards off. In 1861, my friend Mr. W. H. Simpson succeeded in taking with his own hands a pair of eggs, believed to belong to the same birds as these, the nest being within a mile of the spot. The present eggs were taken by some men living in the district, one of whom descended by a rope to get them, and were obtained by my informant on the following day. They are large specimens, and of the same character as Mr. Simpson's, one of them being almost uniformly freckled with deeply coloured spots on a white ground, and the other being similar, but with fewer markings.]

AQUILA MOGILNIK (S. Gmelin).

IMPERIAL EAGLE.

[§ 56. *One.*—From M. E. Verreaux's Collection, 1863.]

AQUILA CLANGA, Pallas[1].

SIBERIAN EAGLE.

[§ 57. *One.*—"Sarepta." From Herr H. F. Möschler's Collection, 1862.]

[1] [It would be quite out of place here to discuss the specific value of the asserted differences between Eastern and Western examples of the *Falco nævius* of Linnæus.

[§ 58. *One.*—"South Russia." From Herr A. Heinke of Kamuschin, through Dr. Albert Günther, 1863.]

AQUILA NÆVIA (Gmelin).

SPOTTED EAGLE.

§ 59. *One.*—From M. Perrot's Collection, 1847.

Hewitson, 'Eggs of British Birds,' ed. 3, pl. v.

§ 60. *One.*—Pomerania (?). From M. Parzudaki's Collection, 1856.

§ 61. *Two.*—Pomerania, 9 May, 1854. From Dr. T. Krüper's Collection, through Pastor P. W. Theobald.

Given to me at Copenhagen by Pastor Theobald, having been received by him from his friend Dr. Krüper, with the information that the bird always builds in trees.

[Dr. Krüper's accounts of the nesting of this and other species of Eagles in Pomerania are published in the 'Naumannia,' 1852, ii. 1. 61; and 1853, iii. 39.]

[§ 62. *One.*—From M. Nager-Donazain's Collection, through Dr. R. T. Frere, 1861.]

AQUILA BONELLII (Temminck).

BONELLI'S EAGLE.

[§ 63. *One.*—From M. E. Verreaux's Collection, 1861.]

I have had few opportunities of forming an opinion on the subject; I therefore now separate them more as a matter of convenience than anything else. Those who are interested in the question will find the distinction of the Eastern bird (*Aquila clanga*, Pall.) forcibly maintained by Professor Blasius in the supplementary continuation of Naumann's excellent work (Vög. Deutschl. vol. xiii. part ii. p. 10), to which is added an account of its breeding by Dr. Baldamus. Professor Schlegel (who, however, identifies the *A. clanga* of Pallas with the *F. nævioides* of Cuvier, and consequently with the *F. rapax* of Temminck) has also some able remarks on the subject (Muséum des Pays-Bas, *Aquila*, pp. 3, 4). In bestowing an English name on the Eastern form, I have endeavoured to devise one which seems to be less objectionable than many that might be suggested.—ED.]

AQUILA PENNATA (Gmelin).

BOOTED EAGLE.

[§ 64. *One.*—From M. E. Verreaux's Collection, 1861.]

HALIÆETUS ALBICILLA.

WHITE-TAILED EAGLE.

The Sea-Eagle in Scotland generally makes its nest in the high cliffs of the coast, where it lives upon fish, Guillemots, young Herring-Gulls, &c.; but it is also occasionally found breeding inland. In the Shetlands an inaccessible eyrie was pointed out to me on the extreme top of a stack, that is, a steep detached rock; and I have seen another such stack on the north-east coast of Scotland, which was also said to have an eyrie on the top of it. One other instance I have been told of, where a similar apparently exposed spot was chosen; but it is interesting to know that there is often quite a calm at these elevated points, as they are sheltered by the current of air turned upwards by the rock below.

In inland situations, the Sea-Eagle used to be much less common than the Mountain-Eagle, and is still considered a far rarer bird than that. In a place where six or eight eyries might be counted within a circle of as many miles, only one of them would be a Sea-Eagle's. It generally establishes itself upon a rock or island in the middle of a loch. Here it builds upon the ground, or in a tree, a nest whose construction does not at all differ from that of the Golden Eagle, there being always in it a certain amount of *Luzula sylvatica.* The tree need by no means be a large one : I have seen two nests of different years, in separate islands in one loch, each only about four feet from the ground, in very small trees. One of these has been elsewhere described erroneously as belonging to the Fish-Hawk [1], which makes a very different nest. I can at this moment call to mind nine instances where I know the localities of such island eyries in past years. The old birds do not always calculate the depth of the water, as there is one place at least to which a man can wade.

[1] [St. John's 'Tour in Sutherlandshire,' vol. i. p. 37.—Ed.]

Where swimming is necessary, it is often an affair of danger, as the birds will do their best to drown the enemy with their wings; but when once he is out of the water, they have the discretion to keep their distance. In two spots I have seen large Scotch Firs, not on islands, which have been formerly tenanted by Sea Eagles. One was by the side of a loch; but the other was several miles away from any piece of water, in a sort of open wood of similar trees. The nest had been in a fork where three branches met, perhaps twenty high. In other cases, as might be expected, it is the main trunk which bears the weight of the nest. In one instance, the crossed and nearly horizontal trunks of two small trees formed the support. Another, that I have already spoken of, was in a small alder-tree, and had been repaired and often frequented by the Eagles the season I saw it; yet a Hooded Crow had eggs in the upper branches, and Wild Geese and Ducks were sitting in the deep moss and long heather within twenty yards. I have not myself met with an instance of a Golden Eagle building in a tree or on a sea-cliff, but, on the other hand, several of a Sea-Eagle building on a rock inland, many miles from the ocean. Two such nests, within ten miles of the sea, that I visited, were in small rocks of easy approach, in every respect like Golden Eagles', and in one the hen showed the same unwillingness to fly off her eggs. This eyrie was in a low place, in the bosom, as it were, of high crags, not indeed quite accessible without a rope, but you could get very near it from above or below. As we approached the place, two Ravens came out to meet us, which we thought a bad omen; but presently a white tail showed against the grey rock, and the cock bird was seen slowly flapping off. It was an anxious moment; but he began to turn back, and we knew all was right. The nest was very conspicuous, partly supported by the trunk of a Rowan-tree. The site of the other eyrie could scarcely be said to be a rock at all, but rather a rocky bank or 'hanger,' overgrown with small trees. The nest, placed in a sort of great chair of rock, was perfectly accessible from any direction, right or left, above or below; and a man could get within a yard or two from above without in the least disturbing the bird. I went into it on 25th May [1849]; and at that time it was regularly occupied by the Eagle, as was evident from the fresh droppings on every side, and from the very recent castings lying in the nest. Yet there were no eggs or young; and no man had been there, or he must have left some trace of his visit on the young nettles or other tender herbage growing near. A water-spaniel accompanied me into the nest. It had had young ones the previous season; and two eggs were taken from it the following year, 1850. The whole scene would have made a charming picture. It may be the force of fancy, but most Eagle-stations appear to me to be in extremely picturesque situations, and worth going any distance to see.

On the coasts, the Sea-Eagle chooses a roomy and generally sheltered ledge of rock. The egg which Mr. Hewitson figures [Eggs B. B. ed. 3. pl. iv. fig. 2] is one of two which I took on the 23rd April, 1849, on one of the most northern points of our island. The nest was very slightly made of a little grass and fresh heather, loosely put together without any sticks; but two or three 'kek'-stalks were strewn about outside. There was a good thickness of guano-like soil upon the rock, which made much nest unnecessary. Two or three Guillemot's beaks, the only unmanageable part of that bird, were not far off. The eggs were laid two days before, when I went to reconnoitre; and I never shall forget the forbearance which a friend who was with me showed, at my request, as he lay gun in hand with the hen Eagle in full view upon her nest not forty yards below him. Her head was towards the cliff, and concealed from our sight, whilst her broad back and white tail, as she stood bending over her nest on the grassy ledge, with the beautiful sandstone rock and the sea beyond, completed a picture rarely to be forgotten. But our ears and the air we breathe give a finish to nature's pictures which no art can imitate; and here were the 'effects' of the sea, and the heather, and the rocks, the fresh warmth of the northern sun, and the excitement of exercise, while the musical yelping of the male Eagle came from some stand out of our sight. Add to all this the innate feeling of delight connected with the pursuit of wild animals, which no philosopher has yet been able to explain further than as a special gift of our Great Maker, and then say whether it is not almost blasphemy to call such a scene a 'picture'! Upon this occasion, I made some remark to my friend, when the hen Eagle showed her clear eye and big yellow beak, her head full of the expression of wild nature and freedom. She gave us a steady glance, then sprang from the rock, and with "slow winnowing wing"—the flight-feathers turning upwards at every stroke—was soon out at sea. Joined by her mate, she began to sail with him in circles further and further away, till quite out of sight, yelping as long as we could hear them,—Gulls mobbing them all the time. To enjoy the beauties of a wild coast in perfection, let me recommend any man to seat himself in an Eagle's nest. The year before this, I took the young ones out of the same eyrie, late in July. It was my first attempt at an Eagle's stronghold, and I shall never forget the interest of the whole affair:—a thunderstorm coming on just before, making it necessary to cut drains in the peat with our

knives to divert the torrents of water; our councils about the best
mode of attaching the ropes; the impertinence of a young lad, who,
stationed to watch for my signals, was rendered quite useless by
his keen sense of the ridiculous on seeing me, in my inexperience,
twisting round and round at the end of the rope; the extraordinary
grandeur everything assumed from the nest itself; the luxurious
feeling of exultation; the interest of every plant about it—I know
them all now; the heaps of young Herring-Gulls' remains, and the
large fish-bone; but, above all, the Eaglets fully able to fly, and
yet crouching side by side, with their necks stretched out and chins
on the ground, like young fawns, their frightened eyes proving that
they had no intention of showing fight.

Very gently, as a man 'tickles' trout, I passed my hand under
them and tied their legs together, and then tried to confine their
wings. They actually allowed me to fasten a handkerchief round
them, which, however, was soon shaken off when they began to be
pulled up. When the men had raised me, the string attached to my
waist lifted one Eaglet, and presently the second came to the length
of his tether. Great was the flapping of wings and clutching at
rocks and grass. I had many fears that the string or the birds' legs
must give way; but, after much hard pulling, I got them safely to
the top, and they are now (1853) alive at Matlock amongst rocks,
where I hope they may breed; but, though five years old this season,
they have not yet quite completed the adult plumage. Their dutiful
parents never came near them in their difficulties; but I am happy
to say that, in 1850 (the year after I took their eggs), they carried off
their young, through the interest I was able to exert in their favour.
They had shifted their position; and they changed again in 1851 to a
rock with an aspect quite different, and more than a mile away. In
1847, to please the shepherds, the young were shot in the nest, which
was built in the spot where I visited it the two following years. There
was no sea-weed about this nest, either time that I saw it; but a
friend writes me word that two which he examined last year on the
sea-cliffs of this island, and which he carefully described to me, were
principally made of that material, as Mr. Hewitson also had found
them in the Shetland Islands. On one of these two occasions, the old
Eagle made a dash near my informant, with a "fearful scream;" and
such was the tremendous character of the rocks, that his "hair gets
strong" when he thinks of them. These two nests, both occupied,
were not more than a mile and a half apart.

The White-tailed Eagle is about a week or a fortnight later than
the Golden Eagle in laying its eggs. These are, I believe, generally

smaller and of rather coarser texture than those of the other kind. The one Mr. Hewitson figures [§ 67] is somewhat above the average size. I have not known an egg with any true colour upon it which I could ascertain beyond doubt to have been laid by this bird[1]. Two eggs which I took myself are uniformly stained, but not, I think, with proper colouring matter. Eggs of a kind of Penguin are brought home by the guano vessels, and show green to the light, and, being about the right size and shape, are frequently called White-tailed Eagles'.

The young of this species are wanderers on the face of the earth. In most winters, birds of the first year are killed in England; but it has long ceased to breed with us. It formerly built in Whinfield Park, in Westmoreland, where the nests were protected by the then Countess of Pembroke, as Willughby tells us [Ornithol. 1676, p. 17]; and about the year 1692, either this or the Golden Eagle had an eyrie upon "Willow Cragg," in the parish of Bampton, in the same county ['Correspondence of John Ray,' edited by Dr. Lankester for the Ray Society, 1848, p. 257]. About a century later, Dr. Heysham informed Dr. Latham [Gen. Syn., Supp. 1, p. 11] of a nest near Keswick in Cumberland; and the nest mentioned by Dr. Moore [Mag. Nat. Hist. ser. 2, vol. i. p. 114], on Dewerstone Rock, near Plymouth, to which allusion has before been made, probably belonged to this bird. In Ireland there are a good many spots where it still maintains its position, as appears from Mr. Thompson's work [B. Ireland, vol. i. pp. 14–29]; and that gentleman says that, in July 1835, he saw two Eagles, of which he could not determine the species, in the [English] lake-district, but which he considers were probably breeding in that quarter. In Scotland it has been rapidly retiring. It used to build on the Bass Rock, and long ago had two breeding-places in Dumfries-shire [Mag. Nat. Hist. ser. 2, vol. i. pp. 119 & 444], and even near Glasgow; but now its stations are almost confined to the north and west, and the islands. Every Deer-stalker knows to whose share is allotted the "gralloch" of a Stag; and too many Highland game-keepers have learned how they can easily catch either kind of Eagle. It is therefore a melancholy reflection that they can scarcely exist much longer. The White-tailed Eagle, in its sea-girt fortresses, will

---

[1] [Mr. Hewitson has twice figured a specimen as that of the White-tailed Eagle, upon which are some slight markings of reddish yellow (Brit. Ool. pl. xlv., and Eggs B. B. ed. 1, pl. ii. fig. 2). I believe it is from Mr. J. Hancock's collection, and that nothing more is known of its history than that it came from Hoy in the Orkneys, an island on which the Golden Eagle used to, and perhaps may still, breed.—ED.]

be the last to disappear; but each inland 'Craig-an-Eulah' will soon be an empty name [1].

§ 65. *One.*—Shetlands, 1847.　From Mr. Graham's Collection, through Mr. Tuke.

On inquiry made in 1848, I find that this egg was brought from Lerwick by a gentleman who told me where it was taken; and others gave me the name of the adventurer who climbed to the nest. On or about 19th June, 1849, I saw an Eagle here, flying straight away, not sailing in circles as they more commonly do. It went towards Scalloway, and I saw it down. The nest on the Noup was that year said to be inaccessible. The Golden Eagle is not in Shetland.

§ 66. *One.*—Sutherlandshire, 27 April, 1848.

Received from a correspondent, who states that there were two eggs in the nest from which the hen bird was shot; and from its being so grey, it was supposed to be very old. The nest was similar to that of a Golden Eagle, but close to the sea. There was part of a salmon on the top of the rock near it, which no doubt had been brought by the male. The other egg was sent to a gentleman said to be connected with the British Museum. They had not been sat on more than eight or ten days. In 1849, 8th June, Mr. Edge and I saw a White-tailed Eagle flying towards the stack from which this egg had been taken the preceding year.

§ 67. *Two.*—Caithness, 23 April, 1849.　"J. W. *ipse.*"

Hewitson, 'Eggs of British Birds,' ed. 3, pl. iv. fig. 2.

These two eggs I took out of the nest on a headland, from which, in 1848, I brought the two young birds, which are now alive at Mr. C. Clarke's at Matlock [2]. On 21st April I visited the headland, but

---

[1] [The above paragraphs, like those which precede the enumeration of the specimens of Golden Eagles' eggs, were written in 1853 for Mr. Hewitson's use, and are here printed from the original notes in my keeping. As in the case just mentioned, much of the information they contain is repeated in the accounts of the particular nests to which it refers; but believing that everything relating to the history of our native breeds of Eagles cannot fail to be interesting, that fact has not induced me to withhold them here. In another place in Mr. Wolley's notes is a suggestion that the "Willow-Cragg," mentioned by Mr. Aubrey in the passage above quoted, may probably be a corruption of the Celtic "Craig-an-Eulah" (more properly Craig-an-Iolair), or Eagle's Crag.—ED.]

[2] [As stated above (p. 46), Mr. Wolley had been in hopes that these Eagles

the lighthouse-keeper there did not think the Eagles had as yet laid. On reaching the place, and looking over, there was the bird on the nest, tail outwards, and head under the ledge. The male was screaming to her from the rock below, where we were standing. I told the man who had my gun not to fire; thereupon she showed her head and started off. She was immediately joined by the male. There were two eggs visible in the nest. The birds sailed with motionless wings in circles more and more distant: screaming Gulls came to bully them, and looked very small in comparison.

On Monday, 23rd April, having borrowed a coil of ropes from some fishermen, I drove over with a companion to the headland, and put up at the lighthouse, whose keeper and two hands, an old sailor and a young labourer, were to meet me at the nest; a fourth, the shepherd, also met me on the road, to take the ropes and the bags. My companion agreed to make the necessary signs. I had a board to sit on, a tie round each thigh, and a piece under my arms. The nest was made of grass and fine fresh heather, very loosely put together, different from all the other nests I saw afterwards. A few large dry "kek" stalks, and some pieces of Guillemot, quite fresh, were lying about near the nest. There were no other bones. In the descent I kept myself from spinning by a walking-stick, occasionally touching the rock. The post of last year was still remaining, but we did not use it, as we had so many hands, though I think it would have been safer to have done so. The site was a considerable grassy ledge, where grew *Statice armeria*, &c., the rock slightly overhanging. The year before, a very heavy thunder-shower happened just before my descent, and a stream of water poured down almost into the nest; the greater part of which we arrested by canals cut in the turf with my knife. The young, fully fledged and grown, crouched with their heads towards the rock, and allowed their legs to be tied without resistance. I fastened them with thick string to my rope; and their additional weight, with an occasional grip they gave to the rock, made the pulling up very hard work for the men. They slipped a silk handkerchief with which I endeavoured to confine their wings. In the nest there were many bones of young Herring-Gulls, and one of a large fish. The old birds did not appear after our first approach. I had many more difficulties on the first descent than on the second,

might be induced to breed in captivity. With this end in view, a large mass of natural rocks was wired over, so as to form a very roomy cage, in which the birds lived contentedly for some five or six years, until one day it was found that the female had killed and eaten half her mate. On this she was transferred to other hands, and, when I last heard of her, was undergoing solitary confinement at Chatsworth,—certainly an agreeable place of detention for a murderess.—ED.]

—the men hesitating, rope twisting, small boy laughing, &c. The
feeling in an Eagle's nest, where I never expected to be again, was
sublime. The sea far below; the storm in the distance; the voices
of men shouting, not to be understood; the expectation of a hostile
visit from the old Eagles, &c. &c.;—not to speak of the sensation,
that the rope might possibly be cut, a knot fail, the men faint, the
post yield, a mass of rock fall down, or the like. Perhaps the rope
might get fixed in a cleft of the rock; the heather and peat might, after
the rain, give way with the men; they might slip; the Eagles might
make a swoop at them; a flash of lightning might terrify them. The
ledge was about eighteen fathoms from the top, and twice as far from
below. The eggs were perfectly fresh and well-tasted.

The following year (1850) these birds shifted their position about
a quarter of a mile to the west of the place where I took their young
and eggs. I was informed that their new nest was quite near the top
of the rock, but far in below a cleft, so that it could not be easily
taken.

§ 68. Sutherlandshire, 2 May, 1849. "J. W. *ipse*" (written
      in nest).

These two eggs are curiously stained, and much smaller than those
I took 23rd April [§ 67]. They were some days sat upon. On
May 1st, as we were walking up a strath, a shepherd told one of
the men who was with me that he had lost a lamb by an Eagle that
very morning. We slept at a shooting-lodge; and another shepherd
said he had lost four or five that season. We started the next morning with his son. As we approached the rock which looks up the
strath, we saw two Ravens, which had evidently a nest, and I feared
this was a bad sign for Eagles. However, immediately afterwards I
saw a noble White-tailed Eagle moving on the face of the rock some
distance off. He flew, but soon took a turn back to the rock, which
convinced me he had a nest. I stopped the men, and proceeded to
stalk. Almost directly, I saw the nest between a Rowan-tree and the
rock. The cock bird flew away in silence. I made a circuit, and
climbed very quietly, yet with the greatest ease, till I was immediately under the nest. Here I cocked my gun and took breath.
Then I shouted, and made all the noise I could; but nothing stirred.
Warned by my experience on a former occasion [§ 26], I kept myself
in readiness, and threw a bit of stick, when out tumbled the Eagle,
clumsily knocking against the tree. I fired, the bird flew on, and
would, I feared, escape. I watched almost in despair, for the shot

was small; but in about a hundred yards she failed, fell over, and lay dead, with her eyes closed. We hid her up till the evening, and I skinned her the next day. She was a large bird, and had a shot through her heart. The male flew about at distance, flapping slowly; but he never cried or screamed, as did the birds on the last occasion.

"On getting above the nest, I can look down into it from about twelve feet, and I see that there are eggs; but it looks impracticable, or nearly so, without a rope. A stake is planted, and soon, with the rope fastened under my arms, I am lowered into the nest, in which I write this account. It appears about five feet in length by three feet in breadth from the rock, on a sort of triangular ledge, the small Rowan touching it in front. The rock is scarcely overhanging. The nest is made chiefly of dead heather-stalks, with a few sticks for the foundation, the largest of which are above an inch in diameter, and two feet long. It is lined with a considerable depth of moss, fern, grass, and *Luzula*, as was the Golden Eagle's before referred to [§ 26], and is nearly as large. The hollow is small for the size of the bird, and very well defined. There is a rank sort of smell, but no animal remains in or near it; several feet below is an old nest."

After having blown the eggs, written upon them, and finished my journal, I climbed up without hauling, going round a corner, which would, however, be impassable without a rope. The men, who had never been in an Eagle's nest, visited it out of curiosity, being properly secured by the rope. I had other Eagle adventures in the course of the day [§ 27]. At night a forester returned, and next morning told me that he had hurried back, having heard of me; for he was to have killed the two old ones, and taken the eggs for the keeper[1].

§ 69. *Two.*—Sutherlandshire, 1849.

These were sent to me from the north, 11th December, 1849, with a live young Golden Eagle. A year and a half afterwards the sender told me the name of the headland where the nest was: it was one of those I had not time to visit when in the district.

§ 70. *Two.*—Sutherlandshire, May, 1850.

These two eggs, as I subsequently discovered, were from a nest to which my dog "Watch" and I climbed the preceding year,

[1] [The hen bird killed by Mr. Wolley from this nest (at the instigation of the shepherds), and which, I believe, was the only one he ever shot in his life, was sent to England to be stuffed, and is now in the possession of Mr. Edge at Strelley, where I saw it in 1856.—ED.]

25th May. Two days before, a shepherd arrived to show me an Eagle's nest. Soon after leaving the inn, we saw one flapping in the wind high over-head, whereupon my guide called her a bad name—to which he applied the epithets "old" and "grey-tailed,"—showing great spite towards her. Some distance off, Eagle-rocks were pointed out by him—one, easily accessible, near where I had taken a Buzzard's nest; another in a loch, where a nest might be for eight or ten years, and then none for eight or ten years more, as he said, on the authority of his father, who had died a very old man. At this last spot the ledge overhung very much, but it seemed almost accessible from below. It had not been tenanted for several years, as was the case with many others about; for the new forester had trapped great numbers of Eagles since he had come into the country, three years before, even as many as fifteen in one quarter of a year. Three noted breeding-places were searched in vain by my emissaries, in all of which there had been nests three years ago. On that day we, too, hunted over the back of a mountain without success, though I subsequently heard that the nest had been found in another place after I left. It looked peculiarly grand and wild in the mist. I fired shots, and climbed part of the way up the ravine, where White-tailed Eagles were said to be, but nothing was seen or heard but Ravens. A story was told me by my attendants of an old man who, near a nest, was attacked by the birds and kept them off with a stick; he was not climbing to it; but another, who was, had his hat carried away and dropped some distance off, whereupon he thought fit to return. The following day, 25th May, I revisited this spot, but after carefully beating the ground I only saw Peregrine Falcons and Ravens, though I fired shots every few hundred yards. There was a loch, near which horses were to meet us; after a long round I came to it, and I saw a huge new-looking Eagle's nest in a rock of very easy access at the end of it. I climbed up: it was rather a steep hillside than a rock, and as I came near the nest I saw an abundance of Eagle's dung and pieces of of white down about; I tried to alarm the bird in vain. I climbed higher, and to my astonishment the nest was empty; but in it were castings, one damp, and ejected that afternoon. They were mostly of lamb's wool; and I had before seen a leg of lamb lying near. I picked up feathers characteristic of the White-tailed Eagle, and, though I saw no spots of blood nor footmarks, I felt sure that the nest had been robbed that very morning. It was perfectly dry, and I could fancy warm, but I was too angry to pay much attention to its structure; but I saw that it had a tree in front, was made of large sticks at the bottom, and lined with moss and *Luzula*. It was probably the largest

nest I had seen, some five feet by four, and perfectly firm. I stood
in it; and "Watch," my dog, followed me. A low rock on one side
completely overlooked it. Altogether it was the seat of a fearless,
undisturbed tyrant. Much sedge or *Luzula* grew near; and the
rocks about had a warm comfortable look, as is usual near Eagles'
nests. I vowed vengeance, and everybody said it was "a dirty
trick;" for the fox-hunter's servant declared that he had visited it
several weeks before, and then thought it was inhabited, but that
it was the surviving Eagle of the last year that frequented it. I
accepted this explanation, though nevertheless, for various reasons,
had my doubts. On 21st May I had put up a single Eagle from near
this spot, and soon afterwards saw, I believe, four soaring together,
with a Raven bullying them. Mr. Dunbar, another day, saw four
together here.

The following year I heard from the person who, according to
Mr. Charles St. John (Tour in Sutherlandshire, i. 16), "looked
like a spider hanging at the end of its thread" when being lowered
after a Peregrine's nest, that early in May he was told by a shepherd
that the Eagle had her nest in the place I have just described. My
informant wished him not to allow anybody else to touch the eggs,
and made an appointment to meet him two days after and take them;
meantime a boy from a neighbouring farm forestalled him, and sold
them to my correspondent, from whom I now have them. My informant was greatly disappointed, and suspected that the same thing
had happened the year before, when I was foiled in my attempt.

A forester, in 1849, wanted to take me to some nests at the back of
another mountain; but I declined from want of time, and foolishly,
for I afterwards drew it blank [§ 48]. They were said to be White-
tailed Eagle's. Some other likely districts also I had not time to
try; but I went, 11th May, in a crazy little boat on Loch Maddie
to visit the nest which Mr. St. John describes (*op. cit.* i. 37) as an
Osprey's. It turned out to be an Eagle's—I believe a White-tailed
Eagle's, both from the accounts of the people and from the appearance of the nest, which was very different from an Osprey's, but just
like that of an Eagle, lined with *Luzula*, &c. I found lying near it
fresh Eagles' feathers, but it was untenanted. I saw an Eagle flying
near the loch in the evening, persecuted as usual. I took the eggs
of a Hooded Crow from a nest in the same tree, near the top.
The Eagle's nest was low down, four or five feet from the ground,
lying on the trunk and horizontal branches. The tree was living,
and, if I remember right, an Alder. On another island further north
in the same loch is a similar nest, but older, equally low down, and

supported by the interlacing of the trunks and main branches of two
trees. Mr. St. John did not visit this last. Some said the Eagles
sometimes built in a neighbouring mountain instead of on the loch;
but I rather think they were speaking of the pair which had their
nest in another loch, on an island amongst the long heather. I
walked to a house within four miles of this spot; but the next day
was wet, and the island was said to be a good swim from the shore;
besides which, the birds had not bred there since the young ones
were taken some years before by a gentleman in a boat. I heard of
this nest from many quarters; it was once robbed by a shepherd in
two tubs, and another time by a man who swam to it. A few
days previously I met at an inn a gentleman to whom I had a letter
of introduction. He wished I had all the Eagles in the country,
considering them very numerous, for he had seen seven together not
very long before. He said there was one which was very destructive
to his lambs. I was able to tell him I had probably shot that bird
[§ 68]. The next day I saw a shepherd who had himself killed
thirty Eagles whilst the rewards were given. When once Eagles
begin to kill lambs they continue to do so, as I also heard in the
Færoes of the Great Skua: they are only said to take them on a
windy day, when they can rise easily with a weight. Several people
told me this.

§ 71. *One.*—Iceland (?).   From Dr. Pitman's Collection, 1852.

This egg, from the inscription upon it, I believe to have come
from Iceland. I had it of Mr. H. F. Walter, it having formed part
of Dr. Pitman's Collection.

§ 72. *Two.*—Sutherlandshire, May, 1852.

§ 73. *One.*—Sutherlandshire, May, 1852.

These three eggs are from two nests in one of the districts I was
unable to visit in 1849. A man who had then been one of my attendants sent them to me, saying as follows:—"The nests were on a
headland, about a mile and a half from each other, as near as I could
judge. I could climb within six yards of one of them without a rope.
I then got the lads at the top to throw it to me, by which means I
reached the nest, and from thence by the rope to the top. The
Eagle was hovering about until I got to the nest, when she came
right along the face of the rock by my side with a most fearful

scream; but I did not see her afterwards. At the second nest I had to go down about twenty fathoms with the rope. The Eagle there was not seen again after she got off. The nests were not at all like those in the mountains; they were made up of sea-weed and heather. In the first I am sure there were the feet and heads of a thousand cormorants, with a great deal of fishes' bones about it. I cannot take upon me to give a description of the wildness of these rocks, only my hair gets strong when I think of them. After being at this place I always felt some dizziness for two or three days. I should not like to try them again, though they were not so ill to get at as the Golden Eagle's of 27th April, 1849 [§ 26]. There were two eggs in each nest; but one I had the misfortune to lose; it went down over thirty yards of rock. I think those in each nest were laid within a day or two of each other; at least, I was not able to find any difference in blowing them. I had to take a man with me; he was to provide ropes, but I am sorry to say neither he nor they were to be depended on for life one minute."

§ 74. *One.*—Argyllshire, 1853.

Received for me in 1853 by Mr. Edge. In 1851 there was pointed out to us an island in a loch where the White-tailed Eagle had its nest every year. It was in a tree. My guide believed that this species never built in rocks; he had known a good many of their nests in islands, one quite on the ground, another or two five, and some twenty feet up in a tree. He shot an Eagle belonging to this loch once, before he knew that it had a nest there. Another time the bird deserted because he climbed up and looked into the nest; and once again she forsook her eggs, after having been shot at by a gentleman. A boat is always kept on the loch. As my guide was once swimming off with some young Eagles, he was nearly drowned by the old one making swoops close to him. He called to his man on shore to fire, but she returned to the charge. After he had landed she kept out of shot.

[§ 75. *Two.*—Shetlands, 1854.

Received by me from a correspondent in the Shetlands, who states that the nest was "in very high and dangerous banks on the sea-coast of one of the islands. There were two eggs, but on returning from the nest the climber, in saving his own life, broke one of them."]

[§ 76. *One.*—Shetlands, 1855.

Received from the same correspondent as the last, but it does not appear whether from the same nest or even the same island.]

[§ 77. *Two.*—Shetlands, April, 1856.

Sent by the same correspondent as the last and preceding entries, but from another island. Both from one nest.]

[§ 78. *One.*—Shetlands, 1861.

From the same island and, as it would seem, the same eyrie as those in the last section. My correspondent informed me that the poor fellow who procured it, "in attempting to go to the nest a second time, lost his hold, and, of course, lost his life."]

[§ 79. *One.*—Shetlands, 1857.

From the same correspondent, but from a third nest, situated on the west side of the island on which he himself resides.]

[§ 80. *Two.*—River Luro, Albania, 17 March, 1857. From Lord Lilford's Collection, 1859.

Lord Lilford (then Mr. Powys), mentioning these specimens in the 'Ibis' for 1860 (vol. ii. p. 5), says—"My Greek servant took two eggs of this species from a nest situate in the top of an old ash-tree in a wood on the banks of the Luro river, which runs into the Gulf of Arta, near the ruins of Nicopolis, and not far from the town of Prevesa: this was on the 17th of March, 1857. The old birds were very bold, and often came within gunshot of us; but I would not fire at them, as I did not want a specimen, and the shepherds begged us not to kill them, as they bred there year after year, and kept away other birds of prey which were destructive to their lambs. When my servant was within a few feet of the nest, a large snake put his head out of a hole and hissed fiercely at him; but he, having implored the aid of St. Spiridione, the patron of Corfu, went boldly in and took the eggs, which are now in the possession of Mr. Alfred Newton."

An account of the taking of this nest is also given in 'Frazer's Magazine,' No. 334, for October, 1857.]

PANDION HALIÆETUS (Linnæus).

OSPREY.

I have seen several nests of the Osprey upon the highest points of ruins in and about lochs in Scotland, and several more upon small isolated rocks projecting out of the water. There is something, in the general appearance of the nest, which reminds one of nests of the wood-ants; it is usually in the form of a cone cut off at the top;

the sticks project very slightly beyond the sides, and are built up with turf and other compact materials; the summit is of moss, very flat and even; and the cavity occupies a comparatively small part of it. I know no other nest at all like it. There was a nest for some years on the sloping trunk of a tree, which several persons have described to me. The birds are very constant, year after year, in returning to their old stations; and even after one or both birds have been killed in the previous season, I have frequently seen individuals flying near the now deserted eyrie [1].

§ 81. *One.*—Sutherlandshire, 17(?) May, 1848. From Mr. W. Dunbar's Collection.

Sent to me with two other Osprey's eggs, from three different nests, by Mr. Dunbar. That from which this one comes contained two eggs, the other being in Mr. John Hancock's Collection. They were taken by Mr. Dunbar in Mr. Charles St. John's company; and that gentleman gives an account of the nest, stating that he shot one of the parent birds (Tour in Sutherlandshire, i. pp. 29 *et seqq.*). Mr. Dunbar wrote to me as follows:—" The eggs were quite fresh, and seemed only to have been deposited the same day, or a day before. Mr. St. John shot the old bird; but, being only severely wounded, it went with the strong wind a long distance, and dropped. We searched in vain amongst the grey rocks, but could not find it. The other bird still kept flying about out of reach of gunshot, while the first entirely disappeared, and was no more seen. We came that way exactly a month afterwards; and I went to see the nest, and found two Ospreys with one egg in it. I took the eggs from the same nest the year before, and shot the female bird; but some time after, I was told that, notwithstanding my having killed her, the other one had in a few days procured a fresh mate, and hatched and brought off the young. It was this circumstance that induced me to call a second time this season at the same nest. Whether it was the male or female that Mr. St. John shot I cannot say; but I have no doubt that it was killed." On another occasion, Mr. Dunbar informed me that the nest was on an island in a loch, similar to those from which the two other eggs he sent me at the same time were obtained, " placed on the top of a rock, and composed of an immense heap of an old white sticks. It had been built in the same spot as long as the oldest in-

[1] [The foregoing remarks were communicated by Mr. Wolley, in 1853, to Mr. Hewitson, to whom I am indebted for leave to quote them here. They will be found at pp. 19 and 20 of the third edition of his well-known work.—Ed.]

habitant could recollect, and, from the difficulty of access, the loch being so deep and the island so far from the shore, could not be got at but by a good swimmer. I swam to it, and got the eggs."

[Of the remaining two eggs sent by Mr. Dunbar to Mr. Wolley, one, taken 20th May, 1848, was given to the late Mr. J. D. Salmon; the other, taken 25th May, 1848, is in Mr. Osbert Salvin's Collection. I cannot find that Mr. Wolley visited any one of these nests, though he was in their immediate neighbourhood.]

§ 82. *Three.*—Sutherlandshire, 5 May, 1849. " J. W. *ipse.*"

O. W. tab. vii. fig. 2.

Now the forester, having carefully extinguished the fire at which I had been warming my Golden Eaglets [§ 26], marched for a loch where he said the "Fishing Gled" always built, and where last year it was robbed by a gentleman in a boat. (It appears from Mr. St. John's 'Tour in Sutherlandshire,' i. p. 89, that Mr. Dunbar took a young one and an egg out of the nest, leaving the old Ospreys undisturbed.) The forester pointed out the wrong rock; but with the glass I readily distinguished on another, of conical shape, the nest, and the head of the bird upon it. After a round of a mile or two we reached the nearest point to it. I saw the white head of the bird, which almost immediately stood up, and then took to flight. It made a turn, and uttered a musical kind of cry. The forester was sure it had eggs. I was thinly clad, and had been alternately hot and cold during the day, in the valley or on the mountain; but I was determined to swim to the nest, in spite of the remonstrances of the forester and of my men, none of whom could do so. Luckily, another of them arrived in time for me to use the string as I had intended; for, as I was getting chilled by the wind, I could not have waited. I immediately stripped, put on the belt, which turned out a very inefficient assistance, and tied the string to the nozzle of it in front, Lord Derby's little basket[1] being fastened by a string behind me. After the first dip, it was so cold that I all but came out again. But I determined not to recede; so on I went, making good way till I came to the first ridge of rocks, some of which were under water. By this time I was very cold, and becoming exhausted. Just as I reached the first rock under water the string was checked, being, as I supposed, come to an end. Knowing how a second plunge, after being on land, would chill me, I almost turned to swim back; for I feared they would let go the string rather than pull me back, when it

¹ [See page 28, *note.*—ED.]

would have been all up with me.   However, to my great satisfaction,
I saw them tying the thin rope to the end of the string.   Then
striking off again, after floundering amongst the sunk rocks, to the
leeward of which, for the sake of the string, I took care to keep
as much as possible, I reached the peak.   It was nearly perpendicular both above and below water, and no landing-place appeared.
However, a bit of rock, twice as big as a walnut, projected; and
higher up I stuck my claws into some roots of *Polypodium*, as in
getting to an Eagle's nest on a former occasion [§ 27].   My arms
had hardly strength to hoist me up; but at last I reached the top and
caught the cutting wind.   At once I saw an egg, and in half a second
two more, a little removed from the first—all beautiful.   To my
surprise, the basket held all three.   I had a little difficulty in tying
the lid on, and even then one rolled out; the handle, too, became
loose.   However, for my life I durst not lose time.   I tried to
descend with my back to the rock, but it was no go, and I fell into
the water.   The peak might be twelve or fourteen feet high.   One
glance at the nest was all I could spare.   It reminded me of a large
wood-ants', large and flat at the top, the sticks not nearly so big as
those of an Eagle's, but the upper part apparently very compact, where
it struck me as being composed entirely of moss—the interstices of the
sticks seeming to be filled up with soil or turf, so as to make an almost
solid mass.   But I could not afford a second look.   In tumbling off,
I did not strike against any sunk rock, so that my fall was easy.
Somehow (I cannot say exactly say how) the handle was quite off the
basket, and my only way of saving it was to carry it in my closed
fist, which very much increased the difficulty of swimming.   As soon
as the men saw me fall into the water, they hauled hard upon the
string; and I, coming across a sunk rock, disappeared beneath the
surface.   This frightened them, and they hauled the harder.   As
soon as I came to the top, I had just breath enough to shout,
"Gently!"   But on they dragged; and the wind blowing the water
into white streaks of foam, the waves washed over me, and the
quantity of water I swallowed was something considerable.   The
pulling almost prevented my swimming, and as the string was
fastened low, it helped me very little through the water; I had long
been afraid of its breaking, till at last I got sufficient breath to throw
my "Gently!" to their ears.   Fortunately, they took the hint, and I
gradually reached the shore quite exhausted, when they found me all
scratched and bloody from the rocks.   They had not guessed my
condition until I was very near them, and they did not understand
the danger of hauling too hard.   All I could say for some time was,

" Worse than an Eagle's nest." When they had dressed me, and
taken the eggs out of my hand, I started running to recover my
circulation; but my legs were insensible, and I soon dropped in the
long heather. Fortunately I saw the forester passing near me, and
gave him a hail. The others came up and held me on each side.
They got me across several streams, and at length into a good road a
few hundred yards from the house where we were expected. Here,
with the assistance of a good fire and three or four tumblers of toddy,
I was soon all right. We all chatted over the day. The forester
wished to take me to one or two Eagles' nests; and named a loch to
the north-west, where the Osprey built, and other places for it in the
parish. He said that here its eggs were more thought of than Eagle's.
The ones I took were quite fresh.

The following day I took the son of my landlord to walk; and our
steps naturally bent towards the Osprey's nest, which is probably
the one from which, the year before, Mr. Dunbar took three young
ones, and Mr. St. John, as he himself relates in his book (Tour in
Sutherlandshire, i. pp. 90–93), shot the old male. Just after leaving
the house, I had a good view of an Osprey hovering over the bay and
stream, with Gulls persecuting it. In hovering, it moved its wings
rather slowly, but it more frequently sailed motionless like a Kite.
We turned along the south side of the bay till we came to some
houses, where we got a little lad to take us to two lochs, one of which
the forester mentioned to me the day before. My guide, who called
the bird in Gaelic " Allan-yasker[1]," soon brought us to one of them;
and there was the rock, about a hundred yards from the bank. The
direction is not, as Mr. St. John says (*loc. cit.*), north-west from
Rhiconnich, nor do I remember such high rocks as he describes or
figures in his engraving (at p. 105). The nest was on the south-west
side of a large stone, loose, or apparently so; and its level was on a
line with the top of the stone. Below the nest was some turf and
grass, and a little shrub growing. It seemed very compact, like an
ants', and at the top was much moss; but disordered, as if not
touched since last year. The landing appeared to be perfectly easy.
The stone looked from the bank to be about five feet high. The nest
seemed to be made of sticks, mixed up with fine turf-soil, and apparently a little heather amongst it. Neither I nor the boys could
reach it with a stone. Just as we were leaving it I heard a musical
cry, which I did not at first recognize as that of the Osprey; however, it turned out to be so, and the bird flew round the loch, afraid
to light on the nest. At the larger loch, near a little isthmus leading

[1] [Corrupted no doubt from " Iolair-an-uisge," Eagle of the Water.—ED.]

to a peninsula in the midst, I was within thirty or forty yards of an old Osprey's nest, not touched this year, and perhaps not inhabited for some time—even since a boat, which I saw rotting on the north shore, was first put on the loch. The nest was made of sticks mixed with pieces of turfy-looking stuff, and built on the north side of the rock, which might have been six feet high, and was very steep. There were streaks of white dung visible on the nest close to the peak, which rather overtopped it; there were also one or two patches of *Polypodium* and patches of close moss or lichen. A likely-looking rock at the far south-west end of the loch I had not time to examine.

The day after, I passed the loch where I had taken the eggs two days before, and saw the old Osprey sitting on the side of her nest.

Later in the month (21st May), I stopped at an old castle on a loch to examine an Osprey's nest, in which a man was said to have shot the bird several years previously, but in which, I have been since assured, there were eggs for many seasons afterwards, and that a bird was killed the year before by Mr. St. John's companion, though that gentleman says nothing about it. Indeed I heard that Lord Ellesmere had expressed his regret that it should have been disturbed. The nest seemed in good condition, placed on the highest point of the ruin, and inaccessible except with ropes or a ladder. It was just like the three others I have described. I waited in the ruin for a shot at the Gulls which continued to pass, when I saw an Osprey flying up. It went by at a little distance without attempting to alight, or seeming to take any interest in the nest.

In a letter which I received in July 1850, from this quarter, I was told that the Osprey had not bred there since 1848; and my informant added that, up to the time of his writing, he had not seen any flying about that year. Another correspondent about the same time assured me of his belief that there was then only one nest in the county of Sutherland, which been taken at the request of an English gentleman.

§ 83. *Two.*—Inverness-shire, 29 April, 1851.

O. W. tab. H.

These two beautiful eggs I obtained from a correspondent, 3 May, 1851, they being the only result of a ten days' nesting expedition undertaken by him. He took them at three o'clock in the morning of 29th April, 1851, at the ruins of an old castle on an island in an Inverness-shire loch. After walking nearly all night, he reached the spot in the midst of a snow-storm; and having tied a cord to his life-preserver, he swam off, leaving the other end in charge of a man on shore. On the island he tied the rope to a stone and climbed up the ruins, slipping about in six inches of snow. Having found two eggs in the nest, he discovered that he had left his cap behind him. He tried one egg in his mouth, but could not breathe with it; and at last he swam ashore on his back with an egg in each hand, the man pulling him with the cord. He blew the eggs in the boat-house, washing out the inside with whisky. He had taken these eggs for four years, and the old birds have always had a second brood. The first or second year an old woman saw him come out of the water, and ran into the cottage; since then he has always gone earlier in the morning, and no one has known anything about it. He was exceedingly anxious that I should go early one morning and see him take the other egg or eggs out of the nest for me; but, considering my position there, I declined—the more so as I suspected the proprietress protected the birds; and I have been since assured that there was a man appointed on purpose to take care of them. After I had finally refused his offer, he mentioned incidentally that Mr. R. Gordon-Cumming had got into a great scrape for harrying this nest some years before. The day after I got these eggs, Mr. Edge and I went to the loch; we got to the side of it most distant from the castle, but we saw the head of the Osprey on the nest looking about it in every direction. The cottage was just beyond the castle, from where we were. We then came back round the loch; and as we got near, the bird rose and left the nest, which was now very conspicuous; but she soon lighted on it again, and settled herself down. The wind was bitterly cold, and it was constantly snowing and hailing. I made a sketch of the place [1]; and whilst I was doing so the cock bird came up and alighted on an adjoining part of the wall, first putting down his long claws. The distance of the castle from the shore might be one hundred and twenty yards : the old doorway was on a level with the water; but the whole loch was then somewhat dammed up by a kind of weir. At one time both the birds were flying at once. We went to the house, and saw the old woman before mentioned, who told us that one morning, several years before, she saw "a chiel'" coming out of the water, who had been to the nest. In the old castle was born, we were told, the first Marquis of Huntly.

§ 84. *Three.*—Inverness-shire, 8 May, 1852.

These three eggs from a nest on the same loch as those last mentioned. My correspondent wrote to me as follows :—"The three

[1] [From this sketch, Mr. Jury has executed the plate (tab. H).—ED.]

eggs I took myself all at once on the night of 8th May 1852, between eleven and twelve o'clock.. As it was very dark, and there was no moon, I had the precaution to take my cousin along with me, and he proved of great service. I took off my clothes, and put on my life-preserver, attaching a cord to the back of it. By the help of a fusee I was able to distinguish that the time I was about to launch my carcase into the water was twenty-five minutes to twelve. I got over quite safe. The cock bird flew away before I reached the island; and after I had climbed up to the top of the ruin, and was just at the nest, I put out my hand to catch the hen, but when she felt me she gave a loud scream and flew away also. On arriving at the island I had fixed the cord to a bush; and on coming back I had some diffi-culty in finding it owing to the darkness of the night; but when I did so, I secured it to my belt and bawled to my cousin to pull, which he did. In the middle I was taken with the cramp, but he succeeded in hauling me out. After dressing we forded the river, which was very high at the time; and on going across with my cousin on my back, I stumbled, and down he went, but he managed to get on his feet; and this put an end to our adventures."

In a former letter he had told me that these eggs were taken after Mr. R. Gordon-Cumming had already been to the nest and taken one egg.

§ 85. *One.*—Inverness-shire, 1851.

This egg, with another which I subsequently gave to Mr. J. D. Salmon, was sent to me by the person from whom I obtained the last two, but not from the same locality. He informed me that the eggs were taken in 1851 by a shepherd, from whom he received them, but that he himself had three times robbed the nest of this pair of birds. The first year he took it from the ruins of a shooting-lodge, the second from a dead Scotch fir tree, and the third year (1850) from the old lodge again, when the hen bird was shot by one of his relations, who lay in wait and shot it with a walking-stick gun, in company with a gentleman, Mr. John Hancock, who sketched it as it lay dead. In 1851 a new lodge was built, close against the old one. There was another nest several years ago in a tree, which my informant knew of, and made a drawing of it, as well as he could, for the same gentleman. The following year my informant sent me an-other egg of the Osprey, but from what locality he was unable to make out. This egg is now in Mr. J. P. Wilmot's Collection. In 1851, I heard from another quarter that one of two Englishmen that year got an Osprey's nest, and shot the bird, from a loch in Ross-shire, where time out of mind it had bred.

§ 86. *Three.*—Æijävaara, East Bothnia, 25 May, 1854. " J. W. *ipse.*"

These eggs were taken by myself from a nest about seven fathoms from the ground, on the top of a tree, a Scotch fir, still feebly living, near Kangas-järwi, on the Muonio-alusta side of the lake. One bird was seen to leave the nest when we were still far away, and the two flew round, whilst we were there, at a good distance, seldom crying. Under the tree was a great mass of sticks—an old nest which had fallen to the ground. I caused myself to be concealed in a heap of fir-branches; and it was not long before one of the old birds came and hovered for a moment just over the nest, then went away, and came back straight into it. Ludwig and Heiki returning a little, she rose on my side. This was repeated a second time, and I then fired just as she left; and she fell at my feet with four or five shots in her body, and a broken leg[1]. Another tree being reared by the side of the one already there, I climbed up to the branches, and then it was easy to go to the top. I let down a string for my tin box, and, when I got it, lowered the three beautiful eggs. The nest was made of good-sized sticks, large at the top, lined with tree-hair and moss. The cock bird came rather near, and cried several times. The Saturday before (20th May), Heiki had been up and found only one egg in the nest: it was probably the one I have marked with a cross, for this only showed the slightest symptoms of having been sat on. This man, as others do hereabouts, believes that the markings are brought out by incubation. We took the nest a little after midnight—in fact, on the 26th May.

Heiki visited this nest in 1855, but it had fallen to the ground. He and another man found a new nest on the same hill that year, about a quarter of a mile (Swedish) from the old one. They discovered it by a fish lying on the ground, but the nest was scarcely visible: it was a large thick tree, he thinks more than a fathom and a half round, and by measurement more than eleven fathoms high.

§ 87. *Three.*—Kangas-järwi, East Bothnia, 23 May, 1854.

Taken by Apoo from the nest he had led me to, 15th May, then

[1] [I believe that the skin of this bird was presented by Mr. Wolley to Mr. Felkin of Beeston: its sternum he gave to my brother. (Osteoth. Newt. *MS. Cat.* No. 1, c.)—Ed.]

empty, but the birds flying about with symptoms of anxiety. The tree was a Scotch fir, and living. Another tree was reared up to form steps.

§ 88. *Three.*—Kangas-järwi, East Bothnia, 26 May, 1855.

O. W. tab. vii. fig. 3.

Brought by Apoo the day that he took them from the nest, which he showed me, and afterwards robbed, the year before [§ 87].

§ 89. *Two.*—Kangas-järwi, East Bothnia, 1855.

Taken by Apoo; probably a second laying in the former nest.

§ 90. *Three.*—Kyrö, Kemi Lappmark, 1854.

Out of seven from four nests, brought by Nikoo on Midsummer Day. As some of them were far away in the woods, he could not spare time to wait for the full layings.

Two of these seven formed lots 1 and 2 at Mr. Stevens's, 26th January 1855, and passed into the possession of Mr. W. H. Simpson and Mr. H. F. Walter respectively. A third is in Mr. G. D. Rowley's collection.

§ 91. *Three* —Muonioniska, East Bothnia, 29 May, 1854.

O. W. tab. vii. fig. 5.

Taken by Salamon on the day he went, with another man, over Pallas-tunturi. Brought to Ludwig, 4th June; slightly sat upon.

§ 92. *Three.*—Saivo-mutka, East Bothnia, 1854.

Apparently Osprey's, though said to be the eggs of *Walkaja Skuolfi, i.e.* Snowy Owl! Taken from a high tree in the same wood that I visited, and brought 2nd July 1854.

§ 93. *Three.*—Saivo-mutka, East Bothnia, 1855.

Taken by Olli, and brought to Ludwig, 2nd June. They were

from the same nest as the last year's [§ 92], which were brought by
Elias as the eggs of *Skuolfi*. Olli said, this year, that they were the
eggs of *Kalasääski, i. e.* Osprey, and that he had said so last year:
the lie was with Elias.

§ 94. *Three.*—Rowajoki, South-west Finmark, Norway, 1855.

O. W. tab. vii. fig. 1., and tab. B.

There were four eggs taken at twice in this nest, by the old man
of Pyha-ota.

[On our way from Skjbotn to Kilpis-järwi, 25th-26th July 1855, we passed
the nest from which these eggs were taken, and I made a sketch of it. It was
in a Scotch fir tree close to the track,—a very large structure of sticks. The
tree stood in a comparatively open space in the forest, and, thus having plenty
of room and air, had preserved its lower branches, presenting a remarkably
symmetrical appearance, very different from other trees of the kind growing
around. My sketch, from which the accompanying plate (tab. B.) is drawn,
though with no pretensions to artistic effect, was considered by my companions
to be characteristic, and therefore I have had it engraved. This nest is also
mentioned in ' Frazer's Magazine,' No. 316, for April 1856.]

§ 95. *Two.*—Rowajoki, South-west Finmark, Norway, 1857.

Received by me from the wife of Pyha-ota, at which place I
subsequently saw the lad who found them. I also saw the nest, the
same I had eggs from in 1855, and which Mr. A. Newton sketched.

§ 96. *Three.*—Lettas-eno, Enontekis Lappmark, 1855.

Near the *Mänty-raja, i. e.* the fir-tree boundary, above Markina
or Enontekis, on the Russian side. Taken by Nälima's boy, helped
by a little lad, Matti.

§ 97. *Two.*—Sardio, East Bothnia, 21 May, 1855.

One of Heiki's nests, all of which were kept carefully distinct by
him.

Heiki told me afterwards (15th March 1857), that in 1855 he
found six Osprey's nests. The first was in Æijävaara, not far from the
great Æijän-paikka, a new nest, probably made by the old cock bird of
that from which, in 1854, I shot the hen [§ 86], with a new mate.

He could hardly get it even with the help of my climbing-irons. He was not there in 1856 to see if there were eggs or not. In 1857, this nest was taken by another man, at two or three o'clock in the morning. The bird was coming home with a fish (a Pike) in its claws. The three eggs now in Mr. Simpson's collection. The second was in Sardio, near Kangasjärwi. He had found it the autumn before. It was in a living tree, not difficult to get up. It was not visited in 1856, being a long way off, a quarter of a mile (Swedish) from Kangasjärwi, and he was alone. There were two eggs. The third was on Kemilaisen-vaara-nenasa. It was first found in the winter. Visible from Särkijärwi, a long way off. A living tree, thick, but not difficult to climb. His finger-nails (*kynsi*) were not wanted. Not inhabited in 1856. But he thinks the owners, that year, built on Terwa-järwen-maa, not more than three hundred fathoms from his own house. A Rough-legged Buzzard was mending the nest as he went to it, but was frightened away. In the summer he saw an Osprey mending it, and it had already made the nest very complete. This nest I myself visited in 1857, in which year he subsequently took two Osprey's eggs from a nest on the same hill. The bird was very angry with, and almost attacked, him. It changed its nest three times that year. It was originally in Terwa-järwen-maa, then on Kemilaisen-vaara (where the eggs, two in number, were taken), and afterwards back again at the first place, upon another nest, which had been begun the year before, in a Scotch fir about eight fathoms high. The fourth nest which Heiki took in 1855 was on Tuorki-särki-vaara, a hill on the other side of Särki-järwi, and about half a mile from the third he found; the tree a Scotch fir, against which another had long ago fallen; the nest about eight or nine fathoms from the ground. There were eggs here in 1856, which he took, as also in 1857, then leaving one as a nest-egg, to which, however, the bird laid no more. In 1856 it made many swoops at him with its claws open, and almost frightened him in such a dangerous place. The fifth nest was in Lappin-kenta-maa; it was found by Heiki and Josa, the latter of whom had probably known something of it before. It was in a living Scotch fir, very difficult to climb. Josa went up with the irons, Heiki helping with a long pole. As he was at the nest, the bird seized the lad's cap, flew some little distance, and then dropped it. He was hurt, too[1]. This place was a little way on the other side of Sieppi. The last nest Heiki took in 1855 was at Jonka-rowa or Kalkion-rowa, somewhat between the two. Josa was again with him, and they found it together. It was on a *honka*, or dead Scotch

---

[1] [To what extent it does not appear.—ED.]

fir. In 1856 Heiki took three eggs (3rd June) from this nest.
The tree was a dangerous one, thin and rickety, so that he was half
afraid of going up. It was on the Ollas-järwi side of Ollas-tunturi,
the first hill from the mountain. Heiki informed me that even
while an Osprey is making its nest, it always goes there to eat a fish
when it has caught one.

§ 98. *Three.*—East Bothnia, 24 May, 1855.

Taken by Heiki, and brought to Ludwig, 1st June. Marked by
both. [See § 97.]

§ 99. *Three.*—East Bothnia, 29 May, 1855.

One of the nests taken by Heiki. [See § 97.]

§ 100. *Three.*—Nikivaara, Sardio, Kemi Lappmark, 26 May,
1855.

Brought by Michael, who took them on Whitsun-eve. About
three weeks later, he took three more eggs from the same nest.

§ 101. *Three.*—Salmo-järwi, East Bothnia, 1855.

Brought by Fetto, 23rd June.

§ 102. *Three.*—Nangi, West Bothnia, 1 June, 1857. "J. W."

O. W. tab. A.

The bird belonging to this nest was first seen to fly over the
Muoniovaara ridge, near Mellavaara, 29th May. The next day I went
with Apoo to the great *Seita* stone to lurk for it. It very soon
appeared far to the south, with a fish in its claws ; and with my glass
I watched it over Nangi, bullied, as I had seen it before (19th May), by
a Rough-legged Buzzard. I even thought that I could see the nest.
31st May and 1st June, I looked for it again in vain, though in the
mean time I had twice seen it fly over the house at Muoniovaara with
a fish. In the evening of the last-mentioned day I went with Josa
to Kimi-lakka, and there we climbed up a tree and watched for a
long time without its appearing, but I thought I could see the nest

in a broad-topped tree. I pointed out the spot to Josa, and, as he found, correctly. He started, and in the course of the night reached the marsh across which it was. A large, very thick tree, and on the trunk *puu merki* [timber-marks], now filled with turpentine, and probably of the last year, made by the Mudos-lombola people. He climbed up with my irons, and said the inside of the nest was easy to come at, owing to the breadth of the tree-top. Anton and Ludwig had seen the bird flying in that direction in 1856. The eggs were perhaps two days incubated, the bird could hardly have been here above a fortnight. Heiki thought the nest had probably been prepared the preceding summer [1].

§ 103. *Three.*—Lebeme-lombola-vaara, Lapland, 18–20 May, 1858.

O. W. tab. vii. fig. 6.

Brought from Kihlangi, 23rd May, by a boy, having been found as above by his father.

§ 104. *Three.*—Wuondis-järwi, Enontekis Lappmark, 1858.

Brought by Heiki, 6th June, from Johan Sieppi; found in a Scotch fir, about twelve fathoms high. The nest was at the top of the tree, about three-eighths of a mile (Swedish) to the north-east of Sieppi.

§ 105. *Two.*—Kielisen-palla, Enontekis Lappmark, 28 May, 1858.

Brought at the same time as the last, from the same man, having

[1] [The "great *Seita* stone," mentioned above, is a huge boulder of gneiss, lying in the forest on Muoniovaara, and, before the conversion of the Lapps to Christianity, was used by them as a place of offering, whereon some of the spoils of the chase were from time to time deposited, in token of thanksgiving. (Cf. Scheffer, ' Lapponia, &c.,' Francofurti, 1673, capp. ix. x.) Access to the top seems to have been gained by means of the trunk of a tree, in which notches were cut to serve as steps; and this rude ladder was still in existence, though much decayed at the lower end, when I made the sketch from which Mr. Jury's plate (tab. A) is taken. The space immediately around has been long ago cleared of trees, excepting the two large Scotch firs standing close to the altar. These, however, had been stripped of their bark to the height of some ten feet, and were dead; their lower branches being plentifully hung with tresses of the *luppu*, or " tree-hair" (*Lichen barbatus* or *L. jubatus*, I believe). But numerous young firs were springing up luxuriantly on every side. This stone now bears an inscription in Runic characters.—ED.]

been found by him as above in a Scotch fir. The nest was about eight fathoms from the ground, and about three-quarters of a mile to the north-west.

§ 106. *Three.*—Lussika-palla, Kemi Lappmark, 11 June, 1858.

O. W. tab. vii. fig. 4.

Found as above by Johan Wassara, and brought by him 19th June. The nest was in a Scotch fir, about six or seven fathoms from the ground.

§ 107. *Three.*—Ranta-sadio, East Bothnia, 4 June 1859.

Found as above by Apoo, near Kangasjärwi, and brought by him 11th June.

§ 108. *Three.*—Vandes-rowa, Enontekis Lappmark, June, 1859.

Brought by Johan Sieppi, 23rd June, having been found by him as above, about three weeks previously.

§ 109. *Two.*—Kieliselde, Enontekis Lappmark, June 1859.

Brought by the same man with the last, having been found by him about ten days before.

[§ 110. *Two.*—Scottish Highlands, prior to 1831. From the late Mr. Yarrell's Collection.

These two eggs I bought at the sale of the late Mr. Yarrell's collection, 5th December 1856, in which they formed part of lot 349. The late Mr. J. D. Salmon, who was present, told me he well remembered to have seen them in Mr. Yarrell's cabinet when he inspected it prior to starting on his expedition to Orkney in 1831. He added that he was nearly sure of their being Scotch specimens, and that at that time so little was known respecting the nidification of the Osprey, that he fully expected to meet with it breeding on the sea-cliffs in either or both of the Orkneys and Shetlands.]

CIRCAETUS GALLICUS (Gmelin).

SHORT-TOED EAGLE.

[§ 111. *One.*—" Germany." From M. E. Verreaux's Collection, 1861.]

[§ 112. *One.*—"South Russia." From Herr A. Heinke, of Kamuschin, through Dr. Albert Günther, 1863.

There may be a mistake in ascribing this specimen to *Circaetus gallicus.* It is a good deal marked with pale rust-coloured blotches, but not as much so as two eggs from Algeria in Mr. Tristram's collection.]

ASTUR PALUMBARIUS (Linnæus).

GOS-HAWK.

[It will be seen from the following notes, that it is not a very uncommon occurrence for the eggs of this species to be somewhat coloured. But the markings of pale olive tint, sometimes of a vermiform character, have not been mentioned by any author that I am aware of, nor do I know that they have ever been observed in any other species of *Accipitres.* That they are to be considered as indications of real colour, and not stains, I do not think there is any reason to doubt.]

§ 113. *Four.*—Palo-joki, Tornea Lappmark, 16 May, 1854.

Taken by a boy, about two weeks before my visit. The boy's father said they were *Koppelo-Haukka* [*i. e.* "Capercally-Hawk"], as there can be little doubt they are. The young inside had bones formed, which were difficult to extract through the moderate-sized holes I have made. They had begun to decompose.

§ 114. *Four.*—Saivo-mutka, West Bothnia, 19 May, 1854.

Taken by the son of a Kätkesuando man. I went to the wood and saw a nest of last year, on the first fork of the tree, not very high. It appeared just like one of the Gos-Hawk's nests near Muoniovaara; there can be no doubt these eggs are Gos-Hawk's.

There are young in them, which in several days would be ready for exclusion. Buzzard here is, I think, never so early.

§ 115. *Three.*—Mudos-järwi, West Bothnia, 28 May, 1854.

These eggs with large young, the fourth hatched. Brought to me at Œfrebyn, by agreement. The man was sure it was *Koppelo-Haukka*. He knows *Piekonna* [*Archibuteo lagopus*] well; but this was quite another kind, which dashes off from its nest and is no more seen. Nothing but birds' bones under the tree. The legs of the young in the nest have no rudiments of feathers, and the fourth toe is much thinner, and its claw much shorter, than the second.

§ 116. *Three.*—Mudos-järwi, West Bothnia, 1855.

Taken from the same nest as the last year's eggs [§ 115], and by the same man. Ludwig got them from him at Muonio-alusta, on the 1st June, as he was working his tar-pit.

§ 117. *Three.*—Alten, West Finmark, N. lat. 69° 52', 29 April, 1855. " J. W. *ipse.*"

These three eggs were taken by myself about a quarter of a mile (Norwegian) south of Jura-holm, or, at least, of the house which is near the point of the islet. I went this morning (the day I am writing), with Knut, to the place where he had seen some bird of prey making its nest in a tree. It had built there for many years, though one season its four young ones were thrown to the ground by a man who climbed up. It was on the east side of the river, and we saw it first from a bank or old raised beach. Then the bird appeared, showing white over the tail. It was long out of sight; but, on our hiding ourselves at a distance, it flew and settled in a large tree. I saw it perfectly with my telescope, even to its yellow eye. The long tail and figure alone would have shown the bird; and its flight, to a falconer, would have been at a glance decisive, while I at once saw the shortness of its wings. It had several kinds of cries. My guide, who has been a great vermin-slayer, did not know whether he should get *skat*[1] for it, as it was not a *falk*. The nest was at a good height, in a large Scotch fir; and I got up to it by making a ladder of a small

---

[1] [The reward given by the local authorities on the production of the heads of certain birds and beasts of prey.—ED.]

tree, which reached to the lower branches when raised against them. I found it to be of prodigious thickness. As I stood on the branches on which its lower part rested, the level of the top was some inches above my head. It was quite like the celebrated Jackdaw's nest at Eton[1], built up to get to a fresh point of support, which in this case was afforded by a large fork. An old nest, or part of this one, had fallen to the ground some time before. At the bottom its diameter was very considerable, and it rose rather spirally upwards. At its side a Squirrel's "drey" had formerly been built into it. The sticks of which it was composed were, in the case of the largest, from half to three-quarters of an inch in diameter, but most of them much smaller. There was a moderate-sized hollow, with a few fresh sprigs of Scotch fir in it, and half-a-dozen small strips of the cuticle of birch-trees. The bird only showed itself once whilst we were at the tree, and then it was after I had descended. It was at a respectable distance, and chattered a good deal. The eggs, perfectly fresh, were probably not yet complete in number. It was a snowy, windy day, but warm. The old snow still deep on the river; but banks exposed to the sun were in some places already bare.

§ 118. *Three.*—Muonio-vaara, West Bothnia, 19 May, 1855. "With feather. L. M. K."

O. W. tab. B.

Found by Ludwig and Anton at the lower end of the hill near Sisnakka-järwi. Anton had seen the nest even last year or the year before; but it looked so small that he had taken it for a Crow's. This spring, as they were going by, he just mentioned it to Ludwig; and the latter thought they might as well get up the tree. As Anton was halfway up, the bird shot out of the nest; and Ludwig heard, now or presently afterwards, the cackling noise which is so different from the cry of the Buzzard. He is most positive as to the bird, little as the eggs are, and small though the nest be. There were big young in the eggs.

P.S.—17th August. I have been with Ludwig and Mr. A. Newton to see the nest, evidently a Gos-Hawk's. We found a Gos-Hawk's feather under it, which Ludwig remembered falling from the bird[2].

---

[1] [The nest described and figured by Mr. Jesse in his 'Scenes and Tales of a Country Life,' (1844) pp. 57–59, and frontispiece.—ED.]

[2] [On this occasion I made a sketch of the nest, from which Mr. Jury has been able to draw the plate above referred to. I only wish it had been in my power to

§ 119. *Four.*—Sardio, Kemi Lappmark, 8 May, 1856. "With bird."

Taken on Palo-vaara by Michel. He caught the bird in an iron trap. It is now before me, and is apparently a female.

[Two of these eggs are marked with true colour. One is blotched decidedly with rusty, more so than any I have ever seen.]

§ 120. *Three.*—Muonio-vaara, West Bothnia, 14 May, 1856. "L. M. K. with bird."

These eggs found by Anton; but the bird, a hen, snared by Ludwig.

§ 121. *One.*—Jeris-järwi, East Bothnia, 21 May, 1856.

This nest, with four eggs, was found by Heiki, on Kutu-nivan-maa, on the banks of Turmas-lombola, just to the west of Jeris-järwi; and the eggs were brought on the 25th May. Heiki says he found this nest in 1855, with young ones in it.

[Three of the eggs from this nest were sold by Mr. Stevens in 1857 to Messrs. Bond, Braikenridge, and Troughton. The remaining specimen now in the collection is a remarkably elongated one.]

§ 122. *Three.*—Kurkio-vaara, 1856. "With bird."

These eggs were written on by Ludwig, after he had seen the bird, which was shot, but not brought to me until the 5th April 1857. Being marked eggs, as well as small ones, they required care in the accepting. One of them is decidedly spotted. The spots on another are also probably natural, but not so satisfactory.

---

have given an illustration of the wonderful and, no doubt, ancient structure, described by Mr. Wolley in the preceding section (§ 117). As an instance of the practice of accurate observation which Mr. Wolley enjoined upon all his collectors, I may add to what he has above said, that as we were going to the nest, and talking with Ludwig of his former visit, when he took the eggs, he mentioned that as the bird dashed off, one of her wing-feathers dropped out. Mr. Wolley remarked that he ought to have preserved it, as it would have served to identify the species to which the nest belonged. The lad replied that, as it was not likely any one had since been there, no doubt we should still find it where it lay. This proved to be the case; and on Mr. Wolley picking it up, he asked Ludwig from which of the bird's wings it was shed. Reflecting a moment, he answered, "The right wing;" and so it was! The feather is now before me, and is undoubtedly a Gos-Hawk's. —ED.]

§ 123. *Four.*—Palo-joki, Enontekis Lappmark, 1856.

Taken in Jankalen-maa by a man of Palo-järwi, but the place is near Palo-joki. Palo-järwi is one mile north of Leppa-järwi. They were brought to Muoniovaara 8th July.

§ 124. *Three.* — Jungki-järwin-maa, East Bothnia, 14 May, 1857.

These eggs, brought to Muoniovaara by my special messenger, Apoo, were taken by Heiki the day before. He blew them at once, not expecting there would be any opportunity of sending or bringing them, as he had been long unwell. They were quite fresh, but he thinks the nest was full. Last year there were young when he found the nest. One egg is very interesting from its most decided markings, even of a vermiform character. Heiki observed that they were the smallest eggs of *Koppelo-Haukka* he had ever seen. It is noticeable that the markings [of a pale olive tint] have the character of those occasionally seen on the eggs of Ducks.

§ 125. *Three.*—Ruona-vaara, Kemi Lappmark, 8 May, 1858.

Brought to Muoniovaara by the finder the following day. They were taken by himself near Mutka-vaara. He saw the bird, which flew from the nest.

[These three eggs are all more or less marked in the singular manner which, in the preceding section, Mr. Wolley has well compared to the blotches of colour which some Ducks' eggs exhibit. But one of them has, in addition to the pale olive markings, some very decided specks of dark brown overlying the former of quite another character, which have a tendency to chip off, as does some of the thickly laid-on colour on the eggs of many Eagles, Buzzards, and Falcons.]

§ 126. *Two.*—Touraine, France. From M. Parzudaki's Collection, 1856.

[§ 127. *One.*—Mr. J. H. Gurney's Menagerie, 1857.

This egg was given to me by Mr. Gurney in 1858, being one of five or six laid by a Gos-Hawk in his possession. The bird evinced a great desire to sit, and some Bantam's eggs were given her for that purpose, but unfortunately nothing came of them.]

[§ 128. *Four.*—Mylenberg, Denmark, April, 1859.   From Herr
    H. C. Erichsen's Collection.

> These eggs were taken by Forester Sörensen in the wood at Mylenberg, near
> Hobro in Jutland, and were given to me by Herr Erichsen at Copenhagen in
> October 1859.]

[§ 129. *Three.*—Mylenberg, Denmark, April, 1859.   From
    Herr H. C. Erichsen's Collection.

> As the last (§ 128), but from another nest.]

ACCIPITER NISUS (Linnæus).

SPARROW-HAWK.

§ 130. *Four.*—England, prior to 1844.

§ 131. *One.*—England, 1836.   From Mr. Harvey.

§ 132. *Six.*—Scotland.   From Mr. W. Dunbar, 1850.

§ 133. *Six.*—England.   From Mr. J. Green, 1851.

§ 134. *Two.*—Ireland.   From Mr. J. Davis's Collection, through
    Dr. R. T. Frere, 1852 [and 1861].

§ 135. *One.*—England.   From Mr. J. Green, 1852.

§ 136. *Two.*—North Finland, 1854.

> Brought by Pekka, the Lapp, as *Nuoli-Haukka* [*i.e.* Bolt-Hawk],
> with the feet of the bird, which I recognized as Sparrow-Hawk's,
> before seeing the eggs.

§ 137. *Four.*—Kangas-järwi, East Bothnia, 21 June, 1857.

> Brought on 23rd June, having been found perhaps a quarter of a
> mile (Swedish) from the village. The nest was of spruce-twigs and
> tree-hair, and described as being just like that of a *Piekonna* [*Archi-*

buteo lagopus], but much less. They seem to be Sparrow-Hawk's. A beautiful nest.

§ 138. *Four.*—Pyha-ota, South-western Finmark, 1857.

From the son of the bad old man. They seem to be Sparrow-Hawk's.

§ 139. *Five.*—Parka-joki, East Bothnia, 1857.

Brought 27th June. They were in a spruce-tree. Beautiful eggs, and apparently Sparrow-Hawk's, being the third nest of this uncommon bird which I have received this summer.

§ 140. *Four.*—Hampshire, 1856. From Mr. A. F. Sealy's Collection.

Given to me at Cambridge, 10th November 1857. Taken at Micklemerst, out of one nest, by Mr. A. Maurice.

§ 141. Kemi Lappmark, 1857.

Brought to Muoniovaara, 25th December 1857, already blown.

§ 142. *Five.*—Ekkes-joki, Kemi Lappmark, 13 June, 1858.

Brought to Muoniovaara on the 19th of the same month. The nest, which was in a spruce, had five eggs.

§ 143. *Five.*—Kemi Lappmark, June, 1858.

Brought to Muoniovaara 24th June, having been found about a fortnight previously. There were five eggs in this nest.

§ 144. *Three.*—Lapland, 1859.

Brought to Muoniovaara on the 21st June, without any particulars.

[§ 145. *One.*—Elveden, 1844.]

[§ 146. *One.*—Stetchworth, Cambridgeshire, 1845.]

[§ 147. *Two.*—Elveden, 7 May, 1851. "E. N."]

[§ 148. *One.*—Methwold, Norfolk, 1851.   From Mr. J. Baker.]

[§ 149. *Five.*—Elveden, 17 May, 1852.]

[§ 150. *Two.*—Elveden, 29 May, 1853.]

[§ 151. *Two.*—Elveden, 1 June, 1853. "E. N."]

[§ 152. *Two.*—Sapiston, Suffolk, 5 May, 1853. "A. N."]

[§ 153. *Two.*—Fakenham, Suffolk, 20 May, 1856.]

[§ 154. *Two.*—Sutherlandshirc, 1857.]

[§ 155. *One.*—Elveden, 1861.]

[§ 156. *Five.*—Convoy, county Donegal, 18 June, 1862. From
    Mr. R. Harvey's Collection.]

TINNUNCULUS ALAUDARIUS, G. R. Gray.

KESTREL.

§ 157. *Four.*—Pity Wood, Derbyshire, prior to 1844.

§ 158. *One.*—Cambridgeshire (?).   From Mr. Osborne, of Ful-
    bourne, 1844.

§ 159. *Five.*—Sutherlandshire, 26 May, 1849. "J. W.   Bird
    shot."

On my way to fish in a little loch, where are Gillaroo Trout, I put
a Kestrel off her nest in a low rock overhanging a curious burn,
partly subterranean. On my return, I shot the female bird from the

nest; and on the next day, or morning following, two men took these eggs out of it, using a rope.

§ 160. *Three.*—Sutherlandshire. From Mr. W. Dunbar, 1850.

§ 161. *One.*—England (?). From Mr. J. Green's Collection, 1851.

§ 162. *Three.*—England (?). From Mr. J. Green's Collection, 1853.

One of these is an interesting egg, from its great resemblance to eggs of the Sparrow-Hawk.

§ 163. *Three.*—England (?), May, 1853. From Mr. J. Green's Collection.

§ 164. *Four.*—Petaja-vaara, Kemi Lappmark, about N. lat. 68°, May, 1857.

On the 23rd of July 1857 Nicolai brought these four eggs and said they belonged to a very shy, strange kind of Hawk, that flies high up from its nest, and that stands in the air in one place, and then changes its place. The nest was in a dry Scotch fir, three or four fathoms from the ground. It was found before the 30th of May. In August, the boy Gustaf has explained to me that it is a Hawk quite strange to the country: he does not know about its hovering, but it flies away from its nest, and sits to watch on a tall tree, in a manner quite different from *Pouta-Haukka* [*Falco æsalon*]. Nicolai had been before asked by me about this bird, and he said he had seen it once or so. On looking at these eggs among some thirty-eight Merlins', I see they are not larger than the largest of them, but are of a yellower red, or at least have a different look.

[On the whole, I have very little doubt that the eggs above-mentioned were rightly assigned by Mr. Wolley to the Kestrel. In his 'Catalogue of Eggs' for 1858 (p. 10), he suggests, and with probability, that the "unusual numbers of several kinds of mice" had attracted this species so far beyond its usual limits. Previously to 1857, he was aware of only one instance of its occurrence north of the Gulf of Bothnia. That happened on the 13th of September 1855, when he and I were approaching Haparanda, on the Swedish

G

side of the Tornea river. We then saw, and for some minutes watched, an
undoubted *Tinnunculus alaudarius* hovering over a corn-field by the road-side.
Its occasionally breeding further north was, however, known to Herr Wallengren (Naumannia, 1855, p. 134).]

§ 165. *Two.*—Elveden, April, 1859.   Given to me by Messrs.
A. and E. Newton.

[§ 166. *One.*—Elveden, 1845.]

[§ 167. *One.*—Stetchworth, Cambridgeshire, 1845.]

[§ 168. *One.*—Chippenham, Cambridgeshire, 1846.   From Mr.
F. Tharp.]

[§ 169. *One.*—Cambridgeshire (?).   From Mr. J. Baker, 1850.]

[§ 170. *Four.*—Icklingham, Suffolk, 8 May, 1851.]

[§ 171. *Four.*—Icklingham, Suffolk, 13 May, 1851.   " E. N."]

[§ 172. *Three.*—Elveden, 31 May, 1851.]

[§ 173. *Two.*—Barnham, Suffolk, 16 May, 1853.]

[§ 174. *One.*—Elveden, May 25, 1853.]

[§ 175. *Two.*—Elveden, April, 1857.]

[§ 176. *Five.*—Convoy, county Donegal, 18 June, 1862.   From
Mr. R. Harvey's Collection.]

[§ 177. *Two.*—Elveden, May, 1863.]

TINNUNCULUS CENCHRIS (Frisch).

LESSER KESTREL.

[§ 178. *Four.*—Bonkhori, Ætolia, 26 May, 1859.   "W. H. S."

Of these eggs, Mr. Simpson informs me that they were a complete sitting,
and " one of several found under the roof of a long line of farm-buildings

forming one side of an extensive square in the village of Vonkhori (more properly Bonkhori), in the province of Ætolia. All the sittings found in this building were placed upon the top of the outer wall, where it is met by the projecting roof; and in one or two instances there was some difficulty in introducing the hand sufficiently far to get at the eggs. There was no regular nest in any case, the eggs being simply placed in a slight depression amongst bits of lime and the remains of *Coleoptera*. The birds were very bold, and came close to us several times, thereby affording a good opportunity for identification."

Mr. Simpson has some general remarks on the nidification of this species as observed by him in Greece, in 'The Ibis' for 1860, pp. 380–81.]

FALCO LANARIUS, Linnæus.

LANNER.

[§ 179. *One.*—From M. E. Verreaux's Collection, 1861.]

[§ 180. *One.* —"Sarepta." From Herr H. F. Möschler's Collection, 1862.]

[§ 181. *One.*—Egypt, 1862. From Mr. S. S. Allen's Collection.

Mr. Allen told me that he obtained several eggs of this bird from the Arabs around the Pyramids. The skins of the birds he brought home were seen by Mr. Gurney, Dr. Sclater, Mr. Tristram, and myself; and I think we all agreed they were those of *Falco lanarius.*]

[§ 182. *One.*—"South Russia." From Herr A. Heinke, of Kamuschin, through Dr. Albert Günther, 1863.]

FALCO SACER, Gmelin.

SAKER.

[§ 183. *One.*—Island opposite Tchernawoda, River Danube, 29 April, 1860. "Bird shot. W. H. S." From Mr. W. H. Simpson's Collection, 1863.

Mr. Simpson has given, in 'The Ibis' for 1860 (pp. 377–78), the following account of his taking the nest which contained this specimen :—

G 2

"On the evening of the 29th [April 1860] another fortunate discovery was made by the same party, and, this time, of the nest of a bird, whose eggs, it is believed, were almost unknown previously in authentic cabinets. We were strolling on a low flat island in the Danube, the edge of which is well covered with tall poplars and other trees. Opposite this belt of trees, and across the river, the Turkish shore rises pretty steeply to a level with the plateau of the Dobrudska, whilst behind, towards the mainland of Wallachia, there stretches an immense tract of low ground, partly swamp, partly forest, and partly open plain. A nest of *Milvus ater* had occupied us for a short time; but on getting close to the river again, where the trees are very tall and not thickly grouped, my friend and *cicerone* drew our attention to a good-sized nest, which was placed about one-third of the way up a tallish poplar. The nest was resting upon a large branch close to the boll of the tree, and appeared exceedingly easy of access. Whilst my friend was climbing towards it, the bird slipped off, and was shot immediately. It proved to be a female *Falco sacer*. Of this I was not quite certain at the time, being then unacquainted with the distinctions between *Falco lanarius* and *Falco sacer*, though the size inclined me to decide in favour of the latter. The nest was not very much larger than those of the numerous Hooded Crows we had already examined, but was deep and comfortably lined, appearing, however, from the outside as like a large Crow's nest as one bundle of sticks is like another. The eggs, four in number, were slightly incubated. In size they seem to be intermediate between those of the Peregrine and the Gyr-falcon, being, however, longer in proportion to their breadth. Two of them are light in colour, the other two much darker. One of the latter is accurately represented in the accompanying plate (Plate XII. fig. 1). It measures 2·2 in. by 1·6 in.

"The male bird was well observed afterwards. Sitting, utterly motionless, on the top of a dead tree, with his head turned over his shoulder, he seemed so mournfully conscious of the catastrophe which had befallen his family, that I felt utterly ashamed of having added murder to robbery in my desire to possess myself of an unknown bird. If the gun had still been in my hand, I could have shot him easily, as he then seemed indifferent to his fate; but it so happened that he flew away before that weapon actually arrived, and thus escaped being involved in the ruin of his household."

Mr. Simpson has since informed me that the island was on the Wallachian side of the main stream of the Danube, almost exactly opposite the Bulgarian village of Tchernawoda, the very tree being visible from some of the houses in the new part of it. I believe he was anticipated by others in this discovery. In 1846, Herr von Woborzil published (Rhea, i. p. 41) an account of a Saker's nest, with five eggs, taken by him, as it seems, on the 2nd of April 1842. Dr. Baldamus also, during his tour in Hungary in 1847, obtained a nest of five eggs, which doubtless belonged to this bird, though, in his description of it, he applies to it the name of *Falco lanarius* (Naumannia, 1851, p. 37). And Messrs. Salvin and Brodrick, in their 'Falconry in the British Isles' (p. 96, *note*), mention a pair of birds "killed in Hungary in 1848, at their eyrie, which was in a tree," and obtained by Mr. A. H. Cochrane "from the person who shot them." But it is unquestionable that properly identified and authenticated eggs of the Saker have long been, and still are, very rarely met with in collections.]

FALCO CANDICANS, Gmelin.

GREENLAND FALCON.

[Mr. Wolley, as I believe is pretty well known, was strongly of opinion that the large Falcons from Greenland, Iceland, and Scandinavia were only local, though always recognizable, races of one and the same species, and he wished to distinguish them by a geographical agnomen. My allegiance, however, to the binomial principle of nomenclature prevents me from following his suggestion. That the characters of the three birds are quite permanent, and in two of them sharply defined, is, I think, now fully admitted by the best authorities on the subject (Hancock, Ann. and Mag. Nat. Hist. 2nd ser. xiii. pp. 110–112; Blasius, Journ. für Orn. 1862, pp. 43–59; and Schlegel, Mus. des Pays-Bas, *Falcones*, pp. 7-14). I myself have never yet seen an adult specimen, even of the two forms that most nearly resemble each other, about the determination of which I had any great difficulty. I therefore consider it most convenient to treat them here as separate species, though I think it more than probable that they have sprung from a common stock.]

§ 184. *One.*—Greenland. "Bird killed." From Captain Holböll's Collection, through Mr. S. Stevens, 1855.

§ 185. *Two.*—Greenland. "Bird killed." From Captain Holböll's Collection, through Mr. S. Stevens, 1855.

These eggs were bought by me, Nov. 12th, of Mr. Stevens. He showed me Holböll's letters and everything. There were two or three eggs professedly added to the lot in Denmark; but all the rest were from Greenland, and apparently carefully separated. The two which are marked "*F. arcticus*" were in a box by themselves, and the one specimen marked "*F. islandicus*" in another box. A number of skins were sent with them, ticketed "*F. islandicus*" and "*F. arcticus*," the former the more marked, and the latter the less marked skins, but all without exception the Greenland Falcon of Mr. Hancock [1].

[1] [A statement of what Capt. Holböll is supposed to have meant by his undescribed "*Falco arcticus*" and "*F. islandicus*" is to be found in 'The Ibis' for 1862 (vol. iv. p. 50, *note*). It does not entirely agree with what Mr. Wolley says in the above passage; but the matter is of very slight consequence in the present instance.—ED.]

FALCO ISLANDICUS, Gmelin.

ICELAND FALCON.

§ 186. *One.*—Iceland.   From Mr. W. Proctor, 1851.

Mr. Proctor states that this egg is from the north side of Iceland, but he cannot say from what place. It was sent to him direct from that country.

§ 187. *One.*—Iceland.   From Mr. John Hancock's Collection, 1853.

I had this of Mr. Hancock, who informed me that he received it from Denmark, but that his correspondent there was "very particular respecting locality," and that this was sent from Iceland.

§ 188. *Two.*—Iceland, 1854.   From Mr. W. Proctor, 1856.

Mr. Proctor tells me that he had these direct from Iceland.

§ 189. *One.*—Iceland, 1855.   From Dr. Kjärbölling's Collection, 1856.

[§ 190. *One.*—Greenland.   From Sysselmand H. Müller's Collection, 1859.

Herr Müller gave me this egg at Copenhagen, and told me that it came to him direct from Greenland; there is therefore a possibility of its being the egg of *Falco candicans*; but, according to Mr. Hancock's belief, *F. islandicus* is the commonest form in the south of that country.]

[§ 191. *One.*—Iceland.   From Dr. Kjärbölling's Collection, 1859.

This egg I bought at Copenhagen. The Doctor assured me he had it direct from Iceland.]

FALCO GYRFALCO, Linnæus.

GYRFALCON.

O. W. tab. C.

[Mr. Wolley was, I believe, the first naturalist able to give from his own observation any particulars of the breeding of this noble bird. I cannot add to the full details which are contained in the following notes. The curious fact that the Gyrfalcon, like so many other *Accipitres,* adapts itself to circumstances, breeding in trees when rocks are wanting near places that abound with food for its offspring, as is the case in the district of Hanhi-järwi-maa, will not escape the student's notice, and will furnish, I think, another good warning against too hasty generalizations with regard to the habits of a bird or other animal. It was not until the fourth summer of Mr. Wolley's residence in Lapland that he became acquainted with this fact, and then, as his remarks show (§ 210), he was justly sceptical concerning it at first. I must, however, call the reader's attention to an error in two of Mr. Wolley's Sale Catalogues. In that for the year 1856, he stated (p. 8) that the Gyrfalcon was "the only species or race of the Great Falcon which occurs in Lapland;" and again in that for the year 1858, he said (p. 10) that "in Scandinavia the forms found in Greenland and Iceland never seem to occur." Each of these assertions requires qualification; for I believe that both *Falco candicans* and *F. islandicus* are occasionally met with in Norway or Sweden, though I am not aware that either has been known to breed in the Scandinavian peninsula. It is therefore necessary to add to each passage, "except as accidental visitors," or words to that effect. I have also here to express my thanks to Mr. Wolf for a beautiful picture, which he was good enough to paint for me from one of the birds to be mentioned hereafter (§ 215). A reduced copy of it, executed by Mr. Jury under the artist's immediate superintendence, embellishes this work (tab. C), and, I think, cannot fail to afford pleasure to naturalists, as, excepting Herr W. von Wright's figure in the 'Tidskrift för Jägare' (I. pl. xii. p. 353), it is the only representation of the adult female Gyrfalcon that has been published. Of its accuracy I need say nothing, for that is guaranteed by the painter's name.]

§ 192. *Four.*—West Finmark, 7 May, 1854.   "J. W. *ipse.*"

O. W. tab. viii. fig. 1.

On my way from Hammerfest, I intended to visit the Falcons' nests of which I had heard from Lassi; but when I got to Kautokeino I was hesitating, for several reasons, whether or not to spare the time that was necessary: the snow might go any day, and I should not get back to Muonioniska; and I had some cause for being uncertain as to the truth of his account. However, I had the good luck to find his *dräng*, who said that his master had the day before pointed out the rock where the nest was. It was only a mile (Norwegian) from the nest, while Lassi lived two miles off, on the way to Kaaressuando, whither, I was told, there was not a Lapp at home who knew the road. Getting three Reindeer, we started at once, and in course of time came to the small cliffs in the narrow valley where the river lay. First I went to a nest of perfectly easy approach, and probably the preceding year's: I thought it was a Buzzard's. A little further on, rather upon a craggy bit of hill than a rock, there were three or four old nests, and near them feathers, some of which I took for Falcons' and others for Buzzards'; abundance also of fresh dung; and one of the nests had been slightly mended. A few steps away lay the haunch of a Reindeer, which the Lapp said had evidently been killed by a Wolf, after being driven to the edge of the little pre-cipice, but not over it. The Wolf's spoor was effaced by more recent snow, but the tracks of Foxes were fresh. We talked a long time about the Lapp murderers of the last winter [1], whom our man had guarded to Alten, and then about midnight got our deer through the deep snow on to the river again, having put on our Lapp clothes, which we had taken off for the climb. Returning, the man showed me the rock where it was thought the nest then might be. The people at the Parsonage would be sitting up; the deer would be ready for the journey; the snow was probably deep; and I all but determined not to try this rock, which was perhaps a quarter a mile from the river. I thought the birds could hardly be there when none had shown themselves. Fortunately I decided to go. We had not long left the track on the river, when a Falcon flew up from the rock where the nest was supposed to be, and soon afterwards, turning back, settled on the trunk of a dead tree, once or twice uttering a cry. I now knew there was a nest, and in a few minutes more I saw it, look-ing very large, and with a black space about it, as though it were in the mouth of a little cave in the face of the rock. This was a joyful moment, but not so much so as when the hen bird flew off with somewhat cramped wings, and settled on a little stump, some thirty yards from the nest. I would not let Ludwig shoot. We were ascending the hill, and might be fifty yards off when she left the nest. I took off my shoes, though there was deep snow everywhere

---

[1] [On the 8th of November 1852, some fanatic Lapps made a sudden and un-provoked attack on the village of Kautokeino, and in their frenzy murdered or ill-treated several of the Norwegian inhabitants. The malefactors were subsequently taken, and after trial two of them were executed at Alten—the rest, some of whom were women, being sentenced to imprisonment for various periods, in pro-portion to their complicity in the crime.—ED.]

except just on the face of the rock, and first tried it from above, but it seemed scarcely practicable. Then I went below, and, with the Lapp to support my feet, and Ludwig to give me additional help with a pole, I managed to climb up. Just at the last bit I had to rest some time. Then I drew myself, and saw the four eggs to my right hand, looking small in the middle of a large nest. Again I waited to get steady for the final reach. I had only a bit of stone to stand upon, not bigger than a walnut, and frozen to the surface of the ledge, which sloped outwards. I put two of the eggs into my cap, and two into my pocket, and cautiously withdrew. The nest appeared to have been quite freshly made, and therefore by the bird herself. The sticks were thick, certainly more so than those used by Ravens or Buzzards, and, unlike the nests of the latter, which I saw the next day, they were barkless and bleached. The only lining was a bundle or two of coarsish dry grass. As I returned, I touched the eggs on a point of rock above me, luckily without injuring them. I handed them down in a glove at the end of a pole, which the Lapp improvised after the fashion of a church col-lecting-bag; and when they were placed in a safe corner, my feet were put in the right places, and I descended in safety. I had luckily brought a box with hay, and on 12th May had the eggs safe at Muo-niovaara. There were young inside, perhaps an inch-and-a-half long, with heads as big as horse-beans. A bird, probably of the preceding year, had been caught in a Grouse-snare at the end of March or beginning of April, and I got its skin [Woll. Don. No. 57] and breast-bone [Osteoth. Newt. *MS. Cat.* No. 369, a].

§ 193. *Three.*—West Finmark, 16th April, 1857.

Ludwig told me this was Lassi's nest, and he desired the other Lapp, Pongo, not to touch; but as he was obliged to leave the neigh-bourhood before Ludwig arrived, Pongo took it as above. Lassi blew the eggs the following day, and delivered them to Ludwig shortly afterwards. It is the same nest I took in 1854 [§ 192], occupied in 1855 and 1856 by Ravens. The eggs were fresh, and, Ludwig thought, not all laid.

§ 194. *One.*—Nyimakka, Enontekis Lappmark, 7 June, 1854. " J. W. *ipse.*"

This egg I took as above, out of a nest in which were three young. Petari took me to the rock at which he had been a week or two before, when some kind of Hawk flew angrily round him. There had been Hawks' nests there for many years. The old spot was covered with good grass. It was a long time before we saw a bird— and then only one, without any cries of alarm. At last the hen came up, with food in her claws, and dashed screaming into a cliff at which I had looked in vain for a nest. A short time before, a man had seen a bird fly out of a low detached cliff; and here was the nest, covered with dung, at a short distance from the ground, in a kind of recess. I could climb so as to touch, but not so as to see more than the heads of two downy young, which were continually chirping. Hoping for a nest-egg, I made various attempts to get a peep; and at last, from above, I was able to see three young ones, perhaps a fortnight old, or nearly so, and an egg. I trebled a string I had in my pocket, and the man let it down for my support. I tied it on, and so was able to reach into the very dirty nest and carry off the egg, which I afterwards found to have a full-sized chick in it, probably dead before I took it, but still not putrid.

[The locality of this nest was shown by Mr. Wolley to Mr. Simpson and myself in 1855, as we were descending the river.]

§ 195. *Four.*—Nyimakka, Enontekis Lappmark, 18 May, 1855.

Taken by Petari, who was with me the preceding year, from the very same nest from which I then took a single egg. There were large young inside.

§ 196. *Four.*—West Finmark, 24 April, 1855.

Just blown by me. They were taken about ten o'clock last night by Lassi, in company with another man, who climbed up to the nest on a perpendicular cliff, by the help of a rope let down from above. The nest, they say, was very old, and had been repaired or used for many years. It was on a little tributary of a stream, in the valley of which I took the nest last year [§ 192]. Very near the nest was a Fox's spoor, and they say the birds had evidently attacked it; for it had hopped about in the snow, and stuck its back in a bush. I have just come from another nest [§ 198] with Lassi; and he says the bird was exactly the same in appearance, voice, &c. The eggs, even at this early time of year, are several days sat upon.

§ 197. *Four.*—West Finmark, 24 April, 1856. "L. M. K."

Taken by Ludwig and Lassi from the same nest out of which the latter got me the eggs last year. They tried for two days to catch the bird, but they could not get it. Ludwig told me that the bird cried out a little at first, and then went and sat on a tree or stake at a distance, all the time they were setting the trap. This nest I have not seen. Ludwig fastened a rope above, and climbed up from below. There was ice on the river beneath. He observed that the sticks were of willow, and without bark.

§ 198. *Three.*—West Finmark, 25 April, 1855. "J. W. *ipse.*"

O. W. tab. viii. figs. 5, 6.

These eggs I took myself, last night, out of a very slight nest in a recess of the cliff overhanging the river. I watched the birds with my glass, and saw the cock perfectly, examining him at a distance of little more than ten yards as he sat on the nest. As we came to the place, the hen left the nest; and whilst we were standing on the other side of the river, the cock flew from a tree close by, and settled on the nest. After looking well at him, I put the gun aside, for Lassi was sure we could get him in a snare. He did not leave till we were very near, though he was in full sight all the time. His breast spotted transversely at the side, his moustache not dark, his back and wings pale slate-colour, with small white spots. His orbits yellow; and his feet, as they hung down when he flew, apparently yellow also. We climbed up, set a snare, and went to watch. After some time, the hen came and crept in by the side of the snare. I sent Lassi at once, but she went out just through it. He set it again, and we watched for an hour or two, the bird sitting on a tree. At last she went away with a low cry, and we, after some time, went also. During the night we returned; but the bird, being probably in a hurry with her fourth egg, had gone elsewhere to lay it. I took the eggs with my own hand, the nest being very easy of access.

The pale egg [tab. viii. fig. 5] was not there when Lassi was at the nest, 21st April: there were then only two. He was there about eight o'clock in the evening; I was there first at midday 25th April. The eggs, of course, perfectly fresh.

§ 199. *Four.*—West Finmark, 1857.

Sent, with another nest [§ 212], by Lassi. Before Ludwig left, Lassi said he knew of a nest in an old place, with one or two eggs. He had to carry the post, and Ludwig sent him word to take the eggs when their number was complete. It was from the upper part of a river, where I tried in 1855 to snare the old bird [§ 198].

§ 200. *Three.*—West Finmark, 27 April, 1855. "J. W. *ipse.*"

O. W. tab. viii. figs. 2, 3.

These eggs from a hill near Pinkisjärwi. I took them in company with Eric. The cliff looked very formidable, but we found it practicable when he had been home to fetch an axe and a rope, by cutting down a tall birch to make such a ladder as enabled me to climb up the cliff and take the eggs myself. Indeed I reached it from the top of the tree. The rock was overhanging. The nest, very large, and with a considerable hollow, was made of fresh sticks, not very big; and inside were a few green willow twigs, and several tufts of sedgy grass. The hen bird flew off long before we came near, and circled away, when she was soon joined by her mate. She looked exactly like the birds of the other nest [§ 198]. It was snowing hard while we were there, very conveniently for me, who had not slept much for several nights, as travelling was thus stopped for a time. Under the nest was much *Cystea* [quære, *Cystopteris*?], and a little *Woodsia*, with several kinds of alpine plants. The rock loose and dangerous. The snowy slope below was very steep, and we shot down it on our backs at a great pace. Our Reindeer were feeding in the distance, but we went to the place on snow-shoes. I preserved a feather found near the nest.

§ 201. *Four.*—Aunas-tunturi, Kemi Lappmark, 1 May, 1855. "Bird snared."

Taken by Piety on a steep cliff on the south side of Aunas-tunturi. It was a very old nest. He set a string with a series of horse-hair nooses; and his brother went to examine it, and took the bird out. Piety skinned it. The other bird then sat upon the eggs. There were small young in them. About the nest were many bones of Grouse, Whimbrels, and smaller birds. It was made of old white sticks. It appears that, in 1854, a Merlin built in this spot, though it had always been occupied before by a Gyrfalcon.

[The skin of the bird killed on this nest is now in the Norwich Museum.]

§ 202. *One.*—West Finmark (?), 1855 (?).

Brought to Muoniovaara by Lassi, 8th April 1856. He thought it was a last year's egg. It had been probably found in a nest exposed to the weather.

§ 203. *Four.*—West Finmark, 19 April, 1856. " L. M. K."

Taken by Ludwig himself. The nest was in a cliff facing south-east, about one hundred feet high, overhanging a lake or enlargement of a small river; so that if he had fallen, he would have been smashed on the ice, which was right beneath the nest. It was a very difficult place, so that a Lapp, whom he took with him, went away and durst not help him. He fastened a rope to a large stone, saw that it would reach the ice, and then let himself down. The stones were very loose. He put the four eggs into his cap, and then slipped down the rope, burning his hands considerably. The nest was in a corner, or little rift of the rock, and made of sticks, mostly bare, he thought,—no large mass, and without a deep hollow for the eggs. The bird was there at first, and flew about once or twice, but went away long before he let himself down to the eggs. The nest might have been three fathoms over the river.

§ 204. *Four.*—West Finmark, 28 April, 1857. " With both birds. L. M. K."

From the same locality as the preceding. Taken by Ludwig, in company with another man. The former wrote as follows :—" I shot one of the birds, and then we laid snares for the other, which was the cock, and very wild. We went to a rock further off, and there I met two boys, who had been and found another nest. They had caught one of the old birds, and tried for a whole day to get the other, but it did not come back any more [§ 208]. My nest was built mostly of old bare birch twigs, and then upon these were some finer birch twigs with bark on, but old and dried up. These were mixed with others, rotten and crumbling, some Grouse feathers and bilberry leaves. The nest was about three ells from the bottom, and the hollow was four inches deep and half an ell across. I shot the hen, took the eggs away, and laid instead a Buzzard's egg, smeared with Reindeer blood. When we came in the evening the cock was hanging on the rock, very fierce. His eyes were blue in the middle, and a greyish-yellow ring round them. His feet were reddish-yellow, and his beak dark blue, but yellowish red at the root. The hen had the same kind of eyes, but with the feet and round the beak more purely yellow."

The birds are now before me, unskinned.

[The male bird from this nest, and the only one of that sex obtained by Mr. Wolley, was given by him to Mr. Gould. The female is in the Norwich Museum.]

§ 205. *Four*.—West Finmark, 22 April, 1856.

Brought to Ludwig the same year, while staying with Lassi.

§ 206. *Three*.—West Finmark, 1856.

Sent by Lassi to Ludwig at Maunu, where he received them, together with another nest of three eggs, 28th July. It seems, from an inquiry made the following year, that both nests were taken at the end of April and beginning of May, from the district where I took one and obtained a second in 1855 [§ 196 and § 198]. These are curious-looking, under-coloured eggs.

[Two from the other nest are now in the collections of Dr. T. M. Brewer and Dr. A. L. Heermann.]

§ 207. *Four*.—West Finmark, 24 April, 1857. "With bird."

These were found by Lassi as above. Ludwig wrote that "he got one of the birds, with much difficulty; but the other flew away, so that it did not come back any more. The cliff was fully twenty ells high, and the nest was about the middle of it, in a little corner on the side, so that it was hard to get at. It was an ell and a quarter over on the outside, and had feathers inside,—some of the bird's own, others of Grouse. It was mostly made of old bare birch twigs. The bird was black just at the end of the bill, then became yellow, and was altogether yellow at the root. The eyelids were yellow; but the eyes themselves blue, with a little grey round them [the iris]. The feet altogether bright yellow, with black claws. Lassi went for half a day after the other bird, but it did not come. The eggs were blown the same day, the young inside with eyes." These four are remarkable eggs, blotched and speckled almost like some Buzzards'.

[The bird from this nest, the female, was selected by Mr. Hancock for his own collection, Mr. Wolley having begged him to choose and keep one.]

§ 208. *Three*.—West Finmark, N. lat. 68° 45'. 28 April, 1857. "With black-headed female."

These are the eggs taken by the lads as before mentioned [§ 204].

Ludwig's note says, " The nest was on a cliff. They snared the hen,
but the cock they could not get. They tried to wait as long as they
possibly could, but he came again no more." The hen is the very
black-headed bird, I suppose the typical *Falco gyrfalco* of Schlegel;
but I take it to be an adult of the first year, both from the dark beak
and the character of the long wing-feathers, whose light interspaces
are not speckled; it has also moulted each fifth pen-feather.

[The bird was given to Mr. Gould by Mr. Wolley.]

§ 209. *Three.*—West Finmark, 29 April, 1857. " With hen
bird."

These were brought by the captor to Ludwig, who writes :—"There
were four eggs, but he broke one to pieces on the way. The night before, he set snares for the birds, and the hen came straightway, but
the cock came not. It was so cold that he could not wait long, lest
the eggs should freeze asunder." One of these is a remarkably
pinky egg.

[The hen bird caught on this nest is now in the British Museum.]

§ 210. *One.*—Hanhi-järwi-maa, Enontekis Lappmark, 18 May,
1857. " From nest in a tree."

Brought to Muoniovaara, 18th June of that year, by a man who
said it was the egg of the middle-sized *Koppelo-Haukka* [*Astur pa-
lumbarius*], and that he found it as above stated. He tried to shoot
the bird, but could not get near enough. The egg was a little
broken, being sprung by the young one. A girl told me at Muoniovaara, 4th August 1857, that she was in company with the finder
and another man when they took this egg. They were on their way
back from a Sunday visit to the two houses in Suontajärwi, which
is a mile and a quarter (Swedish) from Muotkajärwi. The nest
was nearer the former place than the latter; and she said that one
of the men had, two years before, thrown the young out of it. The
tree in which it was is on the edge of a very large marsh, on the
north side of it, with no pines between it and the tree; and the
nest was placed just at the top, which was but a little on one side,
so as to give a place of support. It might be seven fathoms high.
The marsh is called Hanhi-uoma, at least in that part where the
nest was, but it has different names in different places. At about

a furlong off to the west is a high bare-topped hill, but there are marshes between. The bird was whitish underneath, with long wings, but the tail not long. It flew rapidly, not slowly as a *Piekonna* (Rough-legged Buzzard), and had a different voice, more like that of *Pouta-Haukka* (Merlin), but stronger. One of the men climbed up and put the egg in his glove; there was already a hole in it, through which the beak of the young bird appeared. She called to him not to disturb the other young, of which she was not sure whether there were more than two; but he threw them on the ground. They were small and white. It was in 1855 that he or the other man threw the young from the same nest, which was not large, and the sticks old and without bark. She added that it was Erki's-day (St. Eric's) that the egg was taken; and on my asking the day of the week, replied Monday, which agrees with the Almanack—an additional proof of her accuracy. Putting all together, I can hardly doubt the egg is a Gyrfalcon's.

§ 211. *Three.* — Hanhi-järwi-maa, Enontekis Lappmark, 26 April, 1858.

Brought to Muoniovaara, 8th May, by Heiki, from the girl mentioned in the last note. They are from the same place as the one egg taken the year before [§ 210]. The nest was in a tree about seven fathoms from the ground, and three or four hundred fathoms from the spot where the nest was in former years.

§ 212. *Three.*—West Finmark, 28 April, 1857.

Received by me, 26th July, at Maunu, where they had been left by Lassi. Ludwig recognized them at once as eggs of which he had seen two in a nest, and desired another man, who was with him at the time, to take subsequently. On 28th April, he had been with him, and got a nest with both the old birds [§ 204]. They met with two lads, one of whom had got the eggs and bird from another nest, and all went together to search some likely-looking cliffs they knew of, which were about a mile (Swedish) from the first-mentioned nest, with a large lake intervening. They drove from that nest, which was on the west side of the lake and about its middle, keeping on the ice and then a bit on the land. They saw the bird leave the nest, and fly wildly away without coming back. The cliff overlooked a marsh, already bare, the wind having blown away the snow earlier. The nest was scarcely more than a fathom from the top, on a little ledge. He climbed from the side till he had a good look at the two eggs then in it, which seemed to him very beautiful, as they did when they reached me, though not nearly so much so as before. The nest was of the ordinary size and appearance. He left the eggs in it in hope of more being laid, and they were taken afterwards by the man who was then with him.

§ 213. *Four.*—West Finmark, 22 April, 1858.

Brought to Muoniovara 8th May, having been found by Lassi as above. This was a fresh nest, about six ells high.

§ 214. *Four.*—West Finmark, 30 April, 1858.

Brought with the last, and found as above by the same man. The nest about thirty ells high.

§ 215. *Three.*—West Finmark, 27 April, 1859. "With hen bird."

O. W. tab. viii. fig. 4, and tab. C.

Brought, 7th May, to Muoniovara by Heiki, who, in company with Lassi, took them as above, in the same place as the latter found the nest last year [§ 214]. They searched together all the nests in two neighbourhoods, but all were empty save this. They thought that the reason why the Falcons had flown away was, that there were no Grouse to be found, and so they could not get food, but must fly away. Another man shot the hen bird from this nest, and brought it skinned[1].

§ 216. *Three.*—West Finmark, 1 May, 1858. "With ske- leton."

Brought to Muoniovara, 8th May, by Heiki, having been found by Lassi. The nest was ten ells high, on a cliff. The bird was shot, and its bones kept and sent.

---

[1] [The skin is now in the Norwich Museum, and is the original of Mr. Wolf's picture, of which the plate (tab. C) is a reduced copy.—ED.]

H

[§ 217. *Four.*—West Finmark, 1 May, 1861.

From the same nest as those in the last section. One of the eggs is very remarkable, being of a flesh-colour, verging upon pale lilac, spotted with irregularly shaped rusty markings. The rest have the ordinary appearance.]

§ 218. *Three.*—West Finmark, 16 April, 1858.

Brought to Muoniovara by Heiki, and found by Lassi at the same place as the eggs before mentioned, from which both birds were killed in 1857 [§ 203 and § 204]. The nest was about six ells high, in a cliff.

[§ 219. *Four.*—West Finmark, 1 May, 1861. "With hen bird."

From a nest which had been robbed several times before, though none of the eggs taken then are now in my possession. The skin of the bird killed from it accompanied these specimens. It is a truly typical *Falco gyrfalco*, darkly coloured, and having all the look of a very old bird.]

FALCO PEREGRINUS, Gmelin.

PEREGRINE FALCON.

[Besides those mentioned in the following text, Mr. Wolley's note-books show that he visited many other Falcons' breeding-places in Scotland, and a few in England. Several of the nests he saw were quite inaccessible even to him, though possessed of so much nerve for rock-climbing. Others contained young ones, some of which he carried off and brought up. Thus he had a very considerable personal acquaintance with the economy of this species; but the notes are too diffuse for insertion here. In a communication made to Mr. Hewitson in 1853 (Eggs B. B. ed. 3, pp. 24, 25), he states that, on the Continent, it not unfrequently breeds in church-steeples in the thickly peopled centre of a city, and also that it often takes possession of the nest of a Raven in which to lay its eggs. It is indeed remarkable how many times Mr. Wolley observed the Falcon and the Raven tenanting in common the same rocky ledges. In one nest, containing four young ones, on an island off the coast of Sutherlandshire, he mentions besides that he found, among other spoil, the wing of a Kestrel,—a circumstance apparently contradicting the common Scottish proverb that "Hawks dinna pick at Hawks' eyn."

The persistency with which Falcons and other birds of prey continue, during a great number of years, to use one spot for breeding is tolerably well known; but one singular instance I cannot refrain from mentioning here. In 1736, when the French Astronomical Expedition for ascertaining the figure of the earth was sent to Lapland, they had a station at Aawasaksa (Avasaxa), a remarkable hill on the left bank of the Torneå, just opposite Matarengi, which, though situated without the Arctic Circle, is of sufficient height to admit of the sun's being seen from its summit at midnight in summer. Here, it is mentioned in the narrative of their expedition ('Œuvres de Mr. de Maupertuis, &c.,' Lyon, 1756, tome iii. pp. 110, 111), they observed a Falcon's nest. In 1799, Captain Skjöldebrand, then travelling with Signor Acerbi, records his having rediscovered this nest, around which "the birds, frightened by the fall of some pieces of rock which we threw from the top of the mountain, flew, and filled the air with their cries "[1]. In 1853, Mr. Wolley's first year in Lapland, he ascended this hill, and the Falcons once more showed themselves to him. He stated in a letter to me soon after, that they "had the cut of Peregrines," as two years later he proved that they were by finding, in company with Mr. Simpson, their nest containing a dead young one, the skull of which is now before me (Osteoth. Newt. *MS. Cat.* No. 15, f).]

§ 220. *One.*—Isle of Wight. From Mr. J. F. Dawson's Collection, 1845.

Given to me by the Rev. J. F. Dawson, of Ventnor. It was taken in the cliffs of that island, where the bird breeds regularly; see Mr. Bury's notes in the 'Zoologist' [1844, pp. 517–520]. Mr. Dawson brought me this egg to Monk's Wood, where we were collecting insects early in June, especially the caterpillars of the Purple Emperor, and from the Mere the caterpillars of the Large Copper.

§ 221. *One.*—Orkneys. From Mr. George Harvey, of Stromness, 1848.

From a crag near Stromness. Mr. Harvey has had many of their eggs some years. He assured me that he once shot, but could not get, an Iceland Falcon, one of a pair that, as he believed, had a nest in Orkney. I did not understand that he saw the nest. This crag is the rock from which the Falcon flew to attack an Eagle, and broke its wing in so doing; but it stunned the Eagle, and they fell together. Some boatmen, in gratitude for delivering the enemy into their hands, gave the poor bird its liberty to mend its wing as it best could.

§ 222. *Four.*—Sutherlandshire, 28 April, 1849. "J. W."

On the 21st of April 1849, a man at the Dunnet Head Light-

---

[1] [I have not seen Skjöldebrand's work, and quote the above passage from an extract given among the "Literary Selections" in the 'New Annual Register' for 1814 (vol. xxxv. pp. 103, 104). Acerbi mentions the Falcons, but says nothing about the nest ('Travels, &c.,' London, 1802, vol. i. p. 366).—ED.]

house pointed out to me the place where a Falcon's nest had been
last year. I picked up a bit of the shell of an egg, probably robbed
within a day or two by the Grey Crows. On the 23rd I made an
easy climb to a Falcon's nest, apparently quite new, near the top of
the cliff. There was a very broad way to it. The nest was hollowed
out to some depth in the turf of a ledge. One dry bone formed the
principal lining. A bit of rock projected sharply into the bottom, so
that it had probably not been used. The old birds were flying in the
distance with the usual cry of anger, the wings flapping quickly, but
little advance made, the *humeri* being apparently compressed to the
sides.

On the 28th of April I walked, with a man to act as guide and to
carry the thin rope, to a very low rock overlooking a loch, at perhaps
a quarter of a mile from its west shore. A high road, little frequented, however, may be a couple of hundred yards from the rock,
between it and the lake. The rock had a good deal of vegetation,
including ivy, about it; and I climbed about from above for some little
time, till I began to think my informant was wrong, and the nest not
there, when out dashed the Falcon, like an arrow, very near me. I had
to go below to get at the nest. As I climbed, both birds flew about
at a considerable height, with their sharp, quickly repeated cry. I
reached the nest, which was in a retiring, much-sheltered corner,
without a rope.

"It is not more than eighteen or twenty feet from the ground,
on a little platform, with a tree in front, and a great deal of the same
Luzula that was in the Eagle's nest [§ 26] here growing. The
whole platform may be four feet square; the bare place for the nest
eighteen inches. The nest is made of little fragments of sticks and a
multitude of bones, chiefly birds' of various kinds, but also two or
three sheep-bones, probably brought to construct it with, also many
little bits of stone, apparently from the rock itself."

I have little doubt that these bones were so brought, as they were
used in the actual construction of the nest, though they certainly had
the appearance of being raked together, and they might be only
the remains of the rapine of former years brought to that spot to
feed the young. There were four eggs in the nest, quite new-laid.
Whilst at a Buzzard's nest, a few hundred yards off, on the same
day, one of the Falcons came up, peering about at a good height;
and it remained quite motionless overhead, so that my man offered
to bet me it was the "Glead;" but when it began to move its
wings he acknowledged his mistake. Further on we came to a very
low rock in ledges, over the whole of which we could walk. My

man informed me that this was called in Gaelic "The Hawk's Crag," and that he used to destroy a nest of the " Hunting Hawk " there every year. A mile or two on, we came to "The Raven's Crag," about which those birds were barking or croaking angrily. The nest was in full view, but not accessible without strong ropes and men; and though we could get very near it, I did not see into it. In passing this rock on the 10th of May, my companion informed me that it was the place in which Mr. St. John ['Tour in Sutherlandshire,' vol. i. p. 70] found the young Falcons the year before. It is not far from the road, and we went up to it, and saw the two old birds scolding; but, though we had the ropes, I made no attempt at the nest, being convinced that it was dangerous of access for a small force of men, and in all probability it would have young ones in it. These rocks are finely situated for making descents upon the lake.

§ 223. *Three.*—Sutherlandshire, April 1849. From Mr. Dunbar's Collection.

These three eggs I purchased of Mr. Dunbar, at Tongue. He had taken them, a few days before, from a rock which another person pointed out to me. On the 30th of April I saw, near this place, a pair of Falcons flying rapidly past, uttering wild cries, as though they had a nest at no great distance.

§ 224. *Two.*—Isle of Wight, 1851. From Mr. John Evans's Collection, 1853.

These were taken on the cliffs, with the assistance of a rope, by a lighthouse-keeper, from whom Mr. Evans obtained them on his visit there the same year. This man's father lost his life on the same cliff. He had gone out alone, and had secured the rope to a crowbar, but not sufficiently well. It was said that he had not liked to share the eggs with any one else.

§ 225. *Six*—Orkneys, 1851. From Mr. George Harvey.

§ 226. *Two.*—Argyllshire, 2 May, 1852.

Sent to me by the captor, with the Eagle's eggs before mentioned [§ 31].

§ 227. *Three.*—Oggo-vaara, Tornea Lappmark, 14 June, 1854, N. lat. 68° 50'. " Bird snared. J. W."

[The particulars of this capture have been accidentally omitted from Mr. Wolley's note-book, though the eggs were properly inscribed by him, and are referred to in the next section but one.]

§ 228. *Three.*—Hanhi-maa, Enontekis Lappmark, 1854.

Out of nine eggs, apparently Peregrines'; called " *Koppelo-Haukka*" by the lads there. Brought to me, July 11th, just before my journey. The nest was in a remarkable situation on the ground, in a large marsh.

§ 229. *Four.*—Oggo-vaara, Tornea Lappmark, 1855.

From the same hill, near Mukka-uoma, whence I got the eggs with the bird snared last year [§ 227]. But the nest was on the other (the south-east) side of the hill.

§ 230. *Four.*—Iso-uoma, Rowa, East Bothnia, 1857.

On the 22nd July the postman brought eggs from Punsi; but they came to Muoniovara some days later, when I was returned. They were said to have been found in a marsh.

§ 231. *Four.*—Kalko-vaara, East Bothnia, 25–30 May, 1858.

Found as above, by Punsi, upon a hillock overgrown with " Bear-moss" [*Polytrichum commune*].

§ 232. *Four.*—Iso-uoma, Rowa, East Bothnia, 6 June, 1859.

Brought by Nils; found as above, half a mile (Swedish) from the house.

[§ 233. *Four.*—Rowa, East Bothnia, 13 June, 1860.

From the same locality as those mentioned in the last three sections. The nest this time was about a quarter of a mile (Swedish) from the man's house. He said it had been taken for three years before, but the bird, which he called " Little Capercally-Hawk," had on each occasion flown away when the finder was some distance off. I cannot think these are otherwise than eggs of the common Falcon.]

§ 234. *Four.*—Aita-uoma, West Finmark, 8 June, 1859.

Brought from Kätkesuando, June 12th, having been found as above on the ground on a hillock. The finder did not know what eggs they were: he said the bird was a Hawk, grey but somewhat lighter on the neck. It was not angry when he took the eggs, but flew round. It had such a cry as the " Little Capercally-Hawk." Round the nest were many birds' bones.

[These are such large eggs that, were it not that they also happen to be very deeply coloured, I should almost be persuaded they belonged to the Gyrfalcon. One of them measures 2·3 in. by 1·75; and I have some Gyrfalcons' that are considerably less; one is only 2·22 in. by 1·68. Most of the eggs of the common Falcon from Lapland seem to be larger than British specimens, but not all, as, for instance, those in the next section.]

[§ 235. *Two.*—Aita-uoma, West Finmark, 17 June, 1861.

These are from the same place as those in the last section, but, judging from their size, form, and coloration, evidently the produce of a different bird. They are very nearly the smallest eggs of this species I have, measuring 1·87 in. by 1·52, and 1·99 in. by 1·49 respectively, and are besides rather curiously coloured. They were found as above, upon the ground.]

[§ 236. *One.*—Head of Teesdale, 1847.   " W. H. S."   From Mr. W. H. Simpson's Collection, 1854.]

[§ 237. *One.*—Shetlands, 1854.

Sent to me by a correspondent, who says they were found " in the sea-banks, about one hundred and fifty feet high," on the island wherein he lives.]

[§ 238. *Two.*—Kirkcudbrightshire, 1855.

These I received from a gentleman, who took them himself. They are from two nests, one of which was taken on the 18th of April, the other about a month later. The hen-bird was caught on each nest].

[§ 239. *Four.*—Shetlands, May 1856.

These, and the two eggs in the next section, were sent me by the correspondent before mentioned (§ 237); these from the sea-cliffs near a headland on one of the southern isles.]

[§ 240. *Two.*—Shetlands, May 1856.

Two very small eggs, and so abnormally coloured as to lead to the supposition that the mother must have been diseased. From the same island as that in § 237. They measure only 1·77 in. by 1·51, and 1·84 in. by 1·51 respectively.]

[§ 241. *One.*—Shetlands, 1857.

From the same correspondent as the last, but from which of the islands I do not know.]

[§ 242. *One.*—Fiskernæs, Greenland. From Dr. David Walker, R.N., Naturalist to the 'Fox,' R. Y. S.

This egg was obtained during the celebrated voyage of the 'Fox,' under Captain Sir Leopold M'Clintock, R.N. Prof. Reinhardt states his belief ('Ibis,' 1861, p. 5) that "there is no difference between the Peregrine from Greenland and the European one." Sir Leopold mentions (Voy. 'Fox,' p. 197) Peregrine Falcons which were shot at Port Kennedy. These birds I afterwards saw, and one is now in the Norwich Museum. They were, to all appearance, specimens of the true *Falco peregrinus*, not *F. anatum*, being small and light-coloured. This egg is a little one, measuring but 1·89 in. by 1·54.]

FALCO BARBARUS, Linnæus.

BARBARY FALCON.

§ 243. *One.*—Kef Boudjato, Eastern Atlas, 20 April, 1857. "Bird shot." From Mr. W. H. Simpson's Collection.

[This egg, it appears, was taken in the presence of Mr. O. Salvin, who shot one of the parent birds. In some excellent remarks on this species in the 'Ibis,' vol. i. pp. 184-189, he states:—"On the 20th of April an Arab reported that he found a nest of "*Bournee*" in Kef Boudjato, a rock situated no great distance from Kef Laks. I immediately started to the spot, taking with me Mohammed, my gun, and ropes. A successful siege was the result; and I returned to the tents with three eggs and one of the parent birds."]

[§ 244. *One.*—Kef Boudjato, Eastern Atlas, 18 April, 1857. From Mr. O. Salvin's Collection.

Mr. Tristram's party obtained four nests of this species, from two of which a bird was shot. In 1856 he brought home two young ones alive, and in

1857 a third. All these passed into Mr. Gurney's possession: one made its escape not long after; but I believe the other two, supposed to be females, are still living at Catton. The skins of the birds that were shot are now in the Museum at Norwich. This egg was from one of two nests within a hundred yards of each other. It was brought by an Arab; but though Mr. Salvin went immediately to the spot, he was unable to see the bird.]

FALCO ÆSALON, Linnæus.

MERLIN.

[The series of Merlins' eggs recounted in the following notes has been selected from about two hundred trustworthy specimens, more than three-fourths of which have been simultaneously compared in forming it. As it stands, it may therefore be held a fair representation of what the eggs of this species are really like. There are not many specimens in it which, taken singly, could be pronounced from their appearance alone to be certainly Merlins'; but, taken as a whole, a purple tint is seen to be prevalent, which is not discernible in the series of Kestrels' eggs lying in the same drawer, while the average size of these latter is also greater. It will be seen that the Merlin is also one of those birds of prey which are not constant in the choice of a locality for their nests, sometimes breeding (as in the British islands is, I believe, its usual habit) on the ground, at others in trees.]

§ 245. *Three.*—Orkneys, 1851.   From Mr. George Harvey.

Out of seven, some of them beautiful varieties.

§ 246. *Six.*—Sutherlandshire, 1852.

Hewitson's ' Eggs of British Birds,' ed. 3. p. 31.

These beautiful eggs from one of the men who accompanied me when I was there. He says, "The male was one of the wicked-est I ever saw. It was like to pick out my eyes when going to the nest, and convoyed me about a mile on my way home. The nest was among the heather." He also adds that it was about the size of a Thrush; and from his description of the bird, and from the situation of the nest, there can be no doubt it was a Merlin. I am not sure I ever saw this bird whilst I was in Sutherlandshire, but I heard the nest of one described. It certainly is not common there. I think the partial colouring of these eggs remarkably fine.

[Mr. Hewitson mentions (*loc. cit.*) that one of these, sent him by Mr. Wolley, "unfortunately too late to figure, is one of the most beautiful eggs I have ever seen. The ground-colour is of a pure white, thickly blotched with crimson-red." The remaining five, I may add, are of the same character.]

§ 247. *Three.*—Nälima, East Bothnia, June 1853.

Brought to me 26th June. There were young Hawks, perhaps Merlins, inside them. I have seen one or two pairs of small Hawks in the woods hereabouts.

§ 248. *Three.*—Rauhala, Kemi Lappmark, 3 June, 1854.

Out of nine eggs from two nests taken by Matti.

§ 249. *Four*—Kätkia-joki, East Bothnia, 1854.

Out of five. No doubt Merlins'.

§ 250. *Four.*—Marrainen, Tornea Lappmark, 1854.   From Pastor Engelmarck.

Called *Pouta-Haukka* [*i. e.* Dry-weather Hawk], which seems by the Finnish lexicon to be properly Kite. Here it is Merlin.

§ 251. *Two.* — Hans-vaara, South-western Finmark, 1855. "With feet."

Brought, as above, to me at Kaaressuando.

§ 252. *Four.*—Muotka-vaara, Enontekis Lappmark, 1855.

Found on the ground by a little girl, and brought to Ludwig as Cuckow's eggs! One of them is very remarkable for its two shades of colour.

[This last has a cream-coloured ground, partially blotched with deep purplish-red and violet.]

§ 253. *Three.*—Marrainen, Tornea Lappmark, 1855.

Given to me at Kuttainen.

§ 254. *Three.*—Karanes-pahta, Tornea Lappmark, 22 May, 1855. ". With skin of hen from nest."

This is one of the rocks I visited last year near Mukka-uoma.

§ 255. *Four.*—Luspa-vaara, Enontekis Lappmark, 1855.

Taken by Naimakkas Peter.

§ 256. *One.*—Herra-vaara, Tornea Lappmark, 1855. " With cock-bird."

§ 257. *Four.*—Venajan-vaara, Enontekis Lappmark, 1855.

Taken by a Lapp from the place where I went to the old Buzzard's nest, between Naimakka and Mukka-uoma. It is called by the Lapps Karijalla-vaara.

§ 258. *Three.* — Kyrö, Kemi Lappmark, 10 June, 1856. " L. M. K."

Found by Ludwig in a good-sized spruce, a few miles (English) north of Kyrö. He was very hungry and tired, and he threw the eggs down from the tree on the soft ground, knowing they were very hard ; and they did not break.

§ 259. *Six.*—Palo-joki, Enontekis Lappmark, 1856.

One of seven brought on the 14th of June.

§ 260. *Four.*—Nollänki, Meras-järwi, West Bothnia, 1–6 June, 1857.

From a nest in which Hendrik had, a week previously, found three Rough-legged Buzzard's eggs.

> [Two of these were included in the sale of February 23rd, 1858, and were purchased by Mr. Braikenridge, who, when informed of my wish to possess the complete contents of a nest, interesting from the fact mentioned in Mr. Wolley's note, most liberally gave them up to me.]

§ 261. *Four.*—Toras-sieppi, East Bothnia, 6 June, 1857.

Brought by Wollas Lassi.

§ 262. *Four.*—Kotti-palla, Enontekis Lappmark, 7 June, 1857.
Found by Muotka-järwi Johann.

§ 263. *Five.*—Kyrö, Kemi Lappmark, 1857.
Brought by Keimio Johann, June 17th.

§ 264. Pippo-vaara, Kemi Lappmark, 6 June, 1858.
Out of five, brought by Sardio Erik.

§ 265. *Two.*—East Bothnia (?), 1859.

Brought from Kätkesuando on the 12th of June, without any
history.

[§ 266. *Three.*—Kätkesuando, East Bothnia, June 1861.

Out of four brought to Muoniovara 23rd June, having been taken as above
the week before. These are remarkably light-coloured eggs, the white ground
in two of them being less than half covered with blotches of pale red.]

FALCO ELEONORÆ, Gené.

ELEONORA'S FALCON.

[§ 267. *One.*—Cyclades, 13 August, 1862. "Kr." From
Dr. Krüper's Collection, through Pastor Theobald, 1863.

This rare specimen was taken, as above mentioned, by Dr. Krüper, and
"written on with his own hand," as I am assured by the Pastor. The Doctor
states (Journ. für Ornith., 1862, pp. 437–440) the grounds of his belief that
Falco eleonoræ, Gené (Mem. Accad. Torin. ser. 2, ii. p. 41), and *F. dichrous*,
Erhard ('Naumannia,' 1858, p. 25), are identical. The same Journal will probably in due time contain his notes on the breeding of this bird, of which he
then (December 1861) only knew that it took place in August. This egg cor-
responds in size, though not in colour, with the figure on the plate (tab. 1)
illustrating Prof. Gené's paper (*op. cit.*).]

FALCO SUBBUTEO, Linnæus.

HOBBY.

§ 268. *One.*—From Herr J. G. W. Brandt's Collection (?).

§ 269. *One.*—England (?). From Mr. J. Green's Collection, 1844.

§ 270. *Four.*—Valkenswaard, North Brabant, 1851.

[These eggs were sent to me direct from Holland, and Mr. Wolley had them from me.]   .

§ 271. *One.*—Holland (?). From Dr. Frere's Collection, 1852.

§ 272. *One.*—Strelley, Nottinghamshire (?). From Mr. Edge, 1856.

This egg, with another, had been for many years in a case, with a stuffed Hobby, at Strelley. Mr. Edge allowed me to take it out, and gave it to me. The presumption is that the eggs were taken there, with the bird.

§ 273. *Two.*—Sjövik, Œland, 17 June, 1856. "J. W."

Taken by myself in a wood near Knisa-moss, where the nest was first found by Mr. Simpson on the 12th June. About noon of the 17th, I climbed up to it, and had an excellent look at the bird; but there was only a single egg. It was a good-sized oak, just in full leaf, or nearly so. The nest, in a firm fork, was lightly built of thorns and twigs, and had a substantial lining of wool. About six o'clock P.M. we came to the tree again, when the bird flew off crying. As I went up, she went off a second time, having evidently come on as we were standing underneath. There were now two eggs in the nest, one so warm as to have been undoubtedly just dropped. The same day I climbed to another nest found by Mr. Simpson, which was also lightly made of thorns. The next day I found a third nest, of similar structure, but it had no eggs. Hobbies sail about after dragon-flies.

[§ 274. *One.*—Holland.   From Mr. R. Reynolds, 1847.]

[§ 275. *Two.*—Falkenswaard, North Brabant, 1861.   From Mr. Newcome's Collection.

These two eggs were obtained by Mr. Newcome during his visit to Holland, in 1851, to attend the Loo Hawking Meeting.   He brought them over himself, and gave them to my brother and myself.]

[§ 276. *Two.*—Burnt Fen, Mildenhall, Suffolk, 1852.   From Mr. Whitmore Baker.

These eggs were stated to be from different nests, and my brother understood Mr. Baker to say he took them himself.]

[§ 277. *Two.*—Benacre, Suffolk, 2 July, 1853.   "J. F."   From Mr. J. Farr's Collection, 1856.

Mr. Farr, writing to me from Gillingham Rectory, 14th February 1856, says:—"I send you to-day two Hobby's eggs, and hope they will arrive safely.   They are the second pair I took out of the same nest, and are something smaller than the first pair, which I took on the 8th of June, shooting the hen bird.   The male then paired again, and on the 2nd July I took the two eggs I have sent you.   Since 1853 I have not found another nest."]

[§ 278. *Three.*—New Forest, Hampshire, 21 June, 1861.   "With bird."   From Mr. W. Farren.

These I obtained from Mr. Farren in the autumn of the same year, with the skin of the hen bird.]

[§ 279. *One.*—"South Russia."   From Herr A. Heinke, of Kamuschin, through Dr. Albert Günther, 1863.]

FALCO VESPERTINUS, Linnæus.

RED-FOOTED FALCON.

§ 280. *Two.*—From M. Perrot's Collection, 1845.

§ 281. *One.*—Tipa Földwar, Hungary, 2 June, 1850. "A.H.C."
From Mr. A. H. Cochrane's Collection, through Mr.
W. Proctor, 1851.

This egg, and another with a similar mark upon it, I saw in the
University Museum, at Durham, and Mr. Proctor informed me he had
got them from Mr. Cochrane. Two days afterwards I saw half-a-
dozen or more of these eggs with Mr. John Hancock at Newcastle,
and he told me that Mr. Cochrane had obtained the birds very plentifully in Hungary. I accordingly wrote to Mr. Proctor for this
egg, and it arrived the next day.

[In answer to inquiries respecting this and the eggs in the next sections,
which I addressed to him, Mr. Cochrane has kindly written to me, under date
21st May 1863, as follows:—"With regard to the eggs of *Falco rufipes*, I must
have collected some hundreds of them when I was in Hungary, and the name
of the place where I took them is Tipa Földwar. As I usually write the date
and name of the place where I collect any eggs on the eggs, some of which
Mr. Proctor received from me, I have no doubt but that the eggs you mention
have been taken by myself. For particulars of the breeding of *Falco rufipes* I
will refer you to Mr. Hewitson's book, the account of which [Eggs B. B.,
ed. 3. p. 28] was furnished by me."]

§ 282. *One.*—Tipa Földwar, Hungary, 1850. "A. H. C."
From Mr. A. H. Cochrane's Collection, through Mr.
John Evans, 1853.

Mr. Evans procured this from Mr. Roberts, of Scarborough. He
had it from a friend of Mr. Cochrane, whose signature is on the
paper pasted on the egg.

[§ 283. *One.*—Tipa Földwar, Hungary, 1850. From Mr.
A. H. Cochrane's Collection, through Mr. W. Proctor,
1858.

This egg also is certified by the writing on the label. I bought it at Mr.
Stevens's rooms, the sale being that of some of Mr. Proctor's eggs, January
26th, 1858. The curious fact of this species having the habit of nesting in
communities was made known to me some fourteen or fifteen years since by
Mr. Newcome, who derived his information from an old falconer of the Loo
Hawking Club, by name Mollen; and, at my suggestion, Mr. Newcome for-
warded Mr. Hewitson the notice which appears in the last edition of his
work ('Eggs B. B.', ed. 3. p. 29). To Mr. Cochrane, however, I fully believe,
British oologists are indebted for the first authenticated specimens of this
egg.]

§ 284. *One.*—"Sardinia." From M. Parzudaki's Collection, 1856.

§ 285. *One.*—"Tamak, Crimea, May 1857." From M. Parzudaki's Collection, 1858.

§ 286. *One.*—Aïn Oosera, Eastern Atlas, June 1856. From Mr. Tristram's Collection, 1858.

[§ 287. *Two.*—"Sarepta." From Herr F. Möschler's Colleclection, 1862.]

ELANUS CÆRULEUS (Desfontaines).

BLACK-WINGED KITE.

§ 288. *One.* — Tangiers (?). From M. Favier's Collection, through Mr. Williams, 1847.

MILVUS ICTINUS, Savigny.

KITE.

§ 289. *Two.*—Monk's Wood, Huntingdonshire. From Mr. Sadd, 1843.

Obtained in 1843 from Mr. Sadd, of Cambridge, who had them from Monk's Wood. The birds were once very plentiful in that neighbourhood; and Mr. Chapman, of Coney Street, York, informed me that he had had "hundreds" of their eggs when the coaches ran that road. I only saw one of these magnificent birds on the wing in Monk's Wood during the three or four days I spent at Sawtry, in June 1843.

§ 290. *One.*—Huntingdonshire. From Mr. Harvey, of Bait's-bight, 1844.

Kites are becoming very rare near Alconbury Hill. I am not sure

that I saw one this year, during my five days' stay at Sawtry. I saw
a Buzzard over Monk's Wood. The Kite's egg is green on "shining"
it to the light, like eggs of the Harriers.

[On this last observation of Mr. Wolley's I may remark that it is perfectly
correct, but that I perceive not much difference in this respect between the
eggs of the Kite and of the Common Buzzard, though, judging from the specimens of both in the collection, the latter appear to be generally more opake.]

§ 291. *One.*—"Heidelberg." From the Berne Museum, 1846.

§ 292. *One.*—From M. Nager-Donazain's Collection, 1846.

§ 293. *Two.*—Glenmore, Inverness-shire, 1850.　From Mr.
Lewis Dunbar, 1851.

Mr. Dunbar informed me that he took these himself between Loch
Garten and the river Nethy. The bird flew off as he approached the
nest, and sailed overhead as he was climbing up to it.

§ 294. *Three.*—Lincolnshire, 1853.　From Mr. G. Adrian.

These were sent for me to Mr. Edge, who, when he found I was
not returning to England that year, blew them for me.

§ 295. *Three.*—Lincolnshire, 1854.　From Mr. G. Adrian.

§ 296. *Four.*—Djurhavn, Denmark, 24 April, 1855.　From
Pastor Theobald's Collection, 1857.

Given to me by Pastor Theobald at Copenhagen, having been
taken as above by him and Herr Erichsen. Both the birds were
on the nest, and the female would not leave it for some time.

§ 297. *Three.*—"Champagne." From M. Parzudaki's Collection, 1856.

I

§ 298. *Two.*—Bosorup, Denmark, 6 May, 1856. "Theob."
From Pastor Theobald's Collection, 1857.

Given to me at Copenhagen, by the Pastor. He told me he did
not see the birds, but observed Kites' feathers in the nest.

§ 299. *Three.*—Lincolnshire, 14 May, 1856. From Mr. G.
Adrian.

Mr. Adrian found this nest from the birds flying about in its
neighbourhood. Some one had been up the tree already; and as it
was not very easy of access, and night was approaching, he determined to take it.

§ 300. *One.*—Roeskilde, Denmark, 27 April, 1857. "Th."
From Pastor Theobald's Collection.

This was from a nest of three eggs, taken at or near Roeskilde by
the Pastor himself, who twice saw the bird flying near the nest.

§ 301. *One.*—Jutland, 8 May, 1857. From Pastor Theobald's
Collection.

§ 302. *One.*—Kef Laks, Eastern Atlas, 17 May, 1857. From
Mr. H. B. Tristram's Collection.

[§ 303. *One.*—New Forest, Hampshire, 1850. From Mr. E.
Fitton's Collection, through Dr. R. T. Frere, 1861.]

[§ 304. *Two.*—Djebel Dekmar, Eastern Atlas, 6 April, 1857.
From Mr. H. B. Tristram's Collection.

Mr. Tristram's note-book states that these were from a nest of four eggs on
a ledge on the north side of the Kef of Djebel-Dekmar. The nest built of
sticks, with the roots and bottom branches of a small shrub clinging to the
rock. The eggs a few days sat on.
Mr. O. Salvin's note-book also contains the information that this nest was
found by Mr. W. H. Simpson, and that all the party watched the bird while
Mohammed climbed and took the eggs.]

[§ 305. *One.*—Gala el Hamara, Eastern Atlas, 15 April, 1857.
From Mr. H. B. Tristram's Collection.]

§ 306. *Two.*—Vendsyssel, Jutland, 17 May, 1858. From Pastor Theobald's Collection, 1859.

These eggs were taken by Herr Fischer as above, in the wood Paihede.

§ 307. *One.*—Mylenberg, Jutland, April, 1859. From Pastor Theobald's Collection.

[§ 308. *One.*—Holland. From Mr. Newcome's Collection, 1852.]

[§ 309. *One.*—North Devonshire. From Lord Lilford's Collection, 1855.]

[§ 310. *One.*—Lincolnshire, 17 May, 1856. "Female trapped." From Mr. G. Adrian.

The nest from which this egg comes was found by Mr. Adrian on the 14th May, the same day as that on which he took the three eggs sent to Mr. Wolley [§ 299]. In the hope that the bird would lay more, Mr. Adrian left it, but a few hours afterwards heard that a farmer, living near the wood in which the nest was, had, the day before, trapped a Kite, which was subsequently sent to him alive, and proved to be a hen bird. Three days having passed, Mr. Adrian again visited the nest, and, finding it exactly as he had left it, he took the egg. He had no doubt that the bird trapped belonged to this nest.]

[§ 311. *Three.*—Lincolnshire, 6 May, 1857. From Mr. G. Adrian.] .

[§ 312. *One.*—Lincolnshire, 8 May, 1857. From Mr. G. Adrian.

With respect to this egg and those in the last section, Mr. Adrian wrote that he "noticed nothing peculiar. The materials of the nests consisted of decayed branches of oak; and they were built upon the larger boughs of that tree, at a height of about twenty-four or twenty-five feet; the tree in neither instance of very large dimensions."]

[§ 313. *One.*—Lincolnshire, 16 May, 1857. From Mr. G.
Adrian.

> Mr. Adrian informed my brother that the Kites in Lincolnshire were be-
> coming scarcer every year. This he attributed partly to the destruction of
> the birds, and partly to that of their favourite haunts, by the felling and
> stubbing of the woods, in two of which one hundred acres had been cut
> down since the beginning of the year, and this in the best locality. He said
> he found this nest on the 6th of May, then unfinished; on the 16th he called
> to see if there were any eggs in it, and found it had been completed by the
> addition of a few pieces of old rags; but there were no eggs. On making inquiry
> of some boys living in a cottage by the wood-side, he discovered that they
> had been to the nest, and taken out two eggs: one got broken, the other is
> the subject of this note.]

[§ 314. *One.*—"South Russia." From Herr A. Heinke, of Kamuschin, through Dr. Albert Günther, 1863.]

MILVUS MIGRANS (Boddaert).

BLACK KITE.

§ 315. *One.*—Kef Laks, Eastern Atlas, 24 April, 1857. From
Mr. W. H. Simpson's Collection, 1858.

Mr. Simpson took particular care with the eggs of the two species
of Kite.

§ 316. *One.*—Khifan M'srouten, Eastern Atlas, 24 April, 1857.
From Mr. H. B. Tristram's Collection, 1858.

An interesting and well-identified little egg—the only one in the
nest.

§ 317. *Two.*—Khifan M'satka, Eastern Atlas, 25 April, 1857.
From Mr. O. Salvin's Collection.

Two specimens from the same nest, taken by Mr. Simpson himself, and the bird seen. Mr. Salvin tells me that this is probably
the commonest bird of prey in Algeria. It is bolder than the Red
Kite, lighting down close to the tents. It is nearly three weeks

later than that species, the eggs not having been got before the middle of April. In a series they are generally of a richer style of marking and colour than those of the other. The nest is built of sticks, lined with rags of burnous, placed in a rock, and commonly supported by a bush.

[Mr. Salvin's remarks on the nidification of this species will be found in 'The Ibis,' vol. i. p. 184.]

§ 318. *Two.*—Djendeli, Eastern Atlas, 15 May, 1857. From Mr. H. B. Tristram's Collection, 1858.

From different nests.

§ 319. *One.*—Kef Laks, Eastern Atlas, 17 May, 1857. From Mr. W. H. Simpson's Collection, 1858.

[§ 320. *Two.*—Kef Laks, Eastern Atlas, 21 April, 1857. From Mr. O. Salvin's Collection.

From two different nests. Both eggs quite fresh when brought by the Arabs. Mr. Salvin states that "in the neighbourhood of Kef Laks, as far as we could make out, there were three pairs of *Milvus regalis*, all of which we could account for. One nest in Gala el Hamara we took; another in the same rock had young, and one nest in Kef Zaroua was inaccessible; so that I have confidence in all eggs brought from the several rocks which form the edges of the *plateau* of Kef Laks—the highest of them all.

To Mr. Salvin's general remarks on the Black Kite I have already referred (§ 317).]

[§ 321. *One.*—Kef Boudjato, Eastern Atlas, 22 April, 1857. From Mr. H. B. Tristram's Collection.]

[§ 322. *One.*—Khifan M'srouten, Eastern Atlas, 24 April, 1857. From Mr. H. B. Tristram's Collection.

From a nest of two eggs taken by Mr. Simpson.]

[§ 323. *One.*—Djendeli, Eastern Atlas, 15 May, 1857. From Mr. H. B. Tristram's Collection.

Mr. Tristram's note states that this specimen was from a nest containing two eggs, near the nest of *Tadorna rutila*, which was one of the great prizes obtained by the Algerian triumvirate (Ibis, vol. i. p. 362).]

[§ 324. *One.*—"South Russia." From Herr A. Heinke, of Kamuschin, through Dr. Albert Günther, 1863.]

MILVUS ÆGYPTIUS (J. F. Gmelin).

ARABIAN KITE.

[§ 325. *One.*—"Egypte." From M. E. Verreaux's Collection, 1861.]

[§ 326. *One.*—Egypt, 14 April, 1862. "Bird seen." From Mr. S. S. Allen's Collection.

The specimen above mentioned was obtained by Mr. Allen; but that gentleman's notes on the breeding of this species are not as yet published. In due time they will probably appear in the pages of 'The Ibis.']

PERNIS APIVORUS (Linnæus).

HONEY-BUZZARD.

§ 327. *One.*—Wellgrove Wood, Oxfordshire, July, 1838. From Mr. Wilmot's Collection, 1856.

Concerning this egg, just received (11th April, 1856), Mr. Wilmot writes:—"The offering I have just dispatched consists of the fellow Honey-Buzzard's egg to the one figured by Mr. Hewitson [Eggs B. B. ed. 3. pl. xv. fig. 1] * * *. As you will see, it is an under-sized, poorly marked egg, that would be valueless but for its being a veritable British-taken one. Indeed I am not aware that there are any other British-taken eggs still extant, except this pair. You will find the history of them in the 'Zoologist,' p. 437. The egg I have sent you is the one my good friend Mr. G. L. Russell had. He is not prosecuting his collection, and therefore let me have it again without reluctance, as indeed he would anything that he possessed; but I have so arranged that you need not feel the slightest scruple in placing it in the collection, where both eggs ought to be."

[It appears to me that Mr. Wilmot, in the above passage, has rather under-rated this specimen. It is not, I confess, a very richly coloured one, but it is, I think I may say, quite as good as the average in this respect, as it is supe-rior to them in the interest which attaches to it from its history, the parti-culars of which I here subjoin, extracted from the 'Zoologist' for 1844, p. 437.

"Early in the month of July, 1838, a female honey-buzzard was shot off her nest, in Wellgrove-wood, in the parish of Bix, near Henley-on-Thames, by a gamekeeper of Lord Camoy's, named Lowe. The bird, with two eggs taken from the nest, passed into the hands of a bird-stuffer at Henley, of the name of Hewer. I was then resident in the Temple, and being an eager collector of the eggs of British birds, had engaged a young friend, Mr. Ralph Mapleton, then living at Henley, to secure for me any rare eggs that he might have an opportunity of obtaining. Mr. Mapleton communicated to me the above occurrence, and at my request purchased the eggs for me. I afterwards saw the bird at the shop of Mr. Hewer, at Henley. The male bird, which con-tinued to haunt the neighbourhood of the nest, was not long after killed by another of Lord Camoy's gamekeepers. The nest, a very large one, was placed in the fork of a beech tree, and was built of sticks of considerable size, with which were intermixed twigs with the leaves on. The lining was composed of leaves and wool; a great portion of the nest was, I am told, remaining in the tree a short time ago [1844]. I made no note of the occurrence at the time, but since my attention was drawn to the subject by the appearance of the observations before referred to [Mr. W. R. Fisher, 'Zoologist,' 1843, p. 375, and Mr. Hewitson, 'Eggs B. B.,' p. 27], I have assisted my memory by appli-cation to Mr. Hewer, and by his aid am enabled to give the above particulars with confidence as to their accuracy. He informs me that the pair of birds are in the collection of W. Fuller Maitland, Esq., of Park Place, near Henley."

In 1862, Mr. Fuller-Maitland informed me that the birds here mentioned were still in his possession. After mentioning two other recent instances of the Honey-Buzzard breeding in England, Mr. Wilmot proceeds to add (loc. cit. p. 439) —"The nest near Henley contained two eggs only, and the state of the eggs indicated that the bird had accomplished full one half of her period of incu-bation, and had consequently laid her complement. Of these eggs, one [the subject of this note] was inferior in size to the other, less strongly marked, and much more pointed at the smaller end. The largest egg ['Eggs B. B.' ed. 3. pl. 15. fig. 1] is about 2 inches long by 1⅝ inch in breadth, and has the colouring, which has evidently lost somewhat of its brilliancy by incubation, pretty equally distributed over the whole surface. In other respects it re-sembles the specimen figured by Mr. Hewitson ['Eggs B. B.' pl. x.], and when newly laid, must have been a splendid egg."

I cannot refrain from here noticing the pleasing fact that these eggs were the means of Mr. Hewitson and Mr. Wilmot becoming known to each other—with what advantage to oology all egg-collectors recognize, though of the inti-mate friendship into which that acquaintance has ripened few may be aware.

The Honey-Buzzards certainly did not build their nest in Wellgrove Wood to no good purpose.]

§ 328. *One.* — "France."   From Dr. Pitman's Collection, 1845 [?].

§ 329. *One.*—From Mr. J. Green, through Mr. Wilmot, 1846.

§ 330. *One.*—From M. J. Hardy's Collection, 1848.

§ 331. *One.*—From Herr J. G. W. Brandt's Collection, through Dr. R. T. Frere, 1853.

§ 332. *Two.*—From M. Parzudaki's Collection, 1856.

§ 333. *One.*—Nilivaara, East Bothnia [?], 1856.

Came into my hands at the house (a *good* peasant's house) at Nili-vaara.   It remains to be seen what it is—Peregrine, or Honey-Buzzard.

[I can find no further record of this egg, but I know that Mr. Wolley was at last nearly quite satisfied that this egg was a Honey-Buzzard's. The precise situation of the locality I have not been able to discover, but I have very little doubt it is in the district which, in this work, I somewhat arbitrarily term East Bothnia, and at all events may be safely set down as north of lat. 67°, being four degrees beyond the limit assigned to the species by Herr Wallengren ('Naumannia,' 1855, p. 134).]

§ 334. *One.*—Kyrö, Kemi Lappmark, 4–10 June, 1858.

Brought to Muoniovara, 13th July, by Nikoo, who said it was an egg he did not know, but that it was a foreign Hawk's. He had shot the bird, and brought its wings and feet. It was found, between the 4th and 10th of June, in a spruce-top about four fathoms high from the ground.

[The wings and feet of the bird were sent to Mr. Wolley, who told me that he recognized them as a Honey-Buzzard's; but they unfortunately seem to have been lost. I searched in vain for them among the contents of his Lapland boxes at Beeston, before these were transferred by his father to the Museum at Norwich.]

§ 335. *One.*—"France."   From M. Parzudaki's Collection, 1858.

[§ 336. *One.*—"Germany, 1858." From Pastor Theobald's Collection, 1859].

[§ 337. *One.*—From Herr J. G. W. Brandt's Collection, through Dr. R. T. Frere, 1861.

Hewitson, 'Eggs of British Birds,' ed. 3. pl. xv. fig. 2.]

[§ 338. *Two.*—Frame Wood, Hampshire, 10 July, 1861. "With bird. W. F." From Mr. W. Farren.

Mr. Farren's notes on the breeding of the Honey-Buzzard in the New Forest and adjacent woods will be found in the 'Zoologist' for 1862, p. 8159.]

ARCHIBUTEO LAGOPUS (Linnæus).

ROUGH-LEGGED BUZZARD.

[I cannot publish the details of the magnificent series of the eggs of this species which Mr. Wolley's cabinet contains, without adding a few remarks. When he first went to Lapland, in 1853, identified and authenticated specimens were almost, if not quite, unknown to British collectors[1]. He found the bird very plentiful around Muonioniska; but all the nests had hatched, and that season he was only able to secure a few fragments of a single egg. Some months later, he obtained a couple of specimens from the pastor of Kaaresuando, by whom they had been procured for the chance of any one inquiring for them. The following year, 1854, Mr. Wolley applied himself especially to get properly identified examples. He took great pains to discover whether the Common Buzzard (*Buteo vulgaris*) ever visited the district. He spoke to all the persons he employed of the possibility of there being two sorts of *Piekonna* (the name usually applied to the Rough-legged Buzzard by the northern Finns), without giving any indication of the differences between them, merely requiring the feet of one of the birds to be brought, and offering the same reward for either. This plan he continued to follow, until he had thoroughly satisfied himself that the Rough-legged Buzzard alone bred in the far north. However, in his Sale Catalogue of 1855–1856, he stated that one example of the Common Buzzard was "recognized" just within the

---

[1] [It is recorded of this species by the late Mr. W. C. Williamson, of Scarborough (Proc. Zool. Soc., 1836, p. 77), that it "breeds occasionally" near Hackness; and the truth of the statement has been confirmed by Mr. Hewitson ('Eggs B. B.,' p. 26) through his friend, Mr. James Tuke. In Mr. Wolley's Note-book I find the following :—"Sept. 1843, Mr. Williamson informed me that the Rough-legged Buzzard, which used to breed at Hackness, is now extirpated there. He saw the last two on a barn-door two years ago! He has not got the egg."—ED.]

Arctic Circle. I believe that his earnest desire to do justice to the public, by not withholding from them any circumstance that might appear to favour their interests, here led him to do injustice to himself by exaggerating the amount of recognition which the bird obtained in this case. Mr. W. H. Simpson and I myself were with him on the occasion referred to. We were descending the River Muonio in the beginning of September 1855, and came upon a flock of about five-and-twenty or thirty Rough-legged Buzzards, which were then on their autumnal migration. Among them was one of a deep-brown colour all over. To this bird Mr. Wolley drew my attention, as being the first Common Buzzard he had seen in Lapland; and I examined it with my telescope as carefully as I could. It was sitting on a tree by the river-side, with several others, which were, to all appearance, undoubted Rough-legged Buzzards. They all seemed on friendly terms; and when we disturbed them, they took wing and continued in company. I could detect nothing in its carriage or flight different from the rest, and so far Mr. Wolley agreed with me. He also, if I remember right, admitted at the time the impro-bability of a Common Buzzard being found in a flock of the other species. I told him I thought it was only a very dark-plumaged Rough-legged Buzzard, and reminded him that among the many pairs of that bird's feet he had had brought to him, there were some of an almost deep chocolate-colour. I added that this was the prevailing characteristic of the North-American representa-tive of our *Archibuteo lagopus*, and it seemed to me not at all unlikely that the European form should occasionally exhibit a resemblance to the *A. sancti-johannis*. To this he seemed to assent; and I was therefore much surprised when, some months after, I read the unqualified statement in his 'Catalogue.' Subsequently he told me he had come to think I was right, or, at any rate, that he had used by far too strong an expression in saying that a Common Buzzard had been "recognized" in Lapland. This opinion is strengthened by what Herr Wallengren says several times in his valuable series of papers on the "Breeding-zone of Scandinavian Birds," in the 'Naumannia;' but I here need only cite the single assertion (vol. iv. p. 72) that the Common Buzzard "never oversteps the Polar Circle." The statements made by Mr. Wolley in his Sale Catalogues are so carefully worded, that I know of but very few cases in which they are not literally true; these cases, of which the present is one, I, however, feel it my duty to notice as I proceed.

But supplying our collections with undoubtedly genuine eggs of this species was not the only service Mr. Wolley rendered to natural history concerning it. I am not acquainted with any British author who has described the changes of plumage in the Rough-legged Buzzard correctly, or who has figured an adult bird. This can easily be explained by the fact that the ge-nerality of the examples obtained in this country are young birds in their first dress. Until Mr. Wolley's spoils of 1853 were sent home, I did not positively know what the mature plumage was like. It is true it had been represented in some Continental works, among others, Naumann's excellent 'Vögel Deutschlands' (pl. xxxiv. fig. 1); but I had never had an opportunity of satisfying myself that that painstaking naturalist was right. The bird, however, killed from the nest, mentioned in the first of the following sections (§ 339), revealed the truth, and convinced me that in the adults of this species, as in so many other *Accipitres*, the markings are disposed transversely, instead of longitudinally,—in other words, that the young are striped, and the old are barred. This view of the case was confirmed, without a single exception, by all the other skins, or parts of skins, subsequently obtained by Mr. Wolley, most of which are now in the Museum at Norwich. Naumann's figure of the adult Rough-legged Buzzard being so good, and Mr. Gould intending to depict the same stage of plumage in his magnificent 'Birds of Great Britain,' I do not think it necessary to give an illustration here. Mr. Cassin, so far as I know, is the only writer who has noticed the error into which most of the ornithologists of "Western Europe" have fallen ('Baird's B. of N. Am.,' p. 33); but he has not mentioned, as he might have done, that it was to an ornithologist of " Western Europe" that he owed his having been able to avoid the mistake his own countrymen had also made.

Of the series of eggs now in my possession, I can only say that, large as it is, it has been chosen from a much larger number. I have not the smallest doubt of the genuineness of any one specimen; but my first object in making the selection has always been to take those that were most fully identified. The picking out of finely marked or singular varieties has been a secondary consideration, but it is also one I have not neglected. The extent of variation, both in colour and size, is, however, in some degree shown by the dozen which are represented on the accompanying plates. The differences in the latter point are very great. It will be observed that the short diameter of one of the eggs represented (tab. v. fig. 6) is considerably greater than the long diameter of another figured in the same plate (fig. 3); and yet there is nothing of a monstrous character about either. Such discrepancies, I believe, are by no means unusual; and yet there are oologists who think that from perhaps a single specimen they can prescribe the exact measurement of a bird's egg! In colour the variation is quite as great; but I know how impossible it is to characterize in words the shape or tint of the markings. The more minutely a description is attempted, the less does it seem to convey a true idea of the specimen.

It might be imagined that the measures taken by Mr. Wolley to obtain a large series of identified eggs of this species would lead to its utter extirpation; I have therefore to assure those who were unacquainted with him, that he was one of the last persons to have done anything fraught with such a result. Rough-legged Buzzards are the commonest birds of prey in Lapland; and so enormous is the extent of the district from which his specimens were collected, that no sensible diminution whatever was thereby made in their numbers. It must also be remembered that all rapacious birds in Scandinavia are exposed to systematic persecution, premiums for their destruction being offered by the local authorities. Accordingly it was only necessary that he should promise a very trifling sum, in addition to the legal reward, to ensure the bird's feet being brought to him, instead of to the Länsman or other official. After the year 1857, Mr. Wolley ceased to trouble himself with regard to this species, though a few of its eggs were occasionally brought in, chiefly from remote stations, or by collectors, paid by the day, who wished to swell the importance of their captures.]

§ 339. *Fragment.*—Palo-joki, Enontekis Lappmark, 3 July, 1853. " Bird shot. J. W."

This fragment we found under the nest of a Rough-legged Buzzard. I climbed up to the nest, which was in a Scotch fir of no great size. There were in it two young ones—one which was not many days hatched, the other much larger. They were white, and just like young Eaglets. The nest was small, made of old sticks, with two or three sprigs of Scotch fir, and a little of the black hair-like lichen "*luppu*," which hangs so abundantly from trees hereabouts. The old birds flew around with a melancholy cry, just like the Common Buzzard, and they first did so a long way from the nest. I fired several shots at them, without at all frightening them, though one was certainly hit. Theodore shot one at last, whilst I was climbing up the tree. We picked up all the bits of shell we could find under the tree; and this is the result, sufficient to show the character of the eggs. In the nest was a half-eaten vole. The situation was at the edge of a great marsh—or, at least, near the edge; trees all round.

§ 340. *Three.*—Kaaressuando, Tornea Lappmark, 1853.

Obtained 8th December 1853, from Pastor Engelmarck. These were said to be *Kalasääski*, that is, Osprey; but they appear to be Buzzard's, and are, in all probability, Rough-legged Buzzard's. Two of them are highly marked eggs.

§ 341. *One.*—Æija-vaara, East Bothnia, 14 May, 1854.

Taken by Heiki. There was only one egg; he took it, and visited the nest a week afterwards, but it was deserted. I saw it on the 25th. The tree old and quite dead. The nest large, lined with hair-lichen and a little hay. There had been two or three trees cut down, and reared up to climb by. He could have shot the bird, had he had a gun. The egg, of course, quite fresh; and so I was able to select it from the other three with which it had been mixed. If there are two kinds of *Piekonna*, he thinks this egg belongs to the smallest. He knew the nest three years ago.

§ 342. *Three.* — Ollas-järwi, East Bothnia, 17 May, 1854.
    "Bird shot. J. W."

O. W. tab. v. fig. 1.

The nest was found by Wollas Lassie on the 15th May, and was

taken by him, with my assistance, on the 17th. It was in a very
tall and branchless Scotch fir. He went up with my iron claws,
assisted by a rope. The birds made stoops as he was at the nest,
but did not come very close. I would not have him take the eggs
till I had got an old bird, both of which were wailing near. I was
covered up in a hut of fir-branches. The bird settled under the
nest, and I missed; but it came again, and died with a second shot.
Lassie went up again, and lowered the eggs in my tin. They were
quite fresh. The nest was large, and lined with hair-like lichen
and grass. The bird shot was a hen, and had a half-grown egg-
yelk inside.

§ 343. *One.*—Piko-viksi, West Bothnia, 18 May, 1848.

Out of four from a nest near Viksi-järwi, in an old rotten tree,
which was cut down by Lassie Johann of Muonio-alusta. He found
the nest last autumn, as he was squirrel-shooting. The eggs a day
or two sat on. They fell on a soft place in the moss.

§ 344. *Three.*—Kangos-järwi, East Bothnia, 21 May, 1854.

Three eggs of a Buzzard, no doubt Rough-legged, found by Nils
Suiki, a Lapp, between Kangos-järwi and Salmo-järwi, and brought
to Ludwig the 3rd of June. They were rotten. Two of them are
not unlike Cormorants' in the shell.

§ 345. *Four.*—Rowa, East Bothnia, 27 May, 1854. "Bird
        shot."

Brought by Punsi's lads to Ludwig, 3rd June, with the feet of one
of the old birds. I must here make a memorandum, that I have let
no one know (except perhaps Ludwig) that I prefer *Rough-legged* feet.
I have promised the same pay for any Buzzards' feet, but nothing
but Rough-legged have yet come (30th June, 1854).

§ 346. *Four.*—Särki-järwi, Salmo-järwi, East Bothnia, 29 May,
        1854.

Brought to Ludwig, 3rd June, by Wassara the Lapp's lads, of
whom several were bird's-nesting on the same day. Ludwig says

there were small young in these eggs, which he has carefully kept distinct.

§ 347. *Three.*—Kaaressuando, Tornea Lappmark, 2 June, 1854. " Hen shot. J. W. *ipse.*"

I was taken to the nest on the 1st June, by the boy Johann Hendrik, commonly called Fricky, at Hammen-vaara, three quarters of a mile south of Kaaressuando. It was some fifteen or twenty feet from the ground, in a side branch of a Scotch fir, halfway up the hill, and easily accessible. I went up to it several times, and took the eggs on the 2nd or beginning of the 3rd—for it was about midnight. The birds wailed near the nest long before we came up. I caused a hut to be built above the nest, but I believe the bird saw my gun, and would not come. The second visit, my gun being carefully concealed, the bird at last came on to the nest, looking away from me towards where the men were. I fired, and she fell. It was freezing slightly, and there was a cold wind. The nest was made of fir-twigs, lined with grass or *Carex.* In the bird's ovary I counted about a hundred eggs visible on one side only : there would be as many more on the opposite side, besides those in the middle.

§ 348. *Four.*—Nälima, East Bothnia, 5 June, 1854. " Bird shot."

Four eggs, brought on the 10th June by Keimio Michael, with the feet of the bird, which now lie before me carefully labelled by Ludwig.

§ 349. *One.*—Naimakka, Enontekis Lappmark, 15 June, 1854.

Out of three found on the Finnish side ; I suppose, Rough-legged Buzzard's.

§ 350. *One.*—Muonioniska, East Bothnia, 26 June, 1854. " J. W."

From a nest found by myself and men in low ground near Kharto-vaara. The birds betrayed themselves by their wailing cries. The nest was placed just at the top of a Scotch fir, a small tree, and easy to climb up, but the largest in the immediate vicinity. It was made of sticks, lined with black hair-lichen, and of a good size. There was this addled egg, and one young one some days old, with a yellowish cere. By an oversight, I did not examine its legs. I had a good look at the old birds : the dark mark in the middle of the wing, the light upper part of the head, the dark under surface of the body, and the white over the tail, all corresponded with *Buteo lagopus*, so common here last year.

§ 351. *Three.*—Keras-sieppi, Enontekis Lappmark, 1854. "With both birds."

These three eggs brought to me by Hendrik on Midsummer Day, with the skins of the two old birds, complete, but poorly stuffed. They are now before me. The backs of both generally brown, with the edges of the feathers lighter, especially in the scapulars of the male. Top of the head also brown, with light edges to the feathers. Upper part of the tail white; the dark lower part barred in the male, with indications of bars upwards by the sides of the shafts. The throat and neck dull-coloured; crop white; chest dark brown, more mottled in the male. The belly in the latter also somewhat barred. Tail with a nearly black ring towards the end. Feathers of the thighs and legs barred and speckled. Under side of wings white, with speckles and bars, most of the feathers being dark at the ends, and light or white towards the base: hence the primary wing-coverts form a spot in the centre of the wing. Cere and feet yellow.

§ 352. *One.*—Keras-sieppi, Enontekis Lappmark, 1854.

Out of three brought to me at Midsummer by the old man there.

§ 353. *One.*—Sallanki, Kemi Lappmark, 1854.

With eight others, from a lot of eggs blown by himself, and delivered to me by Sallanki Johan, a great rascal. With the lot is a pair of Rough-legged Buzzard's feet. They do not know that I do not care for Common Buzzard; indeed the bird is not found, or not known, here.

§ 354. *Two.*—Palo-joki, Enontekis Lappmark, 1854.

From Heiki Ollen-poika and Zacharias. They called the bird *Poimonen*, a less common name about Muonioniska than *Piekonna*.

§ 355. *Two.*—Kautokeino, West Finmark, 1854.

Among other eggs collected and brought to Kaaressuando by a
Lapp, with a list in which every egg is wrongly named, he having
chosen the names for which I had offered the best prices. These
two he called *Skuolfi, i. e.* Snowy Owl !

§ 356. *Two.*—Palo-joki, Enontekis Lappmark, 1854.

From the side of a lake up in the mountains. Ludwig got them
in July from Matti, who said they were *Kalasääski;* and I have
often found that Rough-legged Buzzards, in common with Ospreys,
go by this name.

§ 357. *Three.*—Kyrö, Kemi Lappmark, 1854.

Out of twelve specimens brought by Kyrö Nikoo. He shot the
birds from three of the nests, and brought the feet and wings of two.
He said the third was just like them. Two pairs of the feet, now lying
before me, are Rough-legged Buzzards', and probably all the eggs
belong to that species. I have hitherto (June 29, 1854) met with
no other kind of Buzzard. He did not know how many nests there
were.

§ 358. *Two.*—Muonio-niska, East Bothnia, 13 May, 1855.

Heiki brought them on the 1st of June.

§ 359. *Two.*—Kilpis-järwi, Enontekis Lappmark, 23 May, 1855.

From between the two lakes which bear the above name.

§ 360. *Four.*—Nangi, West Bothnia, 23 May, 1855. "Cock
    shot. L. M. K."

Ludwig tells me that he and Anton found this nest near Nangi-
järwi. It was in a large Scotch fir. Ludwig went up with the
irons, and saw there were four eggs, and then, with Anton's help,
made a covert. He lay some three hours, when he got out and shot

a bird flying, which turned out to be the cock. Its skin I have examined.

§ 361. *Three.*—Muonio-niska, East Bothnia (?), 25 May, 1855.

Brought by Piko Heiki on 1st June: taken, probably, in the district.

§ 362. *Three.* — Sardio, Kemi Lappmark, 26 May–1 June, 1855. "With bird."

Taken by Michael Sardio himself, not far from his father's house. The skin of the bird which he obtained from this nest is a fine dark specimen. He had marked the eggs in pencil, and kept them separate ever since they were taken.

§ 363. *Three.*—Hetta, Enontekis Lappmark, 1855. "Bird shot."

Brought to Ludwig by Gabriel Muotka-järwi, 25th June, with the feet of the bird, which I have seen. They were called *Skuolfi*, which is Snowy Owl.

§ 364. *Two.*—Palo-joki, Enontekis Lappmark, 1855. "Bird shot."

With another nest of three eggs taken by Johan Matthias and Zacharias, near Palo-joki: a bird shot from each, and the legs and feet kept separate, and inspected by me.

§ 365. *Three.*—Palo-joki, Enontekis Lappmark, 1855. "Bird shot."

The second nest referred to above.

§ 366. *One.*—Ketto-uoma, Kyrö, Kemi Lappmark, 1855.

O. W. tab. v. fig. 5.

This egg the lad Johan Johansson declared he had taken himself

K

out of a nest, with one or two others, which he broke. It is a re-markably large specimen.

§ 367. *Three.*—Kyrö, Kemi Lappmark, 1855.

Out of thirteen others brought by the same lad, and at the same time, as the preceding. They are all marked by the rascal Kyrö Nikoo, and I have thrown away several.

§ 368. *One.*—Bergeby-elv, East Finmark, 1853. From Pastor Sommerfelt's Collection, 1855.

O. W. tab. v. fig. 5.

This egg, given to me by Pastor Sommerfelt, seems to be of un-usual size for *Buteo lagopus*. It is said by Herr Nordvi and the Pastor that large eggs of Buzzard are not uncommon in the Va-ranger district.

§ 369. *Two.*—Tartcha-pahta, Mukka-uoma, Enontekis Lapp-mark, 1855.

Brought by the Lapp, Pehran Pieran Nicolaef.

§ 370. *Three.*—Kuttainen, Tornea Lappmark, 1855.

With two others, out of two nests, taken by Isaac Jatko. They seem to be Rough-legged Buzzards'.

§ 371. *One.*—Palo-joki, Enontekis Lappmark, 1855.

From a nest of three found by Johan Matti and Zacharias.

§ 372. *Three.*—Salmo-järwi, East Bothnia, 1855.

Brought by Fredrick: rather interestingly and finely marked eggs.

§ 373. *Two.*—Neiden, East Finmark, 1855.

With another, which Mr. W. H. Simpson has, from Herr P. C. Ekdahl: apparently Rough-legged Buzzard's.

§ 374. *Two.*—Tromsö, South-western Finmark (?), 1855 (?).

[These two eggs were sent to me in 1856, by Herr Ebeltofft of Tromsö, whom Mr. Wolley had previously requested to receive eggs brought by the Lapps for me. They are marked ' *Boimas,*' which I believe to be the Lapp name for the Rough-legged Buzzard, and I take them to be the eggs of that bird. They are rather small specimens.]

§ 375. *One.*—Kurkio-vaara, Kyrö, Kemi Lappmark, 6 June, 1856. "L. M. K."

First shown by Michael to Ludwig, who took the eggs. He saw no bird. The nest was at the top of a low Scotch fir.

§ 376. *Four.*—Kyrö, Kemi Lappmark, 7 June, 1856. "L. M. K."

Taken by Ludwig one mile (Swedish) south of Kyrö. He was under the nest before the bird flew. As it got up, it hung its legs down, and he saw distinctly that they were feathered to the toes. The nest was four fathoms up in a Scotch fir. Ludwig made a watch-house, and shot at the bird (which cried around) once or twice, to no effect.

§ 377. *Three.*—Akka-rowa, East Bothnia, 7 June, 1856.

O. W. tab. v. fig. 5.

Brought to Muoniovara, 23rd June, by Fredrick Salmo-järwi.

§ 378. *Five.*—Keras-sieppi, Enontekis Lappmark, 14 June, 1856. "L. M. K."

Five eggs from a nest three fathoms above the ground, on the branch of a dead Scotch fir. Ludwig and Sieppi shot several times at the bird, and the latter even watched three hours. The old man began to suggest it was the Devil. At last, with a shot from Ludwig, it came down, and lay with its feet in the air. The old man called out, "Is it the right kind?" (they had before talked of my belief iu two kinds of *Piekonna*): Ludwig said, "Yes; but it is all alive still." As he spoke, the bird got up, flew away, and was no more seen. The old man said it was the Devil himself!

K 2

§ 379. *Two.*—Enontekis Lappmark (?), 1856.

O. W. tab. v. fig. 4.

Received by Ludwig at Kaaressuando, the beginning of July, from the Nyimakka´man.   Found by Rastin Piety.   Well-marked eggs.

§ 380. *One.*—Sardio, Kemi Lappmark, 1856.

Seems to be a Rough-legged Buzzard's, though the Sardio lads said it was *Koppelo-Haukka, i. e.* Gos-Hawk.   It is a well-marked egg.

§ 381. *Two.*—Sardio, Kemi Lappmark, 1856.   "With foot."

Brought by Michael, with three others, and the foot of a Rough-legged Buzzard, now before me, which he said belonged to two of the eggs—he could not say which, but probably those which are larger than the rest, and otherwise unlike them.

§ 382. *Three.*—Pulju, Kemi Lappmark, 1856.

The feet of the bird from this nest lie before me, carefully labelled, as are the other pairs of feet.   This pair is dark, and thickly spotted. The eggs are small.   The nest was said by Piety to be in Ollituna-rowa.

§ 383. *Five.*—Tepasto-lombola, Kemi Lappmark, 1856.   "With feet."

Brought to Ludwig by Piety.   The feet before me are closely spotted.

§ 384. *One.*—Tepasto-lombola, Kemi Lappmark, 1856.

Brought to Ludwig by Piety, who had the egg, with the feet of the bird, from Lombola Hendrik.   The feet, now before me, are rather faintly spotted.

§ 385. *One.*—Palo-joki, Enontekis Lappmark, 1856.

One of sixteen specimens.

§ 386. *Four.*—Akka-mella, West Bothnia, 1857. "Cock shot.
J. W. *ipse.*"

A. *Two.*—19 May.

This nest I first found on the 11th, as I was measuring the river.
I was going up the wooded bank, Mella-vaara, when one of the
birds came and sat in a tree near. I saw it very clearly: it made its
usual cry, and we almost at once saw the nest in a young Scotch fir.
Johan Keimio was eager, and climbed up. The nest was empty.
On the 19th I drove my Reindeer " Kokko-julma " on the river; both
birds showed and screamed. I brought down the two eggs in my
cap. The nest lined with *luppu* and sedge. I left in it two old Golden-
eye's eggs filled with sand, and having large holes open. The
name is from *Akka,* a kind of Lapp divinity (*vide* Leemius) [De
Lapp. Comment. p. 420], and *mella,* a sandhill. Here is an old
burying-place, still used.

B. *Two.*—28 May.

On this day I took two more eggs. The Golden-eye's had been
carried off, one to the Buzzard's ordinary feeding-place, the wooden
rail of the burial-ground.

§ 387. *Four.*—Muonio-niska, East Bothnia, 26 May, 1857.
" J. W."

Yesterday, or rather last night, I went with Wollas Lassi to take
this nest, which he had found more than a week ago. The cock, as
usual, was on the wing some time before we came to the nest. It
was in a youngish Scotch fir, five or six fathoms from the ground,
and had been occupied last year. Lassi climbed up. It was in his
own woodcutting ground. The hen sat on the edge of the nest for
a little time before she took to flight, and was in full moult. She
sat on a tree at some distance. Both birds were rather shy. The
cry of the hen stronger than that of the cock. The eggs were let
down in a botanical tin, and blown on the spot; small young ($\frac{3}{4}$ inch)
inside.

§ 388. *Four.*—Nollänki, Meras-järwi, West Bothnia, 24–30
        May, 1857.

From Nollänki, a place two miles and a quarter from Meras-järwi.

Hendrik brought them, 15th June, under the name *Kalasääski.* He
said he saw the bird, which was spotted with black, and cried " *Bii,
bii.*" They look almost as if they were from two nests ; but he only
spoke of one. Two of them are rather smaller, and have darker
spots than the others, one of which is a beautiful egg. There can be
little doubt they are Rough-legged Buzzards'.

§ 389. *Four.*—Nilsi-vaara, Enontekis Lappmark, 30 May, 1857.

Taken by Jon Pehrsson Pilto, half a mile (Swedish) above Mukka-
uoma, on Kommaens.

§ 390. *Three.*—Muotka-järwi, Enontekis Lappmark, 2 June,
      1857.

This nest was in a long *honka* [1], ten fathoms from the ground, in
Honga-vaara-etalan-paasa. Taken by Maria's brother, Elias, in her
presence.

§ 391. *Four.*—Sieppi-Kerro, East Bothnia, 2 June, 1857.

O. W. tab. vi. fig. 2.

Found by Apo in a dead pine, about four fathoms from the ground.
The nest was lined with *luppu* and was on a branch not close to the
trunk. Both birds were seen, and believed by Apo (an honest man)
to be the same as those of which I shot one on Akka-mella [§ 386],
in his company. The eggs carefully kept separate in the botanical
tin.

§ 392. *Four.*—Kaakkari-järwi, Enontekis Lappmark, 2 June,
      1857. " With feet."

O. W. tab. vi. fig. 4.

The bird, shot or trapped from the nest, as Maria said, and, as is
evident from the feet, was a cock. Kaakkari-järwi is near or in Aita-
selka, three-quarters of a Swedish mile to the east of Muotka-järwi.
Beautiful and strongly marked eggs. In the same tree was a *Sotka's*
(*Clangula glaucion*) nest.

---

[1] [Dead Scotch fir.—ED.]

§ 393. *Four.*—Lehti-rowa, East Bothnia, 2 June, 1857.

These four eggs found by Heiki, on the morning of 2nd June, in an old Osprey's nest which he found about April this spring. He does not know whether or not it was inhabited last year; but it was a very good nest on the top of a pine, some ten fathoms high. The birds came crying round, and Heiki is certain they were the common *Piekonna.* He distinctly saw that the cock was white over the tail. He cut down a *honka* to help him to the branches.

§ 394. *Four.*—Hutta-vaara, East Finmark, 2 June, 1857. From Pastor Sommerfeldt's collection.

O. W. tab. vi. fig. 5.

§ 395. *Four.*—Pieto-maski, Mukka-uoma, Enontekis Lappmark, 3 June, 1857. "L. M. K."

Taken by Ludwig, on his journey to Pera-vaara, a couple of Swedish miles from Mukka-uoma, to the eastward. He could neither snare nor shoot the bird.

§ 396. *Four.*—Peldo-uoma, Kemi Lappmark, 4 June, 1857.

This, with another nest of three eggs, was found by Erik Sardio in one day, on his way to Peldo-uoma, and deposited there against my arrival. They were taken to Muoniovara, 4th August, by Michael, untouched in the basket, as I had left them ready blown in June.

§ 397. *Four.*—Peldo-uoma, Kemi Lappmark, 1857.

A fine nest. As the last, but found by Johan Yli-tallon. At Peldo-uoma I declined to receive several nests of *Piekonna.*

§ 398. *Five.* — Toipalen, Mukka-uoma, Tornea Lappmark, 6 June, 1857. "With feet."

Brought to Ludwig, with the bird's feet, 7th June, by Jon Pehrsson Pilto. The nest was taken three-quarters of a mile to the north of Mukka-uoma.

§ 399. *One.*—Makki-hukio-vaara, Kurkio-vaara, Kemi Lappmark, 11 June, 1857.

A long egg. Out of five; the other four given to Messrs. F. and
P. Godman. Brought by Heiki, with particulars. In the same tree
was another nest, that of a *Pistee-tiainen* [*Parus cinctus*].

§ 400. *Three.*—Ruata-joki, Enontekis Lappmark, 12 June, 1857.
"J. W."

These eggs found by myself, but taken by one of my men as I
stood under the tree, a Scotch fir, in sight of the banks of the little
river which, flowing from Ounas-tunturi by Keras-sieppi, is joined
by the Lieppa-joki, and, being replenished in Utkojärwi by the Nälima water, after passing through Nullus-järwi, takes the name of
Utko-joki till it runs into the Muonio.

§ 401. *One.*—Hirsi-maa, Enontekis Lappmark, 23 June, 1857.

Taken by the girl Maria : big holes, being blown by herself.

§ 402. *One.*—Tanan-anti, Kemi Lappmark, 1857 [?].

[Appears to have been obtained by Mr. Wolley in 1857, on his journey from
Muonio-niska, by Peldo-uoma, to the Varanger Fjord. The locality is on the
upper waters of the River Tana, and Mr. Wolley reached it on the 22nd June.]

§ 403. *Three.*—Lehma-selka (?), Enontekis Lappmark, 1857.

O. W. tab. vi. fig. 1.

. The girl Maria said this was the first nest she found; but she
attributed to it an egg which, from its appearance and a peculiar
black nodule in its yelk, evidently belongs to another nest. Hence
it is possible there may be a mistake in these three eggs being the
ones she took on Lehma-selka; but they are, at all events, apparently
out of some one nest; and as there was only one (and this she well
recognized), of all she took, from which she did not get the bird,
there is no doubt these three eggs were properly identified. The
nest at Lehma-selka was on a branch in the middle of a *honka*—a

dead Scotch fir. The bird, a hen, was trapped by the left foot, which, still fresh, is before me. A very light-coloured example.

§ 404. *Five.*—Kyrö, Kemi Lappmark, 1857.

O. W. tab. v. fig. 3.

These may have belonged to different nests.

§ 405. *Two.*—Kyrö, Kemi Lappmark, 1857.

From Michael Sardio.

§ 406. *Four.*—Sardio, Kemi Lappmark, 1857. "With bird."

From Michael Sardio.

§ 407. *Four.* — Muotka-järwi, Enontekis Lappmark, 1857. "With feet."

O. W. tab. vi. fig. 3.

As placed by the girl Maria. A nest of great beauty. One egg extremely fine. The feet of intermediate colour.

§ 408. *Five.*—Hämma-järwi, Kaaressuando, Tornea Lappmark, 1857.

O. W. tab. vi. fig. 6.

Five beautiful eggs of *Piekonna*, found as above, by Nälima Lassi, in one nest. Blown by the lad, Johan Peter, and washed inside "many times."

§ 409. *Three.*—Marrainen (?), Tornea Lappmark, 1857.

Received, blown, at Kuttainen, probably from Marrainen, and from different nests. One egg is marked like a fine Golden Eagle's.

§ 410. *Three.*—Hanhi-järwi-maa, Enontekis Lappmark, 29 May, 1858.

Brought to Muoniovara, 8th June, by Maria.

§ 411. *Three.*—Wuopio-uoma-ranta, Kemi Lappmark, May, 1858.

Brought to Muoniovara, 19th June, by Kyrö Nikoo, having been taken about a month since.

§ 412. *Two.*—Kota-vaara, Enontekis Lappmark, 1858.

Brought to Muoniovara, 19th Juue, by Sieppinen Johan, having been found two or three weeks before.

§ 413. *Two.*—Muotka-järwi, Enontekis Lappmark, 1858.

Brought to Muoniovara, 26th December 1858, by Maria.

BUTEO VULGARIS, Bechstein.

BUZZARD.

§ 414. *Three.*—Sutherlandshire, 28 April, 1849. " J. W. *ipse.*"

Hewitson, ' Eggs of British Birds,' ed. 3, pl. xiv. fig. 1.

Four or five hundred yards further south [from the Falcon's nest (§ 222)] we saw a Buzzard's nest, or Glead's, as it is here called ; and though it was only about twenty-four feet from the ground, I had great difficulty in getting at it, as the rock was in little broken bits. I tried to climb up with the rope ; but afterwards I climbed from above with the rope under my arms, my man working it round a stake, and all was then easy. There were boys' or men's foot-marks to be seen about it, they not having been able to get at the nest, which was fixed into the roots of a mountain ash, *i. e.* between the trunk and the rock, and made of old heather-stalks, lined with the same *Luzula* as Eagles use. It contained three dirty eggs, one of which was unspotted. They were quite cold, and one was cracked in the nest before I touched it. The nest from below had the appearance of a large Crow's. The bird, soaring far overhead, was quite silent. There was a steep slope down to the edge of the rock, covered with long heather ; but the nest was not more than six or seven feet below the edge. The rock was a resumption of the range whereon was the Peregrine's nest before described [§ 222], one of the birds of which came up peering about at a good height while I was at the Buzzard's.

§ 415. *Three.*—Sutherlandshire, 21 May, 1849.   "J. W. *ipse.*"

Hewitson, 'Eggs of British Birds,' ed. 3, pl. xiv. fig. 2.

In a walk, on the 21st May, to the foot of Quenaig, after having seen an Eagle, I came by some rocks very likely for Eagles, and where Peter has since told me that there used to be an Eagle's nest, easily accessible, the locality of which he showed me. Here I saw a bird I supposed to be an Eagle, and a place like a nest. I fired a shot, and out flew another bird from the nest, as I imagined. The place was very easy for ropes, and I determined to fetch them to it next morning. Luckily I looked again at the supposed nest, and, as it did not seem like one, tried a little climbing. Taking off my shoes, I soon got up to a narrow grassy ledge, along which I went till I suddenly came upon the nest on the ledge, not where I had at first fancied it was. I sprang to it, and saw three beautiful eggs. I rubbed my eyes. They were so small! Surely they were Buzzard's! The nest I looked at again, and the foundation had not sticks big enough for an Eagle. The dead heather-stalks and the sedge (*Luzula*) lining were all right, but they were equally so for a Buzzard. The plaintive cry was now explained; I had thought it odd in an Eagle. It was provoking, but could not be helped. The birds flew within shot as I was at the nest. The eggs, though not far from hatching, are quite clean, and, two of them at least, beautifully marked. I took a bird's-eye view of the little loch, and called at the shepherd's on my way home.

P.S. 1850.—I must here remark that it seems to me very difficult to distinguish a Buzzard from a Golden Eagle in the flight. This year, 1850, I at first thought I was looking at an Eagle overhead, when I afterwards believed it was a Buzzard (this in the Clova Mountains, Glen Phee); and the party subsequently came near a nest, where the birds were making their cat-like mewing. In most cases I have arrived at certainty as to the kind of bird I was looking at, either by the size, the occasional shape into which Buzzards put their wings, or, perhaps best, by the greater length of tail in the Buzzard. The flap is, I think, very similar in both, and so the contour of the wings.

§ 416. *Two.*—Sutherlandshire, 24 May, 1849.   "J. W. *ipse.*"

I went with a man to look for nests of Buzzard and Peregrine in the range of rocks over the inn. He it was who was said to have looked like a spider at the end of its thread last year [St. John, 'Tour in Sutherland,' i. 16] ; but he declared that he was never hanging, and, moreover, that Mr. St. John never saw him, being afraid to look over; and that only one lad held the rope whilst Mr. St. John and his companion tried for a shot at the old birds. I found a nest by firing a shot from below; and I climbed up, my dog 'Watch' after me, to get a proper place above. Ropes were fetched ; but there was so much loose stuff that I could not descend with the gun, and we were obliged to frighten off the bird a second time by a large stone. The man fired at it, and my gun "kicked" him tremendously. The stake being fixed, and three men being at the rope (which was fastened under my arms), and another at the edge to prevent it from cutting, I descended. The last drop, of fourteen feet or so, to the nest was plumb. There were two eggs, poorly marked and hard sat on. The nest was made as usual, lined with *Luzula*, and on a very small ledge, only just big enough to support it. Some sheep, in a spot from which four or five had been lost since Christmas, were rescued by my ropes.

P.S. 1850.—I hear that this Glead's nest is occupied by a Penguin. The Peregrines did not breed in that rock in 1849, but they did in 1848 (*vide* St. John [*loc. cit.*]). This year, 1850, the Buzzards were in a worse place than last. The man who was with me before went and took out three young ones, which died during his temporary absence from home. So that in three successive years the Buzzards have slightly shifted the site of their nest. I may add to the account of my former descent, that the quantity of loose pieces of rock made it a tedious affair; for I either had to kick them away before me, or so to place the ropes as not to touch them. Without this precaution, the descent would have been most dangerous.

§ 417. *Three.*—Inverness-shire, 3 May, 1851. "J. W. *ipse.*"

I took these in a Scotch-fir tree within four or five miles of Carr-bridge. We had found the nest the day before, when the old Buzzard flew off as we stood beneath. It was not accessible without ropes, and even with their help I had great difficulty in reaching it, as it was on a horizontal branch. The keeper said the same nest was occupied by a "Salmon-tailed Kite" [*Milvus ictinus*] the year before. In the same forest I saw and climbed to not less than twenty old nests; but this was the only one with anything in it, though another one was remade this year. According to the keepers, they always reoccupy their old nests, adding a little every year. Three or four years ago Kites and Buzzards were very numerous here, as Mr. Edge had led me to expect. This year we only saw one Kite; but we saw it on two successive days. Its mate may have been sitting; and a nest, which we found near where we saw it, was believed to have been rebuilt this year. Later in the season I was informed that there had been no eggs in it; and in 1852 the keeper wrote to me that he was sorry to say one of the Kites had been trapped.

§ 418. *Two.*—Sutherlandshire, 1851.

Sent to me by a keeper from Assynt. The Kite is unknown in his district, and, I believe, almost so in the county.

§ 419. *Two.*—" Clermont-Ferrand," France. From M. Parzu-daki's Collection, 1856.

§ 420. *Three.*—Lincolnshire, 6 May, 1856. From Mr. G. Adrian.

[These eggs, with those in the next section, were received by me, unblown, from a correspondent of Mr. Wolley's before mentioned (§ 294). He is, I believe, a most respectable man, and I have no reason to doubt his account of of them.]

§ 421. *Three.*—Lincolnshire, 12 May, 1856. From Mr. G. Adrian.

[As the last.]

[§ 422. *One.*—" Cumberland." From Mr. Robert Reynolds, 1846.]

[§ 423. *Two.*—Holland, 1851.

Sent to me direct from a Dutch correspondent.]

[§ 424. *Three.*—From Dr. R. T. Frere's Collection, 1852.]

[§ 425. *Two.*—Blois, France, 1859.   From M. Souchay's Collection.

These my brother Edward obtained, at Blois, from M. Souchay, who is a bird-stuffer there, and said they were taken in the neighbourhood.]

[§ 426. *One*—Switzerland (?).   From M. Nager-Donazain's Collection, 1859.]

[§ 427. *One.*—"Burwell, Cambridgeshire."   From Mr. E. Fitton's Collection, through Dr. R. T. Frere, 1861.]

BUTEO FEROX (S. G. Gmelin).

LONG-LEGGED BUZZARD.

[§ 428. *One.*—"Sarepta," Southern Russia (?).

This egg I picked out of a lot which had been sent to Mr. Stevens's auction-rooms. The name is written on it in a foreign hand, and, I dare say, is right.]

[§ 429. *Four.* "Sarepta," Southern Russia.   From Herr H. F. Möschler's Collection, 1862.

These eggs I received direct from Herr Möschler, who, himself one of the United Brethren, carries on an extensive ornithological trade with the Moravian settlement at Sarepta, on the Lower Volga. His notes on the habits of this species (under the synonym of *Butaëtos leucurus,* Naumann) will be found in the 'Naumannia' for 1853 (pp. 296–303). From them I extract the following passage relating to its breeding in that district :—"It builds its nest on the projections of the declivities of the vales with which the Steppe is everywhere intersected, or above on the ground close to the declivities. Whether it also nests on hillocks is yet uncertain. The nest is about 1½ Rhenish foot [rather more than the English one] in diameter. The depression therein is not far from the size of the crown of a hat. It is built of dry grass, straw, hair, fur, bits of skin, and the like, on a foundation of thick stalks, brushwood, &c. From the middle of April one finds therein three to four, seldom five, eggs." ('Naumannia,' 1853, p. 301.)]

[§ 430. *One.*—"South Russia." From Herr A. Heinke, of Kamuschin, through Dr. Albert Günther, 1863.

Though this egg came to me marked "*Falco buteo*," I refer it as above, not only on account of its large size, but because Herr Möschler states that the Common Buzzard is a rare bird on the Lower Volga, and he is doubtful if that species breeds in the district. ('Naumannia,' 1853, p. 303.)]

CIRCUS ÆRUGINOSUS (Linnæus).

MOOR-BUZZARD.

§ 431. *Four.*—Whittlesea Mere, Huntingdonshire, May 1843. From Mr. Harvey, of Bait's-bight.

Hewitson, 'Eggs of British Birds,' ed. 3. pl. xvi. fig. 1 (?).

I bought these, which were said to be from the same nest, from Mr. Harvey, of Bait's-bight, near Cambridge, in May 1843. He knows the egg well, and had just received them from the neighbourhood of Whittlesea Mere. He engages a keeper who lives near Wood-Walton, and a man, Will Scarr, who keeps a small shop at Ramsey Hern, to send him all the uncommon eggs they can collect from fenmen or otherwise. I have seen and conversed with both the persons in question, and slept one night in the best and only inn, "The Red Cow," at Ramsey Hern, where I was asked the extravagant sum of sixpence for my night's lodging.

P.S. 1854. One of these eggs has been in Mr. Hewitson's hands, and perhaps he has drawn from it.

[Ramsey Mere was drained more than thirty years ago, and Whittlesea Mere in 1851. I do not think the Moor Buzzard has bred in the fens of the Bedford Level since the latter date.]

§ 432. *One.*—1852. From Mr. Green's Collection.

This egg is one of two from the other side of the sea, which Mr. Green had, on May 7th, lately blown. He had the bird with them, I had seen him engaged in stuffing another Moor-Buzzard (which had been trapped) a few days previously. I do not know whether they came from Amsterdam or Hamburg.

§ 433. *Two.*—North Brabant, 1854. From Mr. Newcome's Collection.

Sent to Mr. Newcome, at his desire, from Valkenswaard, with others ; all the eggs correctly named.

§ 434. *One.*—Denmark, 1856.   From Herr Erichsen's Collection, 1857.

Taken by Herr Erichsen.

§ 435. *One.*—Furö Sö, Denmark, 10 May, 1857.   "Theob." From Pastor Theobald's Collection.

Taken as above by the Pastor in a boat.   One egg only was as yet laid.   He saw the bird.

§ 436. *Two.*—Roeskilde, Denmark, May 1857.   From Pastor Theobald's Collection.

Taken near Roeskilde, but not by the Pastor himself.

[§ 437. *One.*—Whittlesea Mere, Huntingdonshire.   From Mr. R. Reynolds, about 1844.]

[§ 438. *One.*—Whittlesea Mere, Huntingdonshire, 1850. From Mr. J. Baker.]

[§ 439. *Four.*—North Brabant, 1854.   From Mr. J. Baker.]

[§ 440. *One.*—"Devonshire."   From Lord Lilford's Collection, 1855.]

[§ 441. *Two.*—"Monk's Wood, Huntingdonshire."   From Mr. T. V. Wollaston's Collection, through Dr. R. T. Frere, 1861.]

[§ 442. *One.*—"Quy Fen, Cambridgeshire."   From Mr. E. W. Dowell's Collection, through Dr. R. T. Frere.]

CIRCUS CYANEUS (Linnæus).

HEN-HARRIER.

§ 443. *One.*—England (?).   From Mr. R. Mansfield, 1844.

§ 444. *Two.*—Eastern England.   From Mr. Harvey, of Bait's-bight, 1844.

These two eggs out of the same nest, in which there were six—an unusual number according to Mr. Harvey.   One of them is spotted, the only one amongst them, and in fact the only spotted one I have ever seen.   These are said to have been from Whittlesea Mere, in the middle of May.

§ 445. *One.*—Orkneys, 1848.

§ 446. *One.*—Sutherlandshire, 1850.

Sent by a game-keeper under the name of " Hen-Harrier."

§ 447. *Three.*—Carr Bridge, Inverness-shire, 1850.

These eggs, originally four in number, from a game-keeper near the place named, who sent them the year after they were taken.

§ 448. *Fifteen.*—Orkneys, 1851.

Out of nineteen sent me by Mr. George Harvey, of Stromness.

§ 449. *Six.*—Rabbit Island, Kyle of Tongue, Sutherlandshire, 1852.

Sent me as those of the "Hunting Hawk," by a correspondent, who says that he took them himself as above.   If I remember right, the island is a low one, rather easily got at.   The bird generally known as the " Hunting Hawk " is, as I believe, the Peregrine Falcon; and so my correspondent understands it.   He evidently mistook them for Peregrine's eggs.   I saw the Hen-Harrier in Sutherlandshire, and so did the Messrs. Milner ('Zoologist,' 1848, p. 2014).   These eggs

L

were deeply stained when they arrived, mostly upon one side, but I do not remember then to have observed the groups of yellowish spots near the holes of several. Can these have been caused by the *larvæ* of moths, which may have attacked the sheep's wool in which I have left them since their arrival?

§ 450. *Two.*—Argyllshire, 13 May, 1852.

These were sent to me by a forester, under the name of the "Ring-tail or Hen-Harrier." As he failed in catching the young birds for me, I must for the present remain in doubt as to whether they are the Common or Montagu's Harrier.

[In 1854 I received from the same locality a pair of young Harriers, which I kept alive for some time. They were undoubtedly *Circus cyaneus*; and though Sir William Milner mentions that he procured *Circus cineraceus* in Sutherlandshire ('Zoologist,' 1848, p. 2014), I question much if that species is ever found breeding in Scotland.]

§ 451. *Four.*—Eastern England.

Hewitson, 'Eggs of British Birds,' ed. 3. pl. xvi. fig. 2.

These are most probably from Mr. Harvey, of Bait's-bight, but perhaps from Mr. Osborne, of Fulbourn, or Tom Rawlinson. From the mode of blowing, and the improbability of my having got them from any other source without recollecting it, I have no doubt they are British specimens.

[One of the above-mentioned eggs is, as stated, the original of Mr. Hewitson's figure. I should think it likely that Mr. Wolley did not obtain them later than 1845; but they seem to have lain in his cabinet without being properly marked for ten years or more. Mr. Wolley's character of Tom Rawlinson will be found in 'The Zoologist' for 1847, p. 1822.]

§ 452. *One.*—Lincolnshire, 14 May, 1856. From Mr. G. Adrian.

[This egg was received by me from Mr. Wolley, together with the Kites' of the same year before mentioned (§ 299 and § 310).]

§ 453. *Three.*—Konna-järwi, Maunu, Tornea Lappmark, 1857.

These eggs were said by the Mortanen lads to belong to the Hawk which is white on the wings[!], but whose name they did not know[1].

[1] [The name by which the Hen-Harrier is commonly called in northern Lapland is, I believe, *Sammakko-Haukka, i. e.* 'Frog-Hawk.'—ED.]

They were found on the ground near Konna-järwi, and are doubtless Hen-Harrier's—the only Harrier I have seen up here; and they are the first of its eggs I have met with. The birds were unusually abundant this spring.

[§ 454. *One.*—West Norfolk. From Mr. Newcome's Collection, 1853.

Taken either in Hockwold or Feltwell Fen " many years ago."]

[§ 455. *Two.*—Argyllshire, 1855.

From the forester who sent Mr. Wolley the eggs before mentioned, from the same locality (§ 450).]

[§ 456. *Two.*—Sutherlandshire, 6 May, 1859.

From a correspondent already several times mentioned in these pages (§§ 48, 49, 50, 55).]

[§ 457. *Three.*—Burwell, Cambridgeshire. From Dr. R. T. Frere's Collection, 1861.

Probably taken nearly twenty years before they came into my possession. They are so large that, but for Dr. Frere's positive assurance, I should have supposed them to be Moor-Buzzards'.]

[§ 458. *One.*—Feltwell Fen, Norfolk, 1840. From Mr. Newcome's Collection, 1863.

A finely spotted example.]

CIRCUS SWAINSONI, A. Smith.

SWAINSON'S HARRIER.

[§ 459. *One.*—" Wolga." From M. E. Verreaux's Collection, 1861.]

CIRCUS CINERACEUS (Montagu).

ASH-COLOURED HARRIER.

§ 460. *One.*—England (?).   From Mr. R. Mansfield, 1844.

Mr. Mansfield said he was certain that this egg was a Montagu's Harrier. I believe it to be so from its size. This species is commoner than is generally supposed, being overlooked from its near resemblance to the Hen-Harrier.

[This last remark of Mr. Wolley's, written now nearly twenty years ago, and at a time when *Circus cineraceus* was usually considered to be a rare bird in England, I believe to be quite correct. In the fens of the Eastern Counties, as, in 1853, I had the pleasure of informing Mr. Hewitson ('Eggs, B. B.' ed. 3. p. 44), it certainly maintained its ground longer than either of the other two British species; and, from the inquiries I have made, I suspect it was there always the most abundant of them. Feltwell Fen, in Norfolk, as I have learned from Mr. Newcome, was a favourite place of resort in former days for the Ash-coloured Harrier.]

§ 461. *Two.*—Whittlesea, Huntingdonshire, 1845.

These two specimens I had from Mr. Osborne, of Fulbourn. He knows the birds well, and I have not the slightest doubt of their authenticity. They were probably taken out of a nest in Wood-Walton Fen, near Whittlesea Mere, for the express purpose of seeing which, and a Hen-Harrier's nest, I went over from Cambridge. The eggs were gone out of both. The former was made of leaves of dried grass, and was slight; but not so slight as, and of less coarse material than, the Hen-Harrier's. On going down the river [Cam] to Burwell Fen one day last May or June [1845] (the former month, I believe), we rowed past Vipers, of Upware, who was coming up in a punt. As we returned from Burwell, he told me he had in the boat with him a Montagu's Harrier and three eggs. He also told me there were two pairs breeding in Wicken Fen this year—a very rare thing now. He hoped to get the other pair, and would let me have them for a pound, and sixpence for each egg. I had seen the birds soaring about; but on my return in a few days, he had not got them. He told me many curious particulars of their habits; their action in choosing a nest, the male selecting a spot, the female approving or disapproving it, as she thought fit; of the male coming to feed the female, and of her sometimes going to meet him, turning on her back and catching the prey thus brought her, which was, however, occasionally dropped on the nest. He also told me of the young pecking one of their fellows to death when bloody; of the habits of the old birds when the nest is approached, their cries, and the like. He described the difference in the situation of the nest of the three species of Harrier. Montagu's Harrier is a migratory bird, the other two not. He had snared many hundreds in his day. As to the bird and eggs mentioned above, when I got up to Bait's-bight, Mrs. Harvey showed me the bird, a beautiful specimen, and I took the three eggs and blew them very neatly and carefully in my rooms—two holes. In a few days Mr. Harvey came and demanded six shillings each! upon which, with the greatest internal reluctance, I gave them up. Mr. Harvey had many specimens from Mr. Seaman, of Ipswich, some of which, if I remember right, were spotted. I gave Mr. Osborne (an honest fellow, I believe, and Mr. Doubleday's correspondent) eighteen pence each for these eggs. He privately assured me afterwards that Mr. Harvey upbraided him greatly in consequence.

§ 462. *One.*—England (?). From Mr. Argent's Collection, 1846.

Mr. Argent has great dealings with the Cambridgeshire fen-men.

§ 463. *One.*—From Mr. Green's Collection, 1852.

A spotted specimen.

[§ 464. *One.*—Feltwell, Norfolk. From Mr. R. Reynolds, prior to 1855.]

[§ 465. *Two.*—Valkenswaard, North Brabant, 1843. From Mr. Newcome's Collection.]

[§ 466. *Two.*—Valkenswaard, North Brabant, 1850. Through Mr. Newcome.]

[§ 467. *Three.*—Feltwell Fen, Norfolk, 9 June, 1854. "Bird shot." From Mr. Whitmore Baker.

On the 16th June, 1854, my brother Edward went over to Feltwell Fen, where he was told that a pair of Ash-coloured Harriers had had a nest, which, after some search, he found. It contained a single egg; but, on taking it up, he perceived it to be a common Fowl's, and discovered a trap set in the nest. On inquiry, he learnt that Mr. Baker, of Stoke-Ferry, had found it a few days before, taken the eggs, and shot the hen-bird. On writing to Mr. Baker, that gentleman expressed his willingness to part with the specimens ; and accordingly, on the 20th, my brother rode over to Stoke and obtained them from him. Mr. Baker imagined that they were Hen-Harrier's, and had written that name on the eggs; but my brother saw the bird which had been killed from the nest, and it was the commoner species—*Circus cineraceus*—as indeed he had been led to believe it would prove. The Fowl's egg and the trap had been put in the nest in the hope of securing the cock-bird—a hope which, I am glad to say, was never fulfilled. To the best of my knowledge, this is the latest instance of a Harrier breeding in Feltwell Fen ; and, judging from the state of the ground, the circumstance is not likely to occur again. The nest was made in the sedge, and on it was lying a feather—one of the *rectrices* of the cock-bird. This is now before me, and is so eminently characteristic that, apart from any other evidence, it would have been quite sufficient to determine the species of the owner.]

[§ 468. *Two.*—Holland, 1855. "With bird." From Mr. John Baker's Collection.]

[§ 469. *Three.*—Eastern England, 1846.   From Mr. Osborne, through Dr. R. T. Frere, 1863.

Dr. Frere tells me that he bought these eggs from Mr. Osborne, 27th May, 1846. They were said to be from a nest of six; but one of them is so differently blown from the other two, that, in spite of the Doctor's positive assurance to the contrary, I suspect there may have been some little confusion here, though I doubt not they belong to this species, and were obtained in the English fens. Mr. Wolley's opinion of Mr. Osborne has been before given (§ 461).]

GLAUCIDIUM PASSERINUM (Linnæus).

SPARROW-OWL.

[§ 470. *One.*—"Greece." From Herr L. Schrader's Collection, through Herr G. T. Keitel, 1861.]

ATHENE NOCTUA (Retzius).

LITTLE OWL.

§ 471. *Two.*—From M. Lefevre's Collection, 1846.

§ 472. *Two*—From M. Hardy's Collection, 1848.

§ 473. *One.*—London (laid in captivity), 1852.　From Mr. J. Green's Collection.

This is one of two eggs laid by one of the Little Owls which Mr. Green had in confinement for a few days. An egg had been laid before he got the birds; and therefore he put a box in the cage, in which they laid two eggs, one yesterday, the other the day before. I saw the birds several days ago, but now there is only one left, Mr. Green having just sent off (May 13th) the other two to a customer. They came in the Ostend boat. The species is the same as that taken near Derby, which I kept so long in confinement, and which is now stuffed at Beeston. This egg I saw blown by Mr. Green's son while I was in the house. Both eggs were precisely similar.

[In the 'Zoologist' for 1848 (p. 2141), Mr. Wolley records the recent death, by an accident, of the Little Owl above alluded to, which he had so long in captivity. Mr. Hewitson, on the authority of Mr. J. J. Briggs, mentions its original capture ('Eggs B. B.,' p. 40), which appears to have been in the spring of 1843; and thus the bird lived just about five years in confinement. Mr. Wolley always suspected that it was one of the Italian specimens imported into this country and liberated in 1842 by Mr. Waterton ('Essays,' 2nd ser. p. 21).]

§ 474. *One.* — Reithoven, North Brabant, 13 May, 1857. "With bird." From Mr. J. Baker's Collection.

This is one of four eggs from a nest on which the bird was caught, says Mr. Baker. He only met with this species in Holland. He says it often builds in holes close to houses, laying generally four eggs, never less than three. He took several nests himself, of which I think he said this was one.

[Mr. W. Bridger has some notes on the breeding-habits of the Little Owl in this district ('Naturalist,' 1855, pp. 271, 272).]

§ 475. *Four.*—Tetsmark, Jutland, 14 May, 1858. From Pastor
   Theobald's Collection, 1859.

Taken from one nest in a church-steeple, as above, by Herr J. C.
H. Fischer.

[§ 476. *Four.*—North Brabant, 1851.

   These were received by me direct from a correspondent in Holland.]

[§ 477. *Two.*—Varen, North Brabant, 2 April, 1858.   From
   Mr. J. Baker's Collection.]

ATHENE PERSICA (Vieillot).

SOUTHERN LITTLE OWL.

[§ 478. *One.*—Chemora, Eastern Atlas, 18 May, 1859.   From
   Mr. O. Salvin's Collection.

   Mr. Salvin's note respecting this specimen is as follows:—"There were six
   eggs in this nest, which was brought to our camp at Aïn Djendeli by an Arab,
   with the old bird, which he had caught on the nest alive."
   Mr. Salvin has some remarks on this supposed species in 'The Ibis' for
   1859 (p. 190). In the same volume Mr. Tristram has also some observations
   (p. 201), whence it appears that, though the light colour of the plumage observable in most specimens of the Little Owl from Algeria is not always
   characteristic of them, yet these are invariably smaller than European examples. On this ground, slight though it be, I enter the southern race here
   under a distinct heading.]

STRIX FLAMMEA, Linnæus.

BARN OWL.

§ 479. *One.*—

This egg was taken by a friend of my brother Charles, who saw
the Owl on its nest.

§ 480. *Two.*—Madingley, Cambridgeshire, 1844.

From Tom Rawlinson. They were found in a tree at Madingley.

§ 481. *Three.*—Eastern England, 1844.

These were sold to me for Short-eared Owl's; but the man had a low price, and told a contradictory story.

§ 482. *One.*—Hutton-Bushell, Yorkshire, 1851.

[§ 483. *One.*—Yorkshire, 1843.]

[§ 484. *Two.*—Barnham, Suffolk, 1847.]

[§ 485. *One.*—Euston, Suffolk, 1851.]

[§ 486. *Two.*—Elveden, 12 May, 1854. From Mr. J. Isaacson's Collection.

From a nest of four, in a hole of a tree, sometimes occupied by *Syrnium aluco.*]

[§ 487. *Four.*—Elveden, 29 April, 1857. "E. N."

My brother's note respecting the above is as follows :—
"These four eggs were found in a hollow elm tree, near the church. On the 25th I put the old bird out from the tree; but it was late in the evening, and I was unable to see the eggs, which were quite at the bottom of the tree. It was not until the morning of the 28th that they were discovered. On the 29th we cut a hole into the side of the tree, and got them out. For the last two years I do not think this species has bred here. The eggs this year were quite fresh. In the tree were three halves of young Rats and half a Long-tailed Field-Mouse; in all four instances it was the 'latter end.' "]

SCOPS GIU (Scopoli).

SCOPS OWL.

§ 488. *One.*—From M. Lefevre's Collection, 1847.

§ 489. *One.*—Madracen, Eastern Atlas, 27 May, 1857. From Mr. O. Salvin's Collection.

From the tombs of Syphax and the Numidian kings, commonly

called Madracen, situated about two-thirds of the way between Constantine and Batna, a little to the east of the road. Mr. Salvin's nests were found in holes of trees—generally Terebinth [*Pistacia atlantica*]. *Strix noctua* is also there, but is an earlier breeder, its eggs being half incubated when those of the Scops are laid. Several of the latter were brought with the birds, but not so in the case of this nest.

[Mr. Salvin's notes on this species, as observed in the Eastern Atlas, are recorded in 'The Ibis,' vol. i. pp. 190, 191.]

§ 490. *One.*—Madracen, Eastern Atlas, 3 June, 1857. From Mr. W. H. Simpson's Collection.

[§ 491. *One.*—Madracen, Eastern Atlas, 4 June, 1857. From Mr. O. Salvin's Collection.

Brought to Mr. Salvin by an Arab.
Mr. Salvin's general observations are referred to above (§ 480).]

ASIO OTUS (Linnæus).

LONG-EARED OWL.

§ 492. *One.*—10 May, 1840. "J. D. S." From Mr. J. D. Salmon's Collection.

§ 493. *One.*—Hackness Wood, Yorkshire, 1851.

§ 494. *One.*—Scotland (?). From Mr. W. Dunbar's Collection.

§ 495. *One.*—Hockwold, Norfolk. From Mr. Newcome's Collection, 1852.

§ 496. *Four.*—Elveden, 2 March, 1852. "Bird seen. E. N."

[Three of these eggs were formerly given to Mr. Wolley. They were found by my brother Edward as above. The nest was an adaptation of an old Squirrel's "drail," built in a spruce. The eggs in it were arranged after this manner, ୦୦୦ On the 10th April, in the preceding year (1851), my brother and I found the young of this pair of Long-eared Owls, and sent them to the Zoological Society. They had fallen out of the nest, which was in a Scotch fir, close to the spruce which contained the nest in 1852.]

[§ 497. *One.*—Elveden, 8 March, 1853. "Both birds seen. A. & E. N."

The produce of the same pair of Owls as the last.]

§ 498. *Three.*—Elveden, April 1855. "Bird seen. A. & E. N."

[Two of these were given to Mr. Wolley. The nest was that of the birds mentioned in the last two sections. It was first found on 11th April, with two eggs in it. Another was laid, and the nest then forsaken.]

§ 499. *Four.*—Elveden, 22 March, 1854.

[Three of these eggs were given by my brother and myself to Mr. Wolley. The nest, which contained originally five, was found and taken by the game-keeper. Later in the season he saw a brood of young Long-eared Owls in the same plantation. The old ones had, therefore, doubtless bred a second time. These eggs are not the offspring of the same pair of birds as those in the last three sections.]

[§ 500. *One.*—Elveden, 1845.]

[§ 501. *One.*—Elveden, 12 March, 1852. "Bird seen. E. N."

Out of a nest of three.]

[§ 502. *One.*—Elveden, 29 March, 1853. "Bird seen. E. N."

This egg is from a nest of five, taken as above by a gamekeeper. It was in a small tree; but the locality was one which we had never before known the Long-eared Owl to frequent; it seemed therefore possible the eggs might be those of some other species. We heard of the capture late in the afternoon, as we were concluding a hard day's bird's-nesting in an exactly opposite direction. My brother, anxious to place the matter beyond all doubt, imme-diately started for the spot; and, reaching it just before dark, was lucky enough to get a satisfactory sight of the old birds, which had not yet aban-doned their plundered dwelling-place.]

[§ 503. *One.*—Elveden, 25 March, 1856. "Bird seen. E. N."

From a nest found by my brother and myself on the 20th March, and then containing three eggs.]

[§ 504. *Four.*—Elveden, 29 March, 1856. " Bird well seen. A. & E. N."

From a nest of five[1]. All the eggs in these last six sections I believe to have the produce of different pairs of birds.]

[§ 505. *Four.*—Wilton, Norfolk, 29 March, 1859. " Bird seen. E. C. N. & E. N."

My brother Edward's note says of these eggs:—"Found by Mr. Newcome on a spruce fir, about fifteen feet from the ground. We both saw the old bird on the nest; and I got and took the eggs, five in number. One of them was fresh, the others more or less incubated,—the bird probably having begun to sit, when the first was laid."]

[§ 506. *Five.*—Wilton, Norfolk, 29 March, 1859. " Bird seen. E. N."

My brother states of these:—"Found on the same occasion as the last, but in another plantation. Mr. Newcome's gamekeeper shook the tree, when the old bird went off. I was at some little distance, and she flew close past me. He then got up to the nest, which was in a spruce fir, about twenty feet from the ground, and reported a young one just hatched, and five eggs. On blowing them, I found they had been incubated for different periods. In two of them the birds had long been dead, and were quite rotten. The male bird was seen, as well as the female (though I saw the latter only). He was sitting on a tree within five yards of the nest-tree, and flew wildly away—which he probably would not have done had he not been close to the nest."]

ASIO CAPENSIS (A. Smith).

CAPE EARED OWL.

§ 507. *One.*—Tangier.   From M. Favier's Collection, 1847.

[1] [I may here perhaps be excused for mentioning that, owing to a slight misprint in a notice of the Long-eared Owl, which I contributed to the last edition of Mr. Hewitson's valuable and well-known work (' Eggs Brit. Birds,' ed. 3. p. 56), my meaning is obscured. The point on which my own experience leads me to differ in opinion from Mr. Tuke is regarding the number of eggs generally laid by this species. If the comma after the word "pair" (line 25) be converted into a semicolon, and the full stop after "edition" (line 27) changed into a comma, the sentence will read correctly.—Ed.]

ASIO BRACHYOTUS (Linnæus).

SHORT-EARED OWL.

§ 508. *One.*—Ross-shire (?).   From Mr. W. Dunbar's Collection, 1851.

Mr. Dunbar wrote to me that this was from " a nest near Loubcroy in the heather. If I mistake not, the Messrs. Milner had one or more of the same nest. I did not get it myself, but the eggs and female were brought to me."

> [In Sir William Milner's account of his expedition in the north of Scotland ('Zoologist,' 1848, pp. 2014–2017) no mention is made of any Short-eared Owls' eggs.]

§ 509. *One.*—Hesleyside, Northumberland, June 1840.   From Mr. J. P. Wilmot's Collection, 1846.

This was obtained, through Mr. Yarrell, from Lovat, the game-keeper at Hesleyside. Mr. Hancock afterwards told me he could be depended upon.

§ 510. *One.*—Sweden.   From Mr. C. J. Andersson's Collection, 1851.

§ 511. *Two.*—Feltwell Fen, Norfolk, 1852. From Mr. J. Baker's Collection.

Mr. Baker tells me there were five eggs in this nest. Last year he shot two birds from the nest in the same fen. There were several nests there—merely holes scraped in the ground for the eggs. This year there was only one nest.

§ 512. *Four.*—Ruana-uoma, Kätkesuando, East Bothnia, 1 July, 1853. " Bird shot.   J. W."

Beating the marsh on the Russian side [of the river] at Kätkesuando, with Ludwig, Theodore, and our two boatmen, the former called out to me to shoot; and I saw almost under me an Owl, squatting on the ground and looking at me. At first I sup-

posed it to be a young Short-eared, but it rose and flew. I shot
it, and it turned out to be an adult bird. At the spot where it left
were three Owlets and four eggs, the latter with the shells just
cracking; so there must have been seven eggs altogether.   The
men called it *Katt-Uggla*, and said it often flies at persons' faces as
they come near its nest. Lying by the nest were four Voles [*Ar-
vicola*, sp. indet.] of the kind which is so numerous in this district
this year—one old one and three young, one of the latter half-eaten.

§ 513. *Six*.—Kaaressuando, Tornea Lappmark, 1853.

These were stated by Pastor Engelmark to have been found in the
bird-boxes; but another account said they were on the ground; and on
comparison they look like Short-eared Owl's eggs.

§ 514. *One*.—Feltwell Fen, Norfolk, April 1849.   " W. H. S."
    From Mr. W. H. Simpson's Collection, 1856.

This was from a nest of four eggs shown *in situ* to Mr. Simpson;
he also saw the birds, one of which was trapped by a man living on
the spot. Not far off was the nest of an Ash-coloured Harrier, with
one egg, which is now in that gentleman's collection.

§ 515. *Seven*.—Maunu, Tornea Lappmark, 1857.

On the 26th July I saw, at a fishing-hut a little below Mukka-
uoma, Johan of Mortainen and two boys of his. He said he had
some eggs at home; and the lads explained that seven of them were
Pumppu-Haukka (*Strix brachyotus*) found all in one nest, on a *palso*
(high tuft or hillock) in Vacker-valle, near their home. Leaving
Maunu on the 26th, I took in the boat a very little boy, landed, and
went with him to their then untenanted house, Mortainen. He climbed
on to the roof, and out of some hole produced, among others, these
eggs ready blown. From the certainty as to the species with which
the brothers had spoken, and bearing in mind it has been plentiful
this year, I have no doubt they are genuine Short-eared Owl's. I
set no higher price on this bird's eggs than on Hawk-Owl's.

§ 516. *Two*.—Autijomen-jankka, Kätkesuando, East Bothnia,
    8 June, 1857.

These were brought to Muoniovara, on the 18th June, by the

sister of the girl who found them as above in a marsh. She said the bird was so fierce, and shrieked so, that she was almost afraid. The date and place of nesting show that these are Short-eared Owl's eggs. It was at the back of Kätkesuando that Ludwig, with me, found the nest in 1853 [§ 512]; but that was behind Pekkola, the southern-most house in the village, while this was behind Aiantajustas—about the northernmost. On the 2nd August the girl told me that there were brown feathers in the nest, such as are on a young Short-eared Owl, which I showed her,—and not grey, as on a Lapp Owl.

§ 517. *One.*—Pinkis-uoma, Palo-joki, Tornea Lappmark, 1857.

Brought to Muoniovara, 24th June. In August, Matti, the finder, relates that he saw the bird leave the egg, which was on a tuft in a marsh. It was like a *Jankka-Haukka* [*lit.* Earth-Hawk]—a large bird with large wings. He did not at that time touch the egg, but the bird deserted. Pinkis-uoma is on the Swedish side, opposite Palo-joki.

[§ 518. *One.*—Feltwell Fen, Norfolk, 1846. From Mr. R. Reynolds.]

[§ 519. *Two.*—Hilgay Fen, Norfolk, 1854. From Mr. J. Baker's Collection.]

[§ 520. *Three.*—Feltwell Fen, 1854. From Mr. Whitmore Baker.

These were obtained by my brother, on the occasion before mentioned (§407), from Mr. Baker, who I believe took them himself.]

[§ 521. *One.*—Feltwell Fen. From Mr. Newcome's Collection, 1863.

A specimen probably at least twenty years old.]

[§ 522. *One.*—" South Russia." From Herr A. Heinke, of Kamuschin, through Dr. Albert Günther, 1863.]

BUBO MAXIMUS, Fleming.

EAGLE-OWL.

§ 523. *One.*—From Dr. Pitman's Collection.

§ 524. *One.*—Upsala-Län.   From Herr C. Åberg's Collection, 1853.

This egg was given me at Upsala by Herr Carl Åberg, this 9th May, 1853, it being one of three in his possession, which he took some five or six years ago from a rock upon some property of his, three or four miles from Upsala in a south-westerly direction.   The bird is hereabouts called by a name [*Uf*] pronounced like our "ugh," which has been given it from the noise it makes.   Early this morning I started, with H H. Åberg and Löfgren, for the spot.   We saw no Owls; but the place where eggs had been, or one just like it, was shown to me.   It was on a shelf above a steep rock, just such a site as that near Gothenburg [1], and with a southern aspect.   Some trees have been cut down where it is.   The nest was there for three years in succession.

§ 525. Åsberg, Angermanland.   20 May, 1853.   "J. W."

This egg I took as above, out of a nest with two young birds.   It had a young one inside, which had made a considerable hole in the shell, through which the beak appeared, and it was chirping loudly. Those already hatched did not seem to have come long into the world. They were quite blind, and covered with white down, having a yellowish tinge.   Their general appearance was that of young Eagles. The nest was scarcely hollowed, and with nothing in addition to the bare ground except the hair and remains of castings of the old birds, some of which remained uncrushed at the side.   There was not more than an inch of earth upon the rock; however, there grew upon it bear-berry, juniper, and a little grass, besides a Scotch fir, some sixteen feet high, with a trunk flattened to the perpendicular rock.   The shelf

---

[1] [This site is described in Mr. Wolley's fragmentary journal of 1853 as follows: —" 22nd April.   After returning to Gothenburg, I went out with a gentleman resident there to look for the nest of an Eagle-Owl across the river.   We came to

was a small one, not quite two feet in width, terminating abruptly soon beyond the nest, but continued on the side by which we approached. Perpendicular rock above and below, but still the access by no means difficult.

There was with me a young man, Peter Ehrson, who had a good idea whereabouts the nest would be. Five young ladies, in wide straw hats, were watching us from below. They imitated very well the " coŏ-hoŏ " of the *Berg-Uf* [Eagle-Owl] in reply to ours. Before we commenced the ascent, while we were debating upon the matter, an Osprey happened to fly along the ridge of rock, upon which one of the Owls gave its beautifully sounding " coŏ," or " ugh "—the same note that I have heard from the birds in the Zoological Gardens, but with a much finer effect, softened as it was by distance. As Ehrson and I came near the part of the rock most frequented by the Owls, we found two Hare's feet and other remains. About this time a *Berg-Uf* sailed below us, giving us a beautiful view of his broad back and mottled wings. He passed in a direction different from that in which we were going, and turned a corner out of sight. A little further on another *Berg-Uf* left the face of the rock, and flew in the other direction, soon settling, and often turning her head to look at us, flying back a short distance, into such a position that I was able to look at her with my glass and see her satisfactorily. A few paces further Ehrson exclaimed, "There is the nest !" and sure enough there were the two young birds and the egg, as mentioned before. We waited an hour in the nest, but the birds did not appear again till we had left the spot. Then the male flew overhead to join the female, and perched upon the extreme top of a spruce-fir, where his

a range of rock, in which a boy pointed out the spot where an old bird and two young ones had been caught last summer. After a little scrambling, I came to the place from above, and found it to be just at the summit of a precipice, in a recess or ledge of some width. The whole of the nest was well rounded and rather deep, but appeared to have been merely scratched in the turf, and to have had no materials added to the natural bed so formed. There were lying in the hollow some bleached bones of rats and of birds of the size of Partridges. It was close under a low piece of rock, which, however, appeared to afford it so little shelter that the water from the melting snow was dripping into the middle of it. It was not at all dissimilar to the spot which a Golden Eagle would select, unless perhaps rather more exposed. The aspect southerly; and Mr. [Duff] assures me that the Eagle-Owl usually lives on the sunny side of a rock. So, as I remember, it was in the case of one at least of the nests which Linnæus mentions in his tour ['*Lachesis Lapponica*,' vol. i. p. 89]. In another rock, which we visited this afternoon, were Ravens and Falcons (no doubt Peregrines); but I had not a good sight of them. This is the rock whence there is so fine a view of the town of Gothenburg. It also has been the resort of Eagle-Owls, which fly out when a gun is fired near it."—ED.]

M

ears were finely relieved against the sky. About this time we heard some more "coö-hoös." Bones of birds, rats, and animals of that size were in the immediate neighbourhood of the nest. Many points of rock within a few hundred yards were white with dung; and it was said that several pairs of Owls frequent this mountain-side. At the inn at Hörnäs, a mile or two back, was a lately trapped *Berg-Uf*, nailed, with spread wings, to the wall. The trap had been baited with a Hare.

[The graphic account of this nest, which Mr. Wolley contributed to Mr. Hewitson's work ('Eggs B. B.' ed. 3. pp. 51–53), was contained in a letter to me, the first I received from him from Scandinavia, dated "Haparanda, 2nd June, 1853." As it gives no more details than will be found above, I abstain from quoting it here, though it is decidedly a more finished production of his pen than these notes, which were probably written down almost in the heat of victory. Mr. Wolley was at this time literally following "in the footsteps of Linnæus," as Mr. Hewitson phrases it. " It was on the 20th May, after climbing to the mysterious cave in Skulaberg," as he wrote to me, that he found this nest. It is a singular coincidence that, according to the Old Style, by which Linnæus reckoned, he, in 1732, also visited this remarkable place on the same day of the same month ('*Lachesis Lapponica*,' vol. i. pp. 52–55, and vol. ii. pp. 242–244).]

§ 526. *Two.*—Salmojärwi, East Bothnia, April 1854.

Found by the boys at Salmo-järwi, two or three days after Easter. They had told me, in the winter, that they knew a breeding-place of this bird on a rock. The eggs were split by the frost, for the birds did not return to the nest after the lads had first visited it. One of them subsequently selected the species of *Huuhkaja* [the name applied about Muonioniska to both the largest Owls] from skins of the Lapp and Eagle-Owl before him. It was of course the latter.

[In 1855 this pair of Eagle-Owls seem to have bred near Särki-lombola, in the same district. The two eggs, taken on the 26th April, passed into the collections of Mr. G. D. Rowley and the late Mr. J. D. Salmon.]

§ 527. *Two.*—Särki-pahta, Salmo-järwi, East Bothnia.   1856.

Brought to Muoniovara, 8th June.

[In April 1856 three other eggs of the Salmo-järwi Eagle-Owls were taken. These are now in the collections of Sir William Milner and Messrs. Bond and Troughton. The two mentioned in the text appear to have been a second laying of the same birds.]

§ 528. *Three.*—Kiwi-luoma, Salmo-järwi, East Bothnia. 14 April, 1857.

Found on a cliff about a quarter of a mile from Särki-pahta, the Tuesday after *Pääsiäisen* [Easter], by Simon Peter, who brought them to Muoniovara the Monday following, as I noted at the time. The *Huuhkaja* which he saw had ears—"smallish ears." The same pair of birds as last year's nests [§ 527, and probably § 526], though they had rather shifted their quarters.

[Several of the eggs laid by the Salmo-järwi Eagle-Owl have the shell very coarse-grained; and this is particularly the case in one of the above lot.]

§ 529. *Three.*—Ækäs-korkion-pahta, East Bothnia. 13 May, 1856.

Brought by Anders Wassara, on the 18th May. He says that he saw the bird, and that it was *Korwa-Huuhkaja* [Eared *Huuhkaja*]. His brother found the nest on the sand under the roots, or just in the spot where the roots had been, of an overturned tree, on a steep hill-side near a force. There are small cliffs or rocks by the river Ækäs-joki.

The following year the nest of this pair of Eagle-Owls was found by the same lad in a similar site, " on the ground, against the up-turned roots of a tree facing the south, on the side of a dell, where he had often heard the birds cry ' hugh, hugh.' He was sure it was the Eared *Huuhkaja*, though he did not see it very distinctly as it flew away. No nest—a mere slight hollow. The bird deserted the two eggs, which were quite fresh. The place was about a quarter of a mile (Swedish) to the east of Ækäs-järwi."

[The eggs of 1857 are in the collections of Sir W. Milner and Mr. Braik-enridge.]

[§ 530. *One.*—1853. Mr. J. H. Gurney's Menagerie.

This is the first egg laid by the female of a pair of birds bred by Mr. Edward Fountaine, whose remarkable success in propagating this fine species in con-finement has been recorded by himself in ' The Ibis,' vol. i. pp. 273–275.]

[§ 531. *Two.*—1857. Mr. J. H. Gurney's Menagerie.

These from the same bird as the last (§ 530). Though she lays and sits every year, she has not hitherto (1858) produced any offspring.]

[§ 532. *One.*—Kemi Lappmark, 3–9 June, 1860.

I have had some doubt about admitting this egg into my series. The finder was Piety, one of the best collectors in the country, and for whose judgment and honesty I have a very great respect. He believed it to be that of *Pieni* (or *Pikku*, which means the same thing) *Huuhkaja*, i. e. *Syrnium lapponicum*. The nest contained this one egg only, the others having been hatched, and was in a tree, three ells from the ground. This fact appears to have made him think as he did; for though he saw the bird, it was at a distance. But instances of Eagle-Owls breeding on trees have been recorded. Here I need only cite one case, on the authority of a most careful observer—the gentleman who prefers being known as "An Old Bushman." He states ('Field,' No. 409, October 27, 1860, p. 351), "I have seen the nest both in a tree and on a rock." The Lapp Owl would seem to be a somewhat later breeder than *Bubo maximus*, and, as a rule, would hardly, I think, have hatched its brood by the time this egg was taken. Besides, the coarser grain of the shell, which in the egg of the Lapp Owl is usually very fine and close, and its size, 2·29 in. by 1·9, induce me to believe that this is an Eagle-Owl's; while, of twenty-nine eggs of *Syrnium lapponicum* out of my series, the longest measures 2·26 in., and the widest 1·81, the average of the whole being 2·054 in. by 1·608. The shortest egg of *Bubo maximus* that I possess measures 2·19 in., and the narrowest 1·67.]

[§ 533. *Three.*—Rota-järwi-pahta, Rowa, East Bothnia.   11 May, 1861.

Brought to Muoniovara, 13th May, by Punsi, who said that they were those of the great *Huuhkaja*, which he himself saw. He found them, as stated above, on the south side of a cliff about half a mile from his house.]

[§ 534. *One.*—"South Russia."   From Herr A. Heinke, of Kamuschin, through Dr. Albert Günther.   1863.]

BUBO ASCALAPHUS, Savigny.

EGYPTIAN EAGLE-OWL.

[§ 535. *One.*—Pyramids of Dashoor, Central Egypt.   3 April, 1863.   "J. H. C." From Mr. H. Cochrane's Collection, through Mr. Leadbeater.

This Mr. Cochrane accompanied Mr. S. S. Allen, of whom mention has before been made in these pages (§ 181 and § 326). I believe they did not find any other large Owl in Egypt. They got plenty of skins of this one, several of which I saw, all unmistakeably *B. ascalaphus*.]

NYCTALE TENGMALMI (Gmelin).

TENGMALM'S OWL.

§ 536. *Four.*—Nälima, East Bothnia. 1856.

O. W. tab. ix. fig. 3. Proc. Zool. Soc. 1857, p. 57.

Brought by Johan Kenta's wife from Nälima, 15th June; taken long before. The bird had been turned out of its *tylla* [1] by a *Sotka* (Golden-eye). Doubtless Tengmalm's Owl.

[One of these eggs was sent by Mr. Wolley for exhibition at the Meeting of the Zoological Society of London, 24th March, 1857.]

§ 537. *Four.*—Helluntai-lauantai, Kyrö, Kemi Lappmark. 30 May, 1857. "Bird killed."

O. W. tab. ix. figs. 1, 2.

Received by myself in Yli-Kyrö, on 14th June, from Johan Johanson, of Ala-Kyrö, who said they were found as above in a *tylla*. As to the species there can be no reasonable doubt; for with them were the foot and wing of the bird.

§ 538. *Three.*—Kätkesuando, East Bothnia. 1858.

O. W. tab. ix. fig. 4.

Brought to Muoniovara, 25th May. Found in a Duck's nest-box.

---

[1] [It is the practice in Lapland to set up in convenient places nest-boxes for the Golden-eye (*Clangula glaucion*) to breed in. These boxes are called in the Muonioniska district by the names *tylla* or *su.* They consist of hollowed-out logs of wood, from three to five feet in length, and closed at either end. In the side a hole is cut to admit the birds. Besides the Golden-eye, the Goosander (*Mergus merganser*) and the Smew (*Mergus albellus*) avail themselves of the accommodation thus afforded. But two species of Owls do the like, and their tenancy is not unnaturally resented as an intrusion by the people who have been at the trouble of making ready the lodgings, as witness the statement of Linnæus ('*Lachesis Lapponica,*' i. p. 93).—ED.]

§ 539. *One.*—Tomi-koski, Tepasto, Kemi Lappmark. 18 May, 1858.

Found as above by Varan Heiki on the Ounas-joki, in a hole made by *Picus martius.*

§ 540. *One.*—Wassara, Kemi Lappmark. 21 May, 1858.

Brought to Muoniovara, 19th June, by one of the Wassara lads. He said that it was *Palokürki* [*Picus martius*], and found as above, a fathom or two from the ground; and that he saw the bird, which was red on the head, and elsewhere black on the body.

> [The above-mentioned egg is certainly not that of *Picus martius*, as the finder thought, though I have no reason to doubt his word that he saw such a bird at or near the nest. It is just one of those cases of mistaken identity as to the parentage of an egg which are constantly occurring, and which are so annoying to the oologist; but I have scarcely any hesitation in placing the specimen in my series of *Nyctale tengmalmi.*]

§ 541. *One.*—Jua-rowa, Särki-järwi, East Bothnia. 2 June, 1858. " With bird."

Brought to Muoniovara, with the bird, 7th June, by Piko Heiki. The nest, with four eggs, was found as above in a hole made by *Picus martius* in a Scotch fir, about a fathom and a half high. Half a mile [Swedish] west of Särki-järwi.

[§ 542. *Four.*— Aha-vaara, Kemi Lappmark. 26–31 May, 1861.

> Brought to Muoniovara, 25th June, having been found as above by Piety Kyrö in an *uu* (nest-box).]

[§ 543. *Four.*— Kippari-saari-ranta, Muotka-järwi, Enontekis Lappmark. June 1861.

> Brought to Muoniovaara 1st July, having been found as above about four weeks previously. These eggs are extremely small (one of them measuring only 1·13 inch by ·97 inch), so that I wrote to Lapland for further inquiries to be made of the finder respecting them. In reply I heard that he thought the bird was like any other *Pikku Pissi* (*Nyctale tengmalmi*). There was no nest in the same hole in 1862. Mr. Wolley never obtained any authentic trace of the occurrence of *Glaucidium passerinum* in Lapland; but it was one of the birds for which he was always on the look-out.]

[§ 544. *Five.*—Kätke-joki, East Bothnia, June 1861.

Brought by the finder to Muoniovara, 14th July. He got them, about a week before Midsummer, in a rotten trunk of a tree. These eggs are also very small, one measuring only 1·37 inch by 1·01 inch.]

[§ 545. *Five.*—Lombola-tunturi, Kyrö, Kemi Lappmark, June 1861.

Brought to Muoniovara, 4th August: found as above, a week after Mid-summer-day.]

[§ 546. *One.*—" Sweden," 1859. From Mr. H. W. Wheel-wright's Collection.]

SURNIA ULULA (Linnæus).

HAWK-OWL [1].

§ 547. *Four.*—Kangos-järwi, East Bothnia, 18–22 April, 1854.

O. W. tab. ix. fig. 5.

Out of eight eggs brought to Muoniovara for me, on the 28th April, by Isaak of Kangos-järwi. With them was a Hawk-Owl, whose wing had been struck off as it made an attack on the intruder, raising a lump on his head. There had been two nests of seven eggs each, of which six were accidentally broken by the frost, having been left in an uninhabited room, as I have just (15th May) learned at Kangos-järwi. One of the nests I visited on my way hither. It was in a hole in a tree, about ten feet from the ground, without any lining. In it, last year, were some kind of Duck's eggs. I saw both the birds still crying near the place, and they were clearly Hawk-Owls. This nest was taken on Easter Tuesday, and the other also from a tree on the following Saturday. From this last, the bird sent me, a male, was killed.

§ 548. *Three.*—Putharla, East Bothnia, 1 May, 1854.

Out of six eggs taken by Isaak Rowtio from an old *tylla* on

[1] [An interesting note on the habits of the Hawk-Owl, by Mr. Wolley, will be found in the 'Zoologist' for 1854 (pp. 4203, 4204). It contains no new information, however, respecting its manner of breeding; so I do not reprint it here.—ED.]

Puthars-puolella, Muonioniska. He said it was exactly the same kind of bird as a specimen of Hawk-Owl which happened to be lying in my room; but he could not catch it, though he and another lad tried to plug it up in its nest with a piece of wood.

[The remaining three eggs of this nest are in the collections of Sir William Milner, Mr. Burney, and Pastor Theobald.]

§ 549. *Two.*—Kurkio-vaara, Kyrö, Kemi Lappmark, 1856.

Ludwig was at the place on the 10th June, and received the eggs unblown. They said they were *Pissi, i. e.* Hawk-Owl.

[Six other eggs from this nest were sold at Mr. Stevens's, 12th May, 1857, to Sir William Milner, the late Mr. J. D. Salmon, Mr. Burney, Mr. A. F. Sealy, and Mr. Braikenridge.]

§ 550. *Six.*—Ollas-rowa, Muonioniska, East Bothnia, 27 April, 1856. " With both birds."

O. W. tab. ix. fig. 6.

Ludwig received these eggs, and wrote of them as follows:— "6th May, Niemi's Johan brought six *Pissi's* eggs taken in Ollas-rowa, 27th April, with both birds. He said that when he went to the nest, the cock came and struck two holes in his ear; but, as he had got a stick in his hand, he struck it on the head, so that it died straightway; and the hen he got fast in the hole, when she came out from the nest." Ludwig relates that the birds made quite a serious attack on Johan. They are both skinned, and I have sent them to England.

§ 551. *Four.*—Kyrö, Kemi Lappmark, 1847.

O. W. tab. ix. fig. 7.

Received by me in Yli-Kyrö, amongst Nikoo's eggs, but said to have been found by Michael's son. Birds being well known in Kyrö, it is probable that these eggs may be depended upon as Hawk-Owl's. One of them is much smaller than the other three.

§ 552. *Six.*—Tepasto, Kemi Lappmark, 1857.

O. W. tab. ix. fig. 8.

Out of thirteen brought, on 5th August, by Ludwig from Ala-

Kyrö, where he had received them from Johan Heiki's wife, who said they had been sent from Tepasto. They were mixed together; but, on blowing them, it was found that six were fresh and seven considerably incubated. These latter also seem to be much yellower than the others, and doubtless belonged to a different nest.

§ 553. *Five.*—Sirka, Kemi Lappmark, 1857.

Brought on 4th August by Carl Nullas-järwi, who had been with the post to Rauhala, where he received them from the Sirka postman, who had brought them thence.

§ 554. *One.*—Keras-sieppi, Enontekis Lappmark, 1857. "With bird's skin."

From this single dirty egg, which nevertheless had a large young one inside it, it appears that the bird was killed; and on such facts the Keras-sieppi men are trustworthy. The skin is before me.

P.S. 16th August, Matthias says his brother Hendrik found this nest, with young.

§ 555. *Three.* — Merta-vaara, Ounas-joki, Kemi Lappmark, 3–9 May, 1857.

This was brought by Heiki, 11th July. He said they were found in a tree. This information, coming from trustworthy sources, leaves no doubt that these eggs are Hawk-Owl's.

§ 556. *Five.*—Palo-vaara, Salmo-järwi, East Bothnia, 11–17 April, 1858.

Out of six brought to Muoniovara, 22nd May, by Hendrik, having been found as above in a tree which a *Palokärki* [*Picus martius*] had used. He saw the bird, and said that the *Pissi* which lays eggs in *tyllas* is less than the common *Pissi*.

[The name *Pissi* is often used in Lapland for all middle-sized and small Owls, but by those who know the difference between them is restricted to *Surnia ulula*, which is certainly the commonest species in the country. The Hendrik mentioned above was probably mistaken as to the size of the bird he saw, and I have little doubt in considering these eggs to be Hawk-Owl's, since they are fully as large as the average of well-identified ones in the series.]

§ 557. *Two.*—Tepasto, Kemi Lappmark, 18 May, 1858.

From a nest of six, found as above, in a hole in a dead stump.

§ 558. *Four.*—Korkala, Kemi Lappmark, 20 May, 1858.

From a nest of six eggs brought to Muoniovara by the man who found them as above in a *tylla* a quarter of a mile (Swedish) from his house.

[§ 559. *Four.*—Rowa, East Bothnia, 20–26 May, 1860.

Brought to Muoniovara, 23rd June, by Johan Erik, who said that he found them as above, about a furlong (Swedish) from his house, at the top of a hollow tree, the nest being about two fathoms and a half high. He said that he knew the kind of bird well.]

[§ 560. *Six.*—Thitalahen-vaara, Kemi Lappmark, 9–15 May, 1861.

Brought to Muoniovara, 23rd June, by Johan Salanki from Kyrö, who said he found them as above in a *tylla* or *uu.*]

SYRNIUM LAPPONICUM (Sparrmann).

LAPP OWL.

[On Mr. Wolley's first arrival at Muoniovara in the summer of 1853, he was pleased to find evidence of the occurrence in the district of this rare species, in the shape of a tailless skin of it, which had been for three or four years used as a plaything by his landlord's children. But his first introduction to the bird alive occurred a few months afterwards; and I trust I may be excused for introducing his account of it here, especially as it describes a curious habit (common, as it would appear, to several species of Owls) which I do not think has been previously noticed by writers. Writing to me from Muoniovara, 23rd September, 1853, he says:—

" Before proceeding to notice your letter further, I must tell you an adventure of this evening. It had rained heavily all day, but it ceased about four o'clock; and I turned out with Ludwig to see if I could shoot a Capercally or two, for I had killed four on the two preceding days, and many come to the wood now that the leaves are off the birch and aspens. I was anxious to try the shot which we had manufactured; for I had only a charge or two left of No. 11 (Swedish).

Having walked for a couple of hours without a ‘bay,’ as they would
say in the Highlands, and having seen nothing but a little Siberian
Titmouse [*Parus cinctus*], which ‘*tchee, tchee, tcheed*’ its ill-omened
note, I turned homewards; for night was coming on more quickly
than usual. I called and whistled the dog; but it was his duty and
his habit to take a very wide beat, and I was not surprised that he did
not come.   A few minutes afterwards, I heard an unusual kind of yelp
in the distance, and then a succession of barks in a peculiar high
key, which I had not known him adopt on any former occasion; for,
you must know, that a Squirrel, for instance, is ‘bayed’ with a very
different kind of bark from a Capercally, and you at once can recognize what kind of game these dogs are after. I said to Ludwig he
was either after some great Owl, or was caught in a snare.   After a
run of nearly a mile over very rough ground, I began to ‘stalk,’ and
there are so many dead twigs that it requires great care.   But I was
still some little distance from where the dog was barking, when a
small Owl flew up from that direction, and perched in a Scotch fir
only a few feet from my head. I had not seen this kind of Owl before; but I knew that *Strix Tengmalmi* was a Lapland bird, and I
had little doubt that one was now before me, though it was too dark
to see it distinctly. I drew back a considerable distance and fired;
but the large shot and the night were against me, and the bird flew a
short way, and settled close to Ludwig, but flew again before I had
time to go up and give him a second barrel. The dog did not run
up as he usually does when he hears a shot, but continued barking.
Approaching him cautiously, with no inconsiderable amount of curiosity, I saw ‘Halli’ standing quite patiently in a footpath, with a
Capercally snare round his neck. Calling Ludwig to join in the
laugh at my dog’s expense, and with every mark of approval of his
good judgment in standing quite still and calling for my assistance,
I proceeded to liberate him, not without some little deprecation of the
setter of the snare, whom I well knew. Just then I saw a great pair
of wings give two or three noiseless flaps, as their owner lightly
settled in a neighbouring tree. Ludwig had scarcely uttered his im-
pressive “See! see!” when I fired my only remaining barrel at the
place where I guessed the bird was. Relieved from all doubt as to
my success, as he fell head foremost down, I sprang forwards and
scarcely glanced at the banded wings and grey back of my victim,
before I turned up his face that I might indulge my joy without risk
of a mistake. It was indeed *Strix Lapponica*! Ludwig danced
with exultation, and stroked the bird’s head and back, calling him
by all the names and titles he could think of—‘Stora Lapp-Uggla,’

'Gamla poika,' 'Kaunis Pissi-Haukka,' 'Vackra Kissa-Pökkö,' 'Musta Huuhkaja,' 'Pikku Huuhkaja,' 'Tcharppis Skuolfi'—the two last the Finnish and Lappish names. * * * * After having secured my capture in a pocket-handkerchief, I excited the dog to bark again, and he soon brought round the small Owl and five or six Short-eared Owls, with perhaps a Hawk-Owl, but no more *Huuhkaja*. Presently, reflecting that I was scarcely improving my dog, I tried some unearthly noises myself, which were, if anything, more successful than the dog's, but still no *Huuhkaja*. Ludwig said that if any man heard me, he would certainly think it was the *Djefoul*. This led to talk on the supernatural, till Ludwig 'shied' at every stump, and I heard several interesting accounts of native superstitions. * * * * Headless men, a glance through the horse-collar, and so forth, all have place in these arctic lands."

For the next two or three years, Mr. Wolley prosecuted his researches into the history of the Lapp Owl without much success. Sir John Richardson had already many years before described ('Fauna Boreali-Americana,' ii. p. 78) the nest of its Transatlantic representative, *Syrnium cinereum*, which is so closely allied to it that I am doubtful whether any real distinction can be made out between them[1]. It also appears from Dr. Brown's statement, quoted by Dr. Brewer ('North American Oology,' p. 71), that Mr. Audubon had seen an egg of the nearctic form. But I do not know that a specimen of either existed in the cabinet of any oologist.

According to Professor Nilsson ('Skandinavisk Fauna,' Foglarna, 3rd edit. vol. i. p. 124), Herr Von Seth, who, in 1842, took a journey into Lulea Lappmark, and visited Quickjock, reported that this species of Owl built a very big nest in a high tree or on a high stub, wherein it laid two or three dirty-white eggs. If I am not mistaken, however, this intelligence was not published until 1858, when the last edition of Professor Nilsson's work appeared. Meantime Herr C. G. Löwenhjelm, who travelled in the same district of Lapland in 1843, communicated to the Royal Academy of Sciences at Stockholm some zoological notes of his journey, in which he says (Kongl. Vetensk. Acad. Handl., 1843, p. 389) that a female Lapp Owl was preserved in the Parsonage at Jockmock by Pastor Ullenius, having been killed in the neighbourhood, in the beginning of June, when sitting on her nest, which she had built in a thick Scotch-fir wood on a stub three ells high. In this, as it was old and rotten inside, a depression was formed, which, without any roof, she had made to serve as her nest. There was one white egg, the size of an Eagle-Owl's, in it, and beneath, on the moss, lay another quite uninjured. This account, though published in 1844, was, I believe, unknown to Mr. Wolley[2];

---

[1] [If they are considered identical, Sparrmann's name, "*lapponicum*," applied to the bird of the Old World, must give way to Gmelin's "*cinereum*."—ED.]

[2] [The discovery of Pastor Ullenius seems to have been also unknown to Professor Nilsson; at least no mention of it is made in the account he gives of this bird. I became aware of it from one of Herr Wallengren's admirable series of

for, on the 16th July 1856, he announced, as a novelty, to the Meeting of Scandinavian Naturalists at Christiania (Forhandl. Skand. Naturf. 7de Möde, p. 221) that " *Strix Lapponica*, according to the report of several trustworthy persons who had seen its nests, lays its eggs in a depression on the top of the stump of a broken-off tree." On the 24th March 1857, he communicated a paper to the Zoological Society of London (' Proc. Zool. Soc.,' 1857, pp. 56, 57), in which he related the actual discovery, by men in his employment, of the two nests from which eggs were brought to him in 1856, as described below (§§ 561 and 562). At that time he thought that three was the usual number of eggs laid, but it will be seen further on that the complement is often greater.]

§ 561. *Two.*—Juonto-selkä-maa, Kello-joki, Kemi Lappmark, 1856.

P. Z. S., 1857, p. 56. O. W. tab. ix. fig. 9.

These, brought home by Piety as *Pikku Huuhkaja*, agree exactly with the Kurkio-vaara eggs [§ 562], from which the bird was shot, and is now here. The place was a little to the north-east of So-dankyla. Piety met with a man there, who said he had shot a Hawk and another bird. Piety went to his house, and saw the bird and the eggs. It was a *Pikku Huuhkaja*, a bird he knows very well. He cut it up, and therein was another egg, not ready to be laid, but just like the two; hence he is certain about the species to which they belong. This nest was on the top of a broken trunk of a Scotch fir, the main part of which hung down; but, from the description, Piety thinks there was some old nest there. He does not remember see-ing any nest made. It was not high up, some two fathoms perhaps; but those which he has seen before were not more than one fathom high. The top of the tree, where it was broken off, was not level, but had a great splinter on one side. The birds are very bold at the nest, and the cry of the cock attracts people to the nest. The cry is three notes drawn out, the first hardest, the second lighter and short, the third lightest and longest of all:—" HU, HU, hu-u-u." They had not before seen this bird at Sodankyla—as they said, at least.

articles, " Breeding-zones of Birds in Scandinavia," in the ' Naumannia,' where (vol. iv. pp. 76, 77) he quotes, as I have done, from Herr Löwenhjelm's paper. —ED.]

§ 562. *Two.*—Merta-vaara, Kyrö, Kemi Lappmark, 28 May, 1856. " With hen bird."

P. Z. S., 1857, pp. 56, 57.   O. W. tab. ix. fig. 10.

Taken, as above, three-quarters of a mile east of Kurkio-vaara. The nest was in a Scotch fir. Kurkio-vaara Matti said that earlier in the year he shot a *Pikku Huuhkaja*, but did not see the nest until after he had done so. He skinned it, and Ludwig saw the skin. When, soon after, on 28th May, he went again to the place, the survivor had a new mate, and there were two eggs in the nest. He thought if he shot the hen he could get another egg from her inside. Unluckily he shot just through the egg, which had a hard shell. The skin of this bird I have sent to England. The eggs are in size about 2 in. by 1·6 in., and 2·1 in. by 1·65 in.

P.S.—Muoniovara, 5th April, 1857. Matti, now here, says that the nest was made of sticks and all kinds of stuff inside, about three fathoms and a half high up in a large Scotch fir, where it divided into several great forks. It was not like a new nest, and he describes it as about two feet in thickness. He was several times at the nest; first no eggs, and so on. He now says, with certainty, that the skin he brings (that of the bird he shot) was a cock, so that it was the hen which got a new husband.

[In his communication to the Zoological Society before referred to, Mr. Wolley, then writing under date of " February 2nd, 1857," states that the first bird killed from this nest " was found to be a female, with eggs inside." He had not then seen the Owl-slayer; but it appears from his postscript of the 5th April, that the second bird had been confounded with the first, which was in reality a cock. I believe the skins of both are in the Museum at Norwich.]

§ 563. *Two.*—Ækka-järwi, Kemi Lappmark, 1857. ' " With both birds."

O. W. tab. ix. fig. 11.

Brought by Michael, on 4th August. He said they were left at his house during his absence from home (probably about Midsummer) by Abraham Korkala, who had related that there were four more eggs inside the hen bird. This man lives at Ækka-järwi, which is about a mile (Swedish) to the east of Sardio. The skins lie before me.

[The skins were, I believe, among those sent to Norwich.]

§ 564. *Four.*—Palo-vaara-laiduu, East Bothnia, 29 May, 1858. " With bird."

O. W. tab. ix. fig. 12.

Brought to Muoniovara, 23rd June, by Punsi, who said he found them as above, on the south side of the mountain, in a great Scotch fir. The nest was about five fathoms from the ground. He also brought the bird, but most grievously stuffed.

[§ 565. *Five.*—Sieppi, Enontekis Lappmark (?), 18 May, 1861. " With bird."

Brought to Muoniovara, 22nd June, having been found as above, in a tree four or five fathoms high. The eggs had young ones in them. The bird was sent to me.]

[§ 566. *Four.*—Kajo-selkä, Kemi Lappmark, 1861. " With bird's feet."

Brought to Muoniovara from Kyrö, 23rd June, having been found about three weeks previously in a tree as above. The feet came also. There had been five eggs, but one got broken.]

[§ 567. *One.* — Poro-vaara, Kyrö, Kemi Lappmark, 1861. " With bird."

Brought to Muoniovara, 25th June, by Piety, who was unable to give further particulars respecting it. The bird is now in Mr. Newcome's Collection.]

[§ 568. *Five.*—Kemi Lappmark (?), 1861.

Brought to Muoniovara, 30th June, by Wollas Erik, having been found, about the 20th, in a tree.]

[§ 569. *Five.*—Kiwi-järwi-Kentta, Kemi Lappmark, 12 May, 1862.

Brought to Muoniovara, 15th May, by Kyrö Nikoo, having been found as above in a Scotch fir, about three fathoms from the ground.]

[§ 570. *Four.*—Ounas-vaara, Kemi Lappmark, 26 April, 1862. " With bird."

Brought as above by Pehr Kyrö. The skin of the bird I have sent to the Smithsonian Institution at Washington.]

[§ 571. *Four.*—Tepasto, Kemi Lappmark, 1862.

> Sent to Muoniovara, 2nd July, by Tepasto Johan, without any particulars.
> I keep these eggs because they are rather elongated in shape, and of a some-
> what rougher surface than is usually seen in this species.]

[§ 572. *Four.*—Æjtasen-maa, Kemi Lappmark, May, 1862.

> Brought to Muoniovara, 9th June, by Rowa Peter, who said they had been
> found about four weeks since in a rotten stub.]

SYRNIUM ALUCO (Linnæus).

TAWNY OWL.

§ 573. *One.*—Eton, Buckinghamshire, 1843.

Obtained by my brother Charles from a man who had the old bird,
which he had killed from the nest.

§ 574. *One.*—From Mr. Sadd, 1843.

§ 575. *Two.*—Scotland (?). From Mr. W. Dunbar, 1850.

§ 576. *One.*—Hutton Bushel, Yorkshire, 1851.

§ 577. *One.* — Pickering, Yorkshire, 1854. From Mr. A.
Robert's Collection.

§ 578. *Two.*—Southern Sweden, 1856.

[§ 579. *One.*—Elveden, 1846.]

§ 580. *Three.*—Elveden, 22 March, 1852. " E. N."

[§ 581. *Two.*—Elveden, 21 March, 1853. "A. & E. N."]

[§ 582. *One.*—Elveden, 16 March, 1854. "A. N."]

§ 583. *Two.*—Elveden, 25 April, 1854. "A. & E. N."

[§ 584. *Three*.—Elveden, 4 April, 1857. "E. N."]

[§ 585. *Four*.—Elveden, 5 April, 1859. "A. & E. N."

The eggs mentioned in this and the preceding six sections were all, I believe, the produce of the same pair of birds, which to my own knowledge from 1844, and probably for a much longer time, had frequented some clumps of old elms near the house at Elveden. There were three of these clumps, in one or the other of which they invariably laid their eggs. The trees were of considerable age, and mostly quite hollow, with an abundance of convenient nesting-places. By waiting quietly about an hour after sunset, my brother Edward or myself could generally discover whereabouts the Owls had taken up their quarters for the season; but it sometimes happened that we did not find the nest until the young were hatched. Throughout the winter the Owls kept pretty much in company; but towards the middle of February they used to separate, the cock bird often passing the day in a tree at some distance from where the hen was. As soon as he came out in the evening to hunt, he announced his presence by a vigorous hoot. Upon this the hen would emerge silently, and, after a short flight, would reply to her mate's summons by a gentle note. He then generally joined her, and they would fly off together to procure their living. The eggs were commonly laid about the second week in March, and the nests were almost always very accessible. I never knew these birds occupy the same hole in two successive years; but, after the interval of two or three years, they would return to the same spot. There were never any materials collected to form a nest, the eggs being always placed on the rotten wood, which in most cases formed a sufficient bedding. If all the eggs were taken, as was the case in 1854, the hen bird laid again in another tree. We never found more than four eggs in the nest. These often, but not always, proved to have been incubated for different lengths of time, showing that the hen bird sometimes began to sit as soon as the first egg was laid; but we could never divine what might be the cause of this irregularity of habit. After the young birds had left the nest, it was some time before they began to shift for themselves; and they used to sit in the shadiest trees for the best part of the summer, uttering a plaintive note, like "keewick," night and day, almost without cessation, to attract the attention of their parents, who would assiduously bring them the spoils of the chase. In 1851, two nestlings from this pair of Owls were sent by us to the Gardens of the Zoological Society, where they lived for more than ten years, and duly assumed the perfectly adult state of plumage so rarely seen among British specimens of the Tawny Owl. Late in the spring of 1859, to the great regret of those who knew them, the old birds suddenly disappeared, and I never succeeded in ascertaining their fate. I think it due to their memory to insert this account of their habits, the more so as I fear the species is daily becoming more uncommon in England.]

N

NYCTEA NIVEA (Daudin).

SNOWY OWL.

[§ 586. *One.* — "Labrador." From Dr. N. Kjærbœlling's Collection, 1859.

This egg I obtained at Copenhagen. I was somewhat sceptical concerning it at first, but I was subsequently led to consider it genuine. It was probably imported to Europe by the correspondents of Herr Möschler.]

[§ 587. *One.*—"Labrador." From Dr. E. Baldamus's Collection, 1861.

Sent to me by Dr. Baldamus in March 1861, with the information that he obtained it from Herr Möschler, who had received it from Labrador.]

[§ 588. *One.*—"North-Eastern Russia." From Dr. E. Baldamus's Collection, 1861.

P. Z. S., 1861, p. 395.

This egg I received at the same time as the last-mentioned. Dr. Baldamus informed me he had got it from Herr Möschler, to whom it was sent from Archangel by Count Centurio Hoffmansegg, as I afterwards learned from Herr Möschler himself.]

[§ 589. *One.*—Okkak, Labrador, 1860. From Herr H. F. Möschler's Collection, 1861.

P. Z. S., 1861, p. 395.

Being very desirous of learning all the particulars I could respecting the many reputed Snowy Owls' eggs which I had seen in various collections, on the 22nd September, 1861, I went to Herrnhut, and had the pleasure of seeing Herr Möschler. He kindly showed me his cabinet, and allowed me to select from it this specimen, which he told me he had the preceding autumn received direct from Labrador, and which he assured me had been in no other hands but his own, he having been himself the first to open the box containing it. Herr Möschler was careful to tell me that he had no positive testimony of the genuineness of this or other presumed eggs of the species which had passed through his hands; but the circumstantial evidence was to my mind convincing. He informed me that he had had in all more than two dozen eggs sent him from Okkak, the most northerly but one of the four missionary stations maintained by the United Brethren on the Labrador coast. These eggs, together with a few received by him from Archangel, of which I have already mentioned one (§ 588), all closely agree in general character. They are about midway in size between those of the Eagle-Owl and the Lapp Owl, or their New World representatives *Bubo virginianus* and *Syrnium cinereum*.

They are also accompanied by a large number of skins of *Nyctea nivea*, showing that that bird is abundant in the quarter whence they come. Herr Möschler also had assurances from his correspondents in Labrador that the Esquimaux, who brought these eggs to the Moravian missionaries as those of the Snowy Owl, reported that the bird always breeds on the ground in bare places, and often lays a considerable number of eggs. This story, as I had the pleasure of stating to the Zoological Society when exhibiting the present specimen, was corroborated by the evidence of various other observers (P. Z. S., 1861, pp. 394, 395), both in Europe and America; but its truth has since been most completely and satisfactorily confirmed by Mr. Wheelwright's discovery, which I shall recount in the next section.]

[§ 590. *Three.*—Wihri-jaur, Lulea Lappmark, 5 June, 1862. From Mr. H. W. Wheelwright's Collection.

I have already, in the communication to the Zoological Society before alluded to, mentioned (P. Z. S., 1861, p. 395) Mr. Wolley's unsuccessful efforts to obtain eggs of the Snowy Owl from Northern Lapland, as well as my own attempts, which up to the past season of 1863 have been equally ineffectual. He several times met with people who had found nests of this bird, and states (Forhandl. Skand. Naturf. 7de Möde, Christiania, 1857, p. 221) that he was told the old birds sometimes attack persons who approach their nests. They commonly seemed to breed in the districts explored by him only when the lemmings are unusually abundant; but even then, from the vast extent and desolate character of the mountainous country they frequent, it is almost a matter of chance for a man to stumble on a nest. From his chief agent, who since Mr. Wolley's death has been in my own employment, I learned that from the 16th to the 24th of May is supposed to be the time when they usually breed; and that in 1860 a Lapp, who, unfortunately, was not one of his regular collectors, found a nest with six eggs, which, instead of preserving, he ate. It was therefore with great pleasure that I heard from Mr. Wheelwright that better luck had attended his endeavours to the same end in a more south-western district. Writing to me from Quickjock, on the 6th June 1862, he says:—

"I thought I should have good news to tell you before I shut up. . . . I sent two Lapps up to the breeding-place of *Strix nyctea*, about ten sea-miles hence (the way was so bad, and the snow so deep on the fells, that they said I could never get there); and this morning they have come back with the nest, six eggs, and the old female (as white as snow) of the Snowy Owl. . . . The nest is nothing more than a layer of reindeer moss and a few feathers—very few, laid on the bare fell; no sticks or anything else. They say they do not believe there is another nest in this district; but still I shall have another try in another locality. The eggs are a little sat on; so six was the full number of this Owl. The egg in my collection, which Liljeborg took on the fells near Hammerfest, was one of nine [1], and considerably smaller than these I have

---

[1] [Mr. Wheelwright was, of course, only writing from memory. A Snowy Owl's nest was found by Herr Liljeborg on the fells between Œsterdal and Guldbrandsdal, and contained seven eggs (Œfversigt af K. Vet.-Akad. Förhandl., 1844,

just got. They are not nearly so round as my eggs of the Eagle-Owl, but nearly as large."

Three of these eggs Mr. Wheelwright was good enough to let me become possessed of. Of the remainder, one has, I believe, passed into the collection of Mr. Braikenridge, another into that of Mr. G. D. Rowley, and the third remains in Mr. Wheelwright's own keeping.

In the 'Field' newspaper, No. 527, for January 31, 1863 (p. 93), is one of a series of articles entitled "A Spring and Summer in Lapland, by an Old Bushman." From it I make the following extract :—

"Owing perhaps to the lemming migrations, which appear to draw all the birds of prey in the north into one focus, the snowy owl has not been rare on the Quickiock fells during the last three seasons; and in 1861 three nests, all containing young birds, were destroyed by the Laps within sixty miles of Quickiock. In no single instance were the old birds killed; but they did not come back to breed in the same localities in 1862, for we carefully examined every old nest. However, in the beginning of June I sent two Laps off to the great lake Wihrigaur. The road was bad, and the snow lay deep on the fells; but they returned within the week, bringing with them a nest and six eggs of the snowy owl, as well as the old female, which they had shot. I was much pleased to see the marked difference between this egg and the egg of any other of the large European owls. It is more elongated and not so round or large as the egg of the eagle owl (but of course perfectly white); and it is larger than that of the Lap owl (*Strix Lapponica*). The egg of the snowy owl measures just the same in length as that of the eagle owl (2¼ inches); its breadth is 1¾ inches, that of the eagle owl being 2 inches full. The nest was nothing more than a large ball of reindeer moss, placed on the ledge of a bare fell. The old birds appeared to guard it most jealously; in fact, the Laps often kill them with a stick when they are robbing the nest."

Some other interesting information respecting the habits of the bird is added by this excellent observer; but, as it does not relate to these eggs, I do not copy it here[1]. I may, however, remark that I do not quite agree with the statement above quoted as regards the comparative size of the Snowy and Eagle-Owl's eggs, so far as I am able to judge from the specimens now in my possession, and included in this Catalogue. Of seven of the first, the longest measures 2·24 in., the shortest 2·14. Of nineteen Eagle-Owls' eggs, all laid by wild birds, the longest is 2·42 in., the shortest 2·19,—giving an average length for *Nyctea nivea* of about 2·204 in., and for *Bubo maximus* of 2·303 in. Wihri-jaur is on the boundary of the kingdoms of Norway and Sweden, almost immediately under Sulitjelma, the highest mountain of Arctic Europe, and, with the adjoining Wasti-jaur, forms the chief reservoir whence the Great Luleå river flows, before entering the lake of the same name.]

---

pp. 212, 213). This was in the beginning of June 1843, and I am not aware that he ever met with another. Perhaps Mr. Wheelwright meant to have written "Lillehammer" for "Hammerfest."—ED.]

[1] [In the volume, lately issued, containing (under the same title as that by which they originally appeared in the 'Field') the whole series of these valuable articles collected and reprinted, it is further stated (p. 258) that "The snowy owl will occasionally make its nest on the large turf hillocks in some of the mosses."—ED.]

LIST OF PLATES IN PART I.

* By mistake, called "fig. 4" in text.   † By mistake, called "fig. 5" in text.

---

* By mistake, called " tab. B " in text.

† These two plates will be referred to in a later portion of this work; but the subject of the first has already been described by Mr. Wolley in the ' Ibis' for 1859 (vol. i. pp. 191–196).

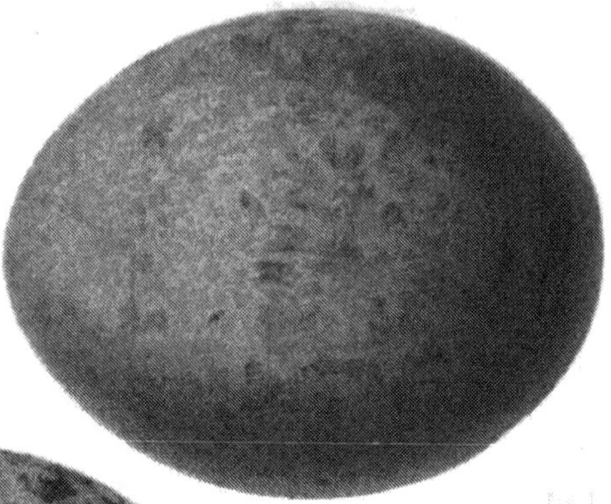

Fig. 1

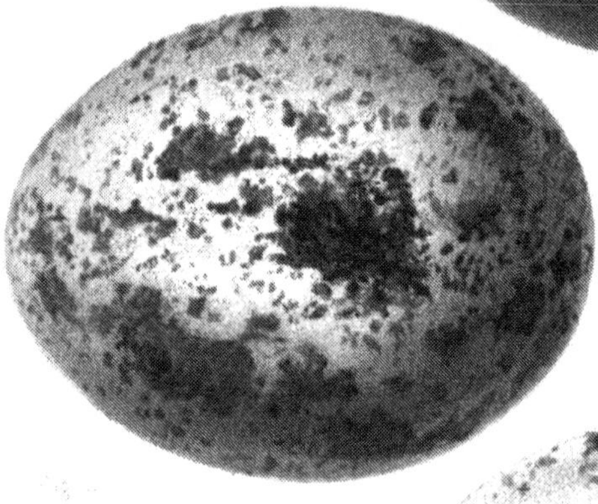

Fig. 2

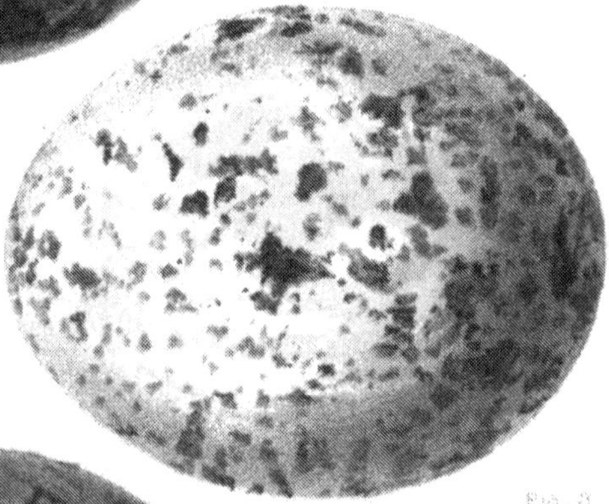

Fig. 3

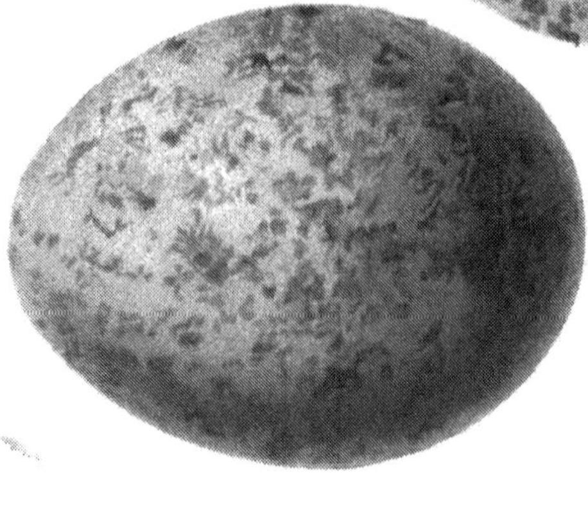

Fig. 4

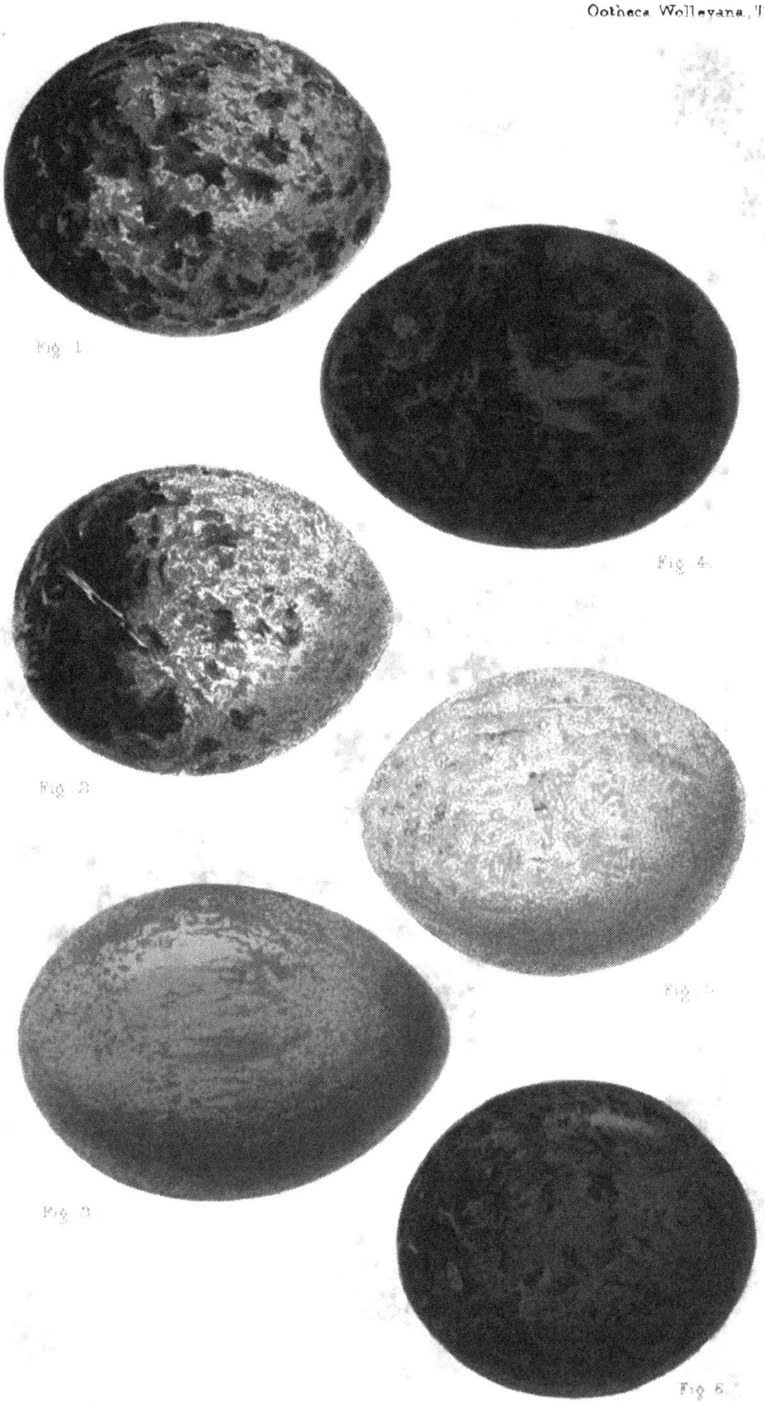
Fig. 1.
Fig. 4.
Fig. 2.
Fig. 5.
Fig. 3.
Fig. 6.

I. Balcomb, del[t]

Hanhart, Chromo lith

John Van Voorst, Paternoster Row, 1862.

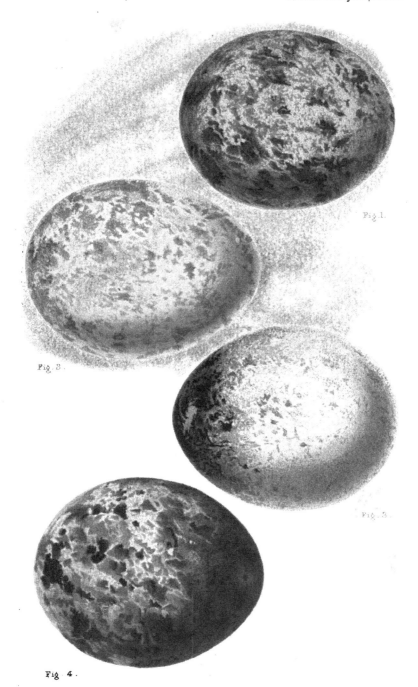

Fig. 1.

Fig. 2.

Fig. 3.

Fig. 4.

J. Halcomb, del.

Hanhart, Chromo-lith.

John Van Voorst, Paternoster Row, 1862.

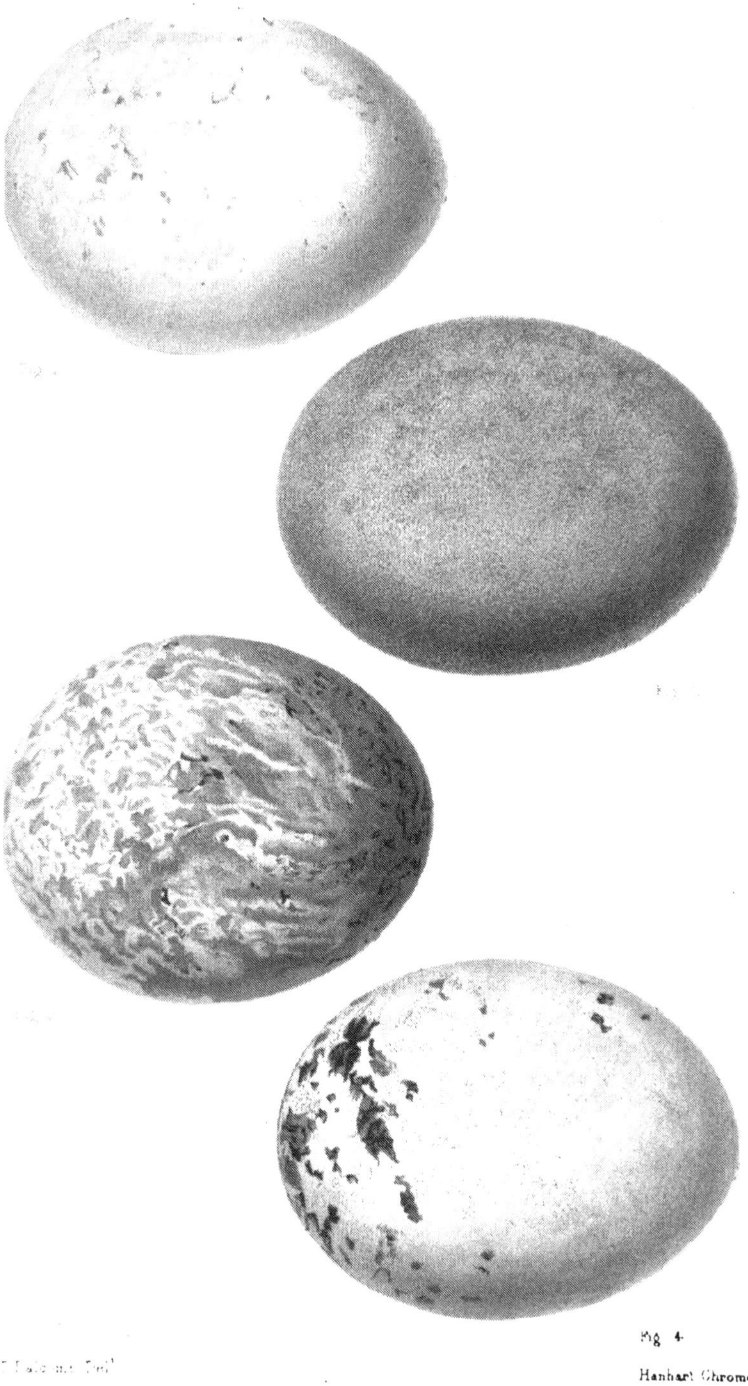

Fig. 4.

Hanhart Chromo-lith.

John Van Voorst, Paternoster Row 1863

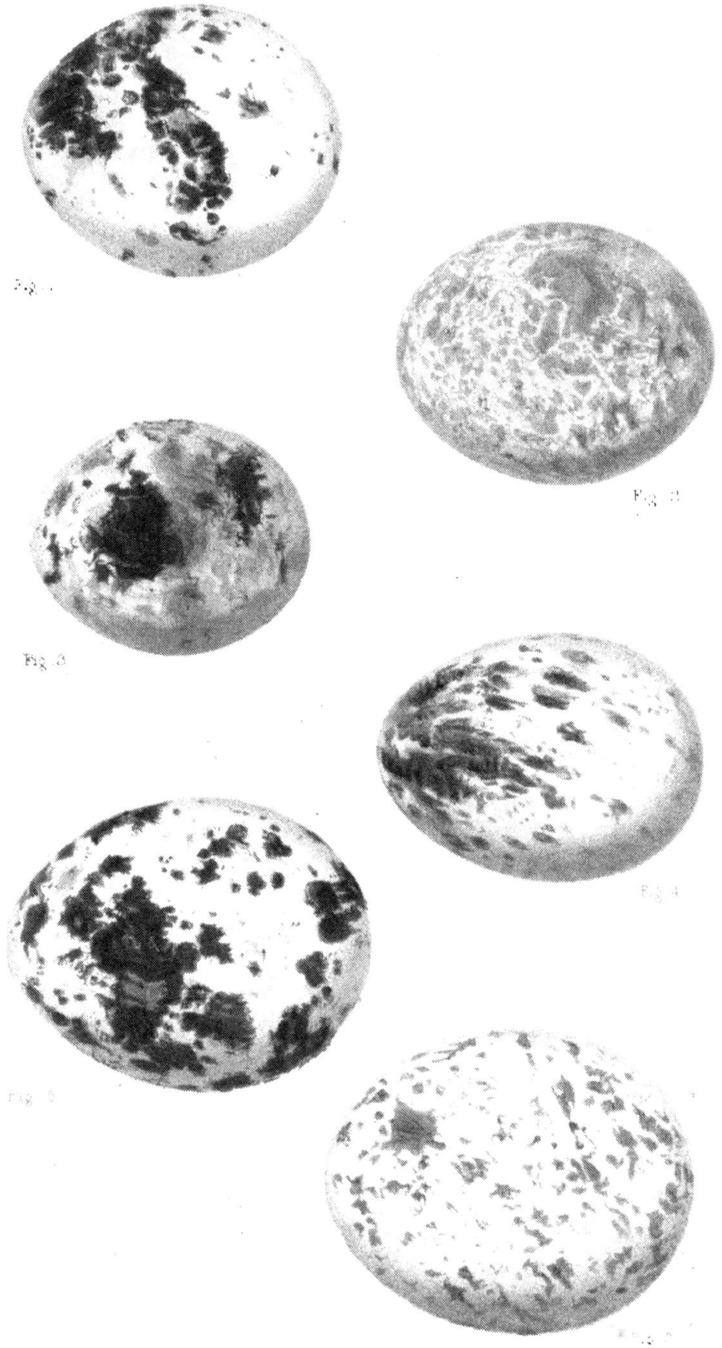
Fig. 2
Fig. 3

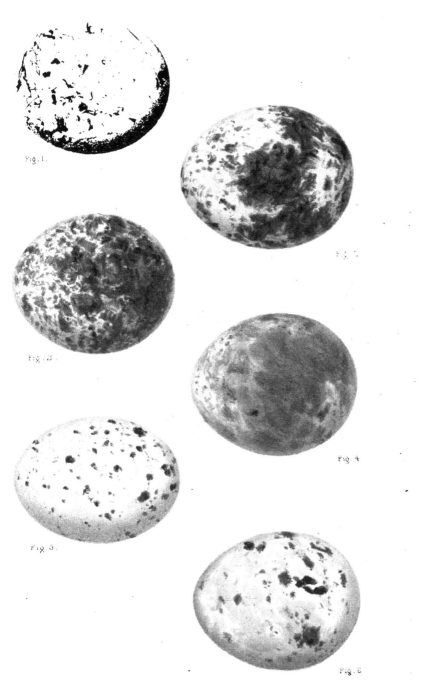

Fig. 1.

Fig. 2.

Fig. 3.

Fig. 4.

Fig. 5.

Fig. 6.

J. Palombe Del.   Bauband imp.

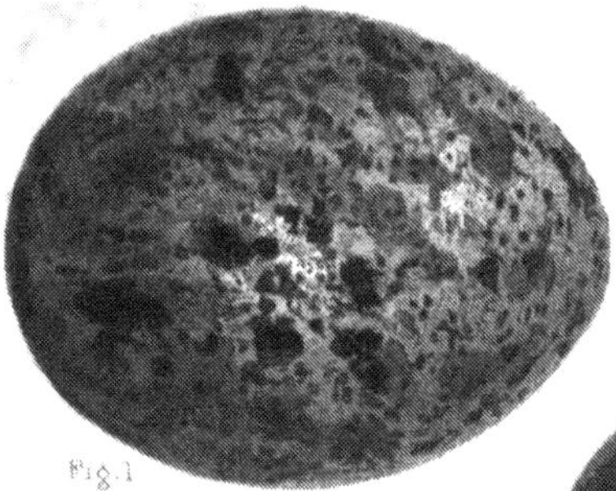

Fig. 1

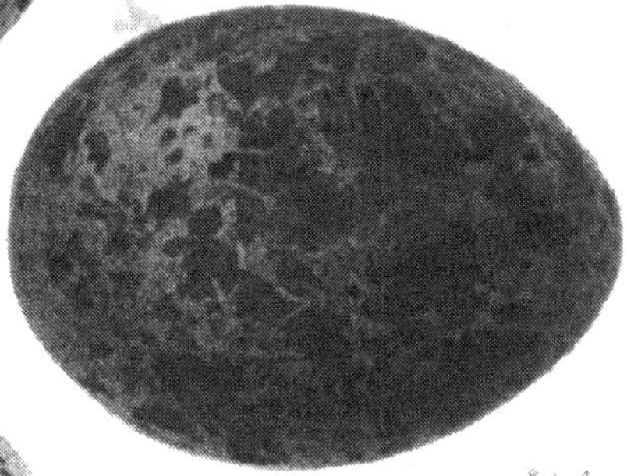

Fig. 4.

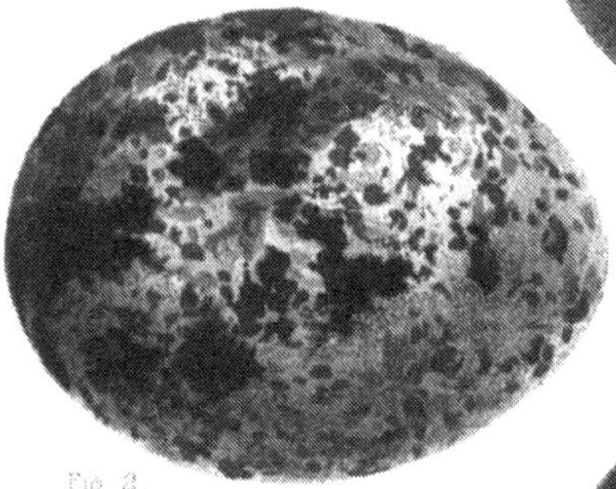

Fig. 2.

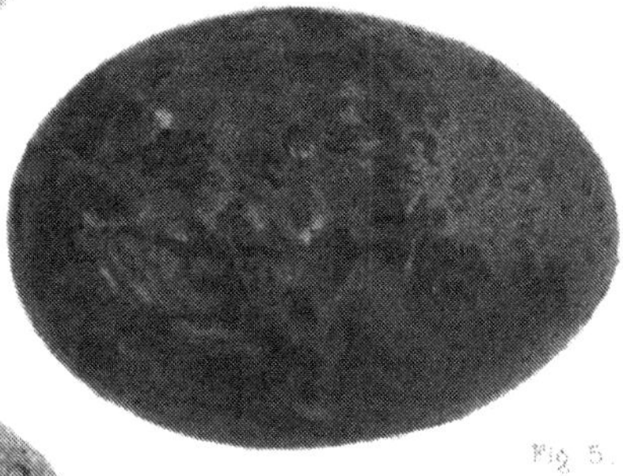

Fig. 5.

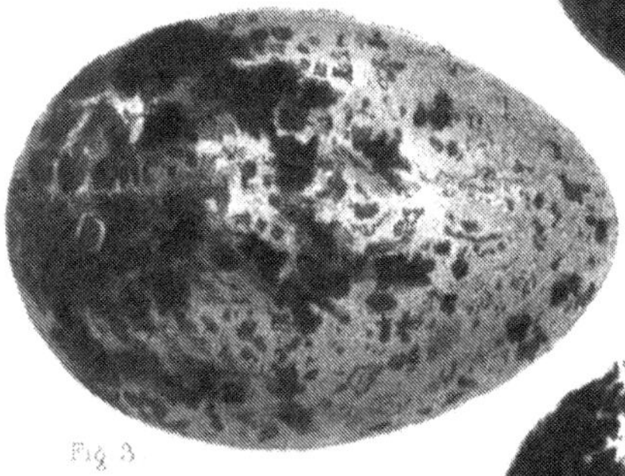

Fig. 3.

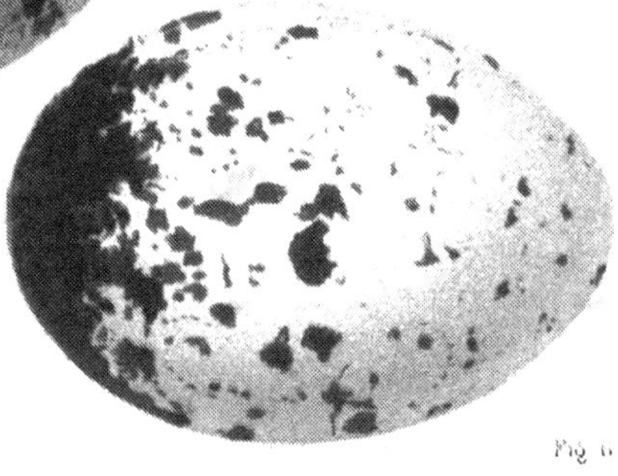

Fig. 6.

J T Balcomb, Del[t]

Fig 1.

Fig 2.

Fig 3.

Fig 4.

Fig 5.

Fig 6.

J.T. Balcomb lith.

Ootheca Wolleyana. Tab. IX.

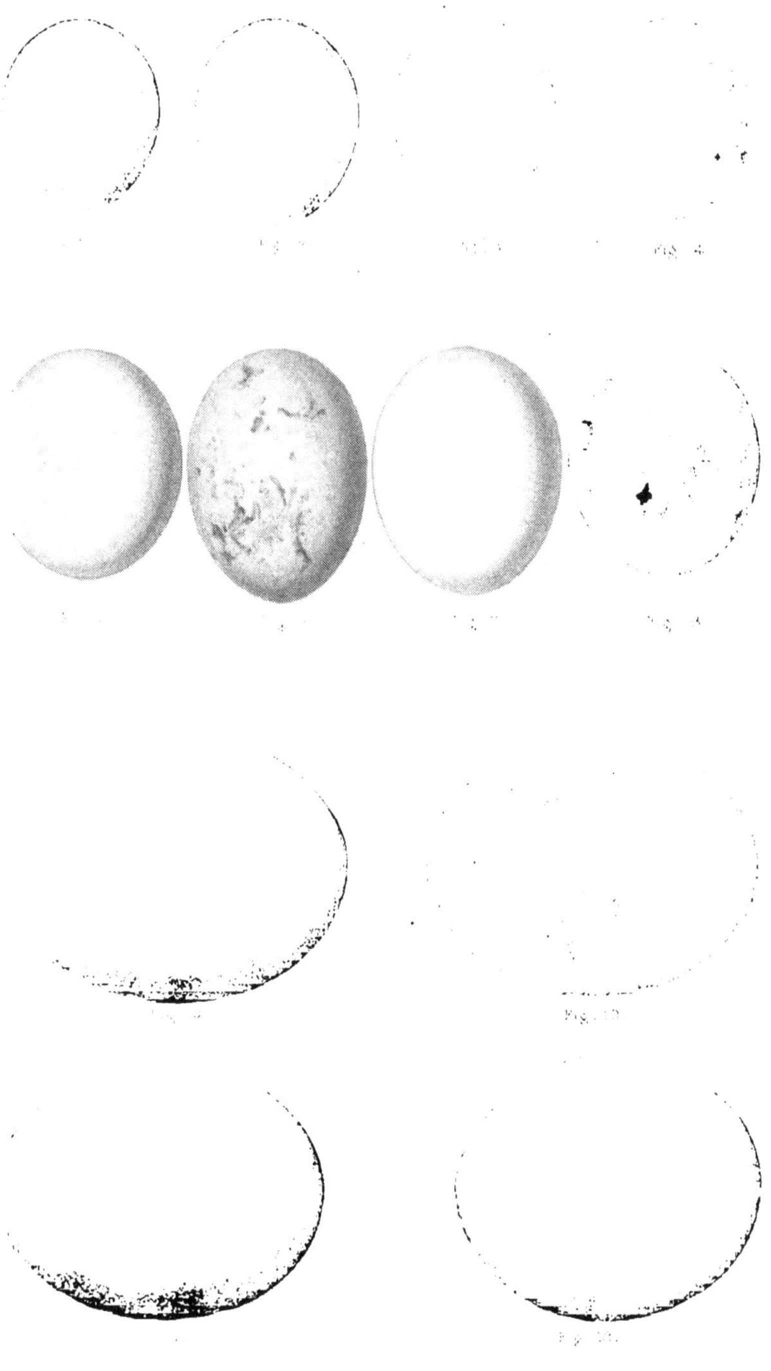

Fig. 4
Fig. 8
Fig. 10

Ootheca Wolleyana , Tab. A.

A.N.ad nat. delin.   Lambart impl   J. Jury lith.

John Van Voorst.Paternoster Row. 1862.

Ootheca Wolleyana. Tab. B.

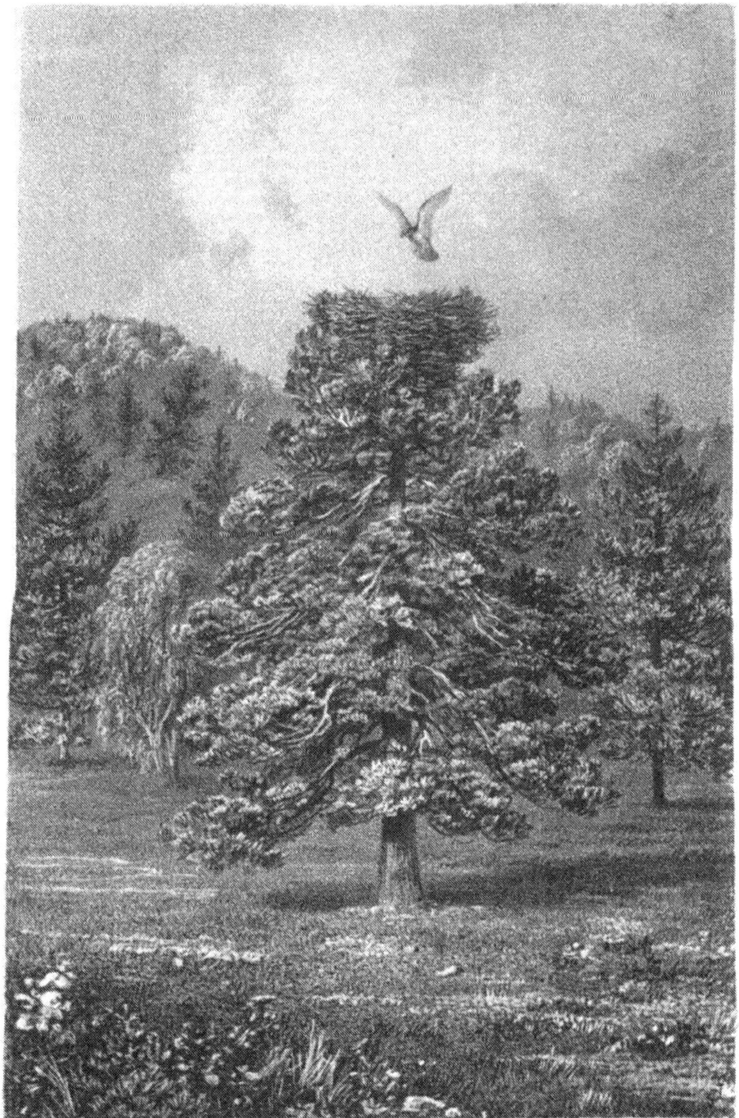

A.N. ad nat. delin. Hanhart, Imp. J. Jury, lith.

John Van Voorst, Paternoster Row, 1862.

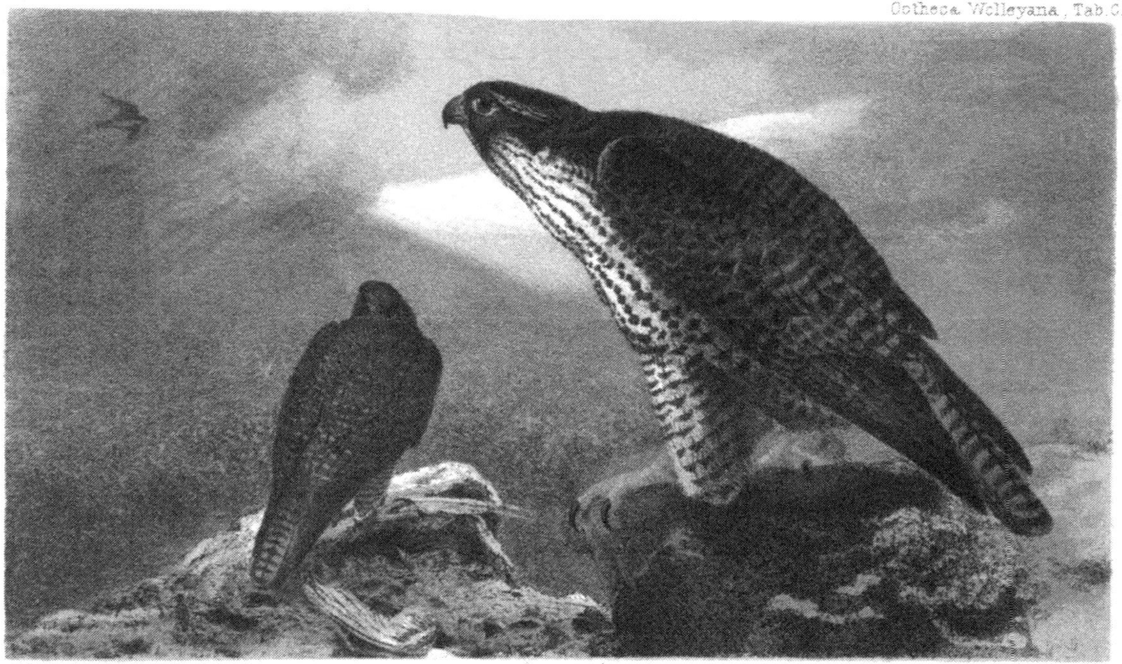

J. Wolf, pinxit. Hanhart, Imp. J. Jury, lith.

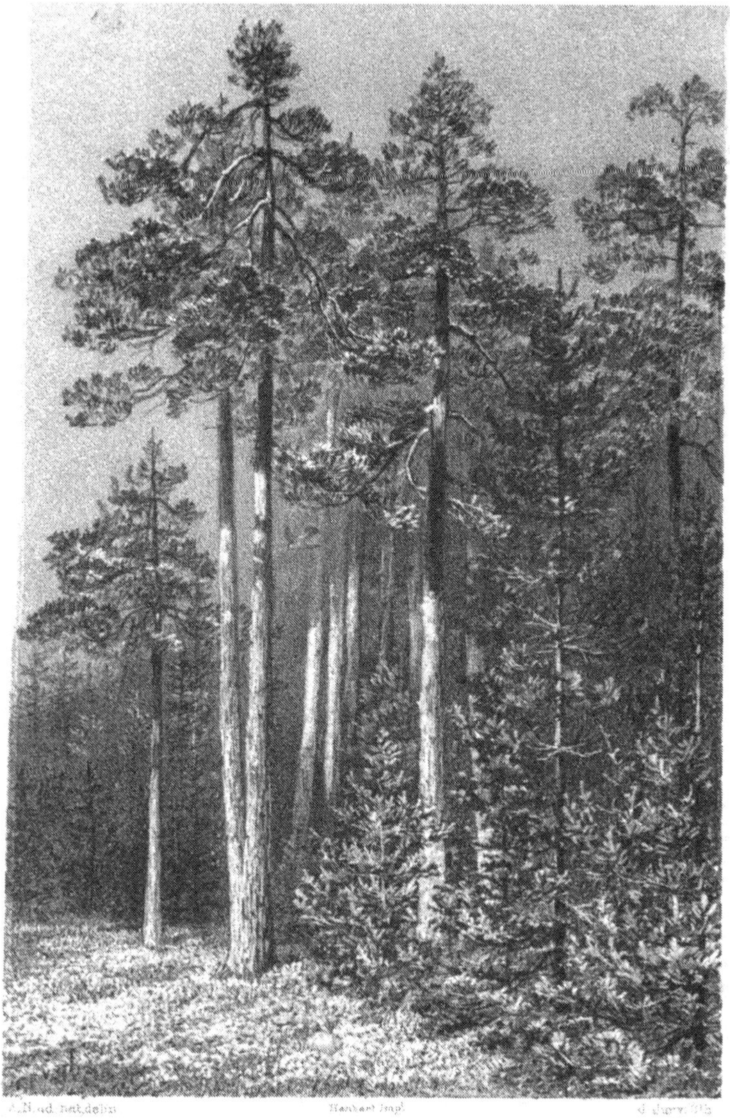

A.N. ad nat. delin. Hanhart Imp. J. Jury lith.

John Van Voorst, Paternoster Row, 1862.

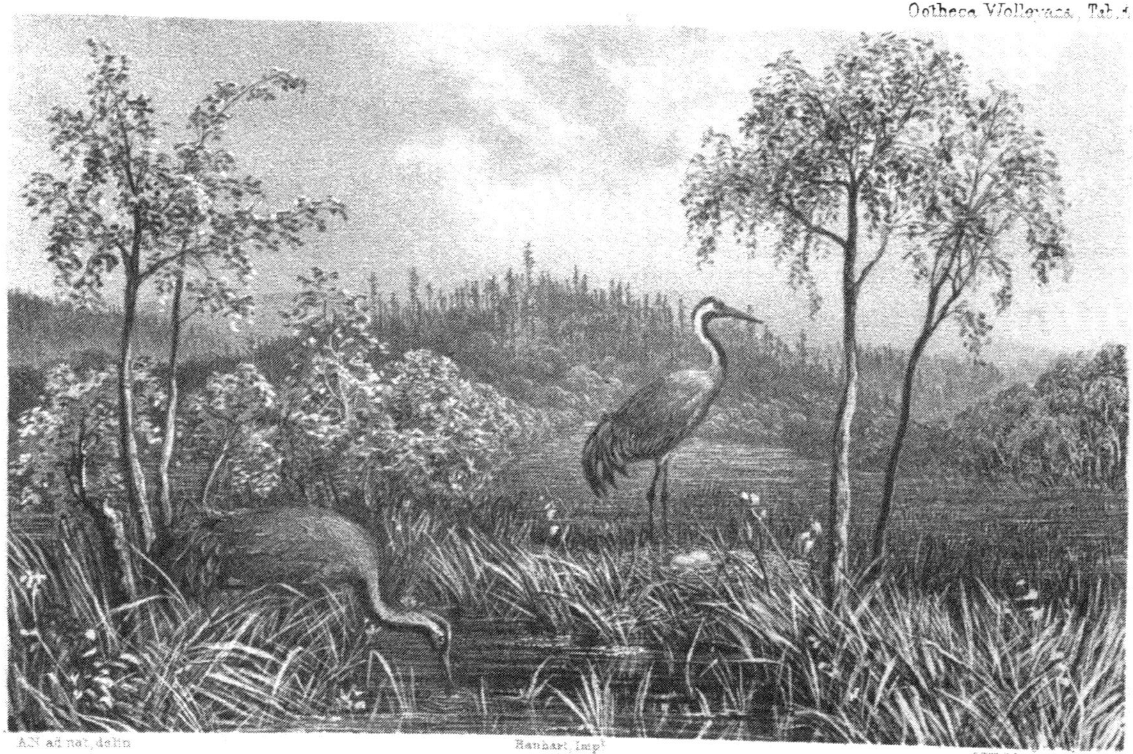

A.N. ad nat. delin. Hanhart, Imp. J. Wolf, et J. Jury, lith.

John Van Voorst, Paternoster Row, 1862.

J. Wolf ad nat. pinxit.   Hanhart Imp.   M. & N. Hanhart lith.

John Van Voorst, Paternoster Row. 1862.

J. Wolf, ad nat. pinxit.   Hanhart, Imp.   J. Jury, lith.

John Van Voorst, Paternoster Row, 1862.

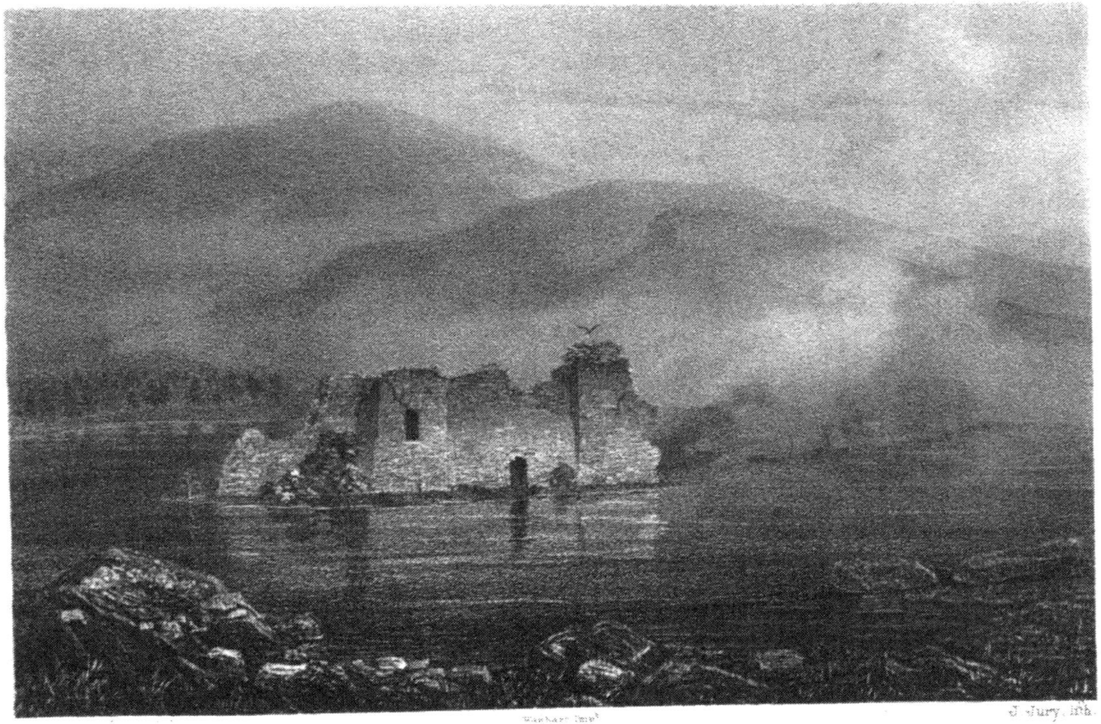

Hanhart Imp.

J. Jury, lith.

Ootheca Wolleyana. Tab. I.

J. Wolley, ad nat. delin.

Hanhart imp!

J. Jury, lith.

John Van Voorst, Paternoster Row, 1842.

.

Lightning Source UK Ltd.
Milton Keynes UK
UKHW022005190319
339471UK00009B/154/P